Aging,
Isolation and
Resocialization

Aging, Isolation and Resocialization

Edited by

Ruth Bennett, Ph.D.

Center for Geriatrics and Gerontology,
Faculty of Medicine,
Columbia University

Foreword by Joseph Zubin, Ph.D.

VNR **VAN NOSTRAND REINHOLD COMPANY**
NEW YORK   CINCINNATI   ATLANTA   DALLAS   SAN FRANCISCO
LONDON   TORONTO   MELBOURNE

Van Nostrand Reinhold Company Regional Offices:
New York   Cincinnati   Atlanta   Dallas   San Francisco

Van Nostrand Reinhold Company International Offices:
London   Toronto   Melbourne

Library of Congress Catalog Card Number: 80-11705
ISBN: 0-442-20661-5

Manufactured in the United States of America

Published by Van Nostrand Reinhold Company
135 West 50th Street, New York, N.Y. 10020

Published simultaneously in Canada by Van Nostrand Reinhold Ltd.

15 14 13 12 11 10 9 8 7 6 5 4 3 2 1

Library of Congress Cataloging in Publication Data
Main entry under title:

Aging, isolation, and resocialization.

   Includes bibliographical references and index.
   1. Gerontology—Addresses, essays, lectures.
2. Social isolation—Addresses, essays, lectures.
3. Socialization—Addresses, essays, lectures.
I. Bennett, Ruth.
HQ1061.A48   305.2′6   80-11705
ISBN 0-442-20661-5

In Memory of

Frederic D. Zeman
Alvin I. Goldfarb

Foreword

Unlike most claims for serendipity, which usually border on the apocryphal, the origin of this book is truly serendipitous. The beginnings of Dr. Bennett's interest in isolation goes back some twenty years when the Biometrics Research Unit of the New York State Department of Mental Hygiene was called upon by its Commissioner, the late Paul H. Hoch, to provide methods for screening the elderly who were seeking admission to the state hospitals in overwhelming numbers and for screening out elderly state hospital residents who no longer needed hospital care. In searching for a homogeneous group of elderly who could serve as a study population for determining high risk indicators for the development of mental disorders of the senium, the Jewish Home and Hospital for the Aged (then called Home for Aged and Infirm Hebrews) was selected. An analysis of the case records of fifty residents who had to be transferred to a mental hospital and fifty matched controls who ended their days peacefully in the institution indicated surprisingly that the most differential factor between the two groups was preadmission isolation. This completely unexpected finding started a series of studies initiated by Dr. Bennett as head of the section of Gerontology of the Biometrics Research Unit and the odyssey of these investigations form the contents of this book. As the work progressed it became clear that isolation was a rather complex concept which could be classified as either voluntary and involuntary and as of early or later development. This gave rise to four types: (1) life long isolates (voluntary), (2) recent or involuntary isolates, (3) early isolates and (4) life long integrated persons (non-isolated).

The fate of these four types, the relation of isolation to adjustment and to mental disorder and the attempts at intervening to reduce isolation constitute the findings reported here.

The future of isolation research is bound up with the parallel research in family relationships and in the newly burgeoning interest in social networks. Though family research has been active for several decades it dealt primarily with interaction between parents and children in situations where isolation was rarely involved. Isolation and its counterpart, the social network of the individual, was rarely spoken of twenty years ago, and it is due in no small measure to Dr. Bennett's pioneering persistence and that of her social science colleagues that the current burgeoning interest in this field has exploded. Perhaps the most dramatic proof of the importance of social network structures and its isolation aspect is the recent studies of Berkman and Syme in which life itself was found to be dependent on one's social network and in which social isolation proved to be one of the most important determinants of mortality among all age groups even when all the other mortality determinants were eliminated.

It is difficult to trace the impact of social science findings on public policy because social science discoveries, unlike discoveries in the physical sciences, get blended into the social fabric of society so that they become invisible in the social matrix that imbeds them. In fact, the validity of social science findings can often be established by noting whether they have become part of the culture. Nevertheless, the entire movement towards care of the elderly including the National Institute of Aging and other agencies of the federal and state governments would not have come so rapidly were it not for the pioneering efforts of the editor of this volume and her colleagues in the social sciences, who developed a sufficient scientific basis and methodology for improving the lot of the elderly that could be incorporated into public policy.

The most important contributions of this book can be summarized as follows: Scientifically, this work presents a quantitative approach to the measurement of degree and type of isolation and its relationship to measurable aspects of adjustment. Practically, it demonstrates that much of the deleterious effects of isolation can be successfully remedied and even prevented. It is for these two reasons that this book is bound to improve our understanding and treatment of the phenomenon of isolation.

With the continued growth of the numbers of elderly, and with the growing tendency for them to continue living in the community, it becomes important to provide methods for discovering those who are vulnerable to isolation and to prevent it from affecting their adjustment. It is now clear that much of the maladjustment which has been attributed in the past to the natural effects of aging is a function of the ecological niche afforded the aged, especially the degree of isolation they suffer. However, not all of the elderly are vulnerable to isolation and it becomes important to develop markers of vulnerability to isolation and to the other noxious social agents. The techniques developed in the studies reported in this book ought to go far in identifying the individuals who are vulnerable to isolation.

In a paper given at a meeting prepared by the Biometrics Research Unit nearly a quarter of a century ago when the studies reported in this volume were in their infancy, our general conclusion was that "something needs to be done during the second half of the 20th century for the last decades of life, similar to what was accomplished for the first decades of life during the first half of this century. Can we through medical, psychological and social techniques develop methods to reduce the mortality rates and increase the release rates? Is it possible that crowding our geriatric cases into a useless existence in our state hospitals is provoking senile marasmus similar to the infantile marasmus which occured in the early years of this century, thereby increasing mortality and decreasing discharge rates? To be sure, success in this direction may prove to be expensive to the state, as it will add to longevity. In fact, in Scandinavian countries, the decrease in mortality rates in the old age group had already added 8 percent to the bed capacities of the hospitals. But release rates, productivity and life enjoyment may also rise in the wake of such improvements. The first decade of life is of concern only to parents. All of us, however, are candidates for the last decades of life. Can we ourselves countenance our own approach to a relatively secure old age, while thousands of our colleagues are doomed to stagnate in our senile wards? And are we ourselves so sure that we will not land in one of them?"

Progress during the last several decades in improving diagnosis and providing alternatives for care has been very rapid, but these advances have not yet changed the lot of the elderly very much. We have reduced the tendencies toward hospitalization by keeping many of the elderly at home. Can we now reduce the dangers such as isolation which living in the community entails?

Joseph Zubin, Ph.D.
Distinguished Research Professor
of Psychiatry, University of
Pittsburgh Medical School
and
Research Career Scientist
V.A. Medical Center, Pittsburgh, Pa.
Formerly, Chief of the Biometrics
Research Unit, New York State
Department of Mental Hygiene

Acknowledgments

First, I would like to thank the authors of the chapters of this book: Lucille Nahemow, Sr. Mary Anne Mulligan, Frances B. Arje, Eugene Barron, Marcella B. Weiner and Lenore Powell. On the first page of each chapter, the authors acknowledge those who helped them in their studies and, therefore, I would like to acknowledge their assistance as well.

Second, I would like to acknowledge the help and support given by my many colleagues at the Biometrics Research Unit of the New York State Department of Mental Hygiene during the early stages of this research. They were: Joseph Zubin, Eugene Burdock, Nechama Tec, Lucille Nahemow, Frances Cheek, Martin Schnall, Joseph Fleiss, Comilda Weinstock, and Samuel Sutton.

Third, I would like to acknowledge the help and support given by some of my current colleagues at the Center for Geriatrics and Gerontology of the Faculty of Medicine of Columbia University, who are: Barry Gurland, David Wilder, Robert Golden and Diana Cook.

Finally, I would like to thank my husband, Michael V. L. Bennett and my children, Nicholas T. Bennett and Elena P. Bennett for their encouragement, support and patience.

Contents

Aging,
Isolation and
Resocialization

PART I
INTRODUCTION:
ISOLATION
AND ADJUSTMENT

1
Introduction
Ruth Bennett, Ph.D.*

With advances made in medicine and the decrease in birth and death rates, the trend toward an increase in the absolute and relative size of aging populations is expected to continue. In a United Nations report (1971), prepared in compliance with a General Assembly resolution, figures show that "the approximately 291 million persons 60 years of age and over, in 1971, throughout the world will increase to nearly 585 million by the year 2000 or by more than 100 percent, while the world's population as a whole will increase from 3.6 to 6.5 thousand million, or by approximately 80 percent" (p. 19).

Importantly, this report notes that for the more developed regions the increase in population as a whole will be 33% from 1970 to 2000, whereas the 60-and-over population will increase by 50%. For the less-developed regions the proportionate increase of the older population is even more pronounced; whereas the population as a whole will increase by 98%, for the 60-and-over population the increase will be approximately 158%. By the middle of the twenty-first century, there may be about 30 million old people in the United States living about 25 years beyond the age of 65. It is of some concern now how they will be supported and cared for. With the trend toward smaller families and divorce, it is clear that many more will be socially isolated. The prevention and reduction of their isolation will become difficult but important problems to deal with.

Isolation of the aged is of general concern throughout the world. In the Secretary General's Report to the General Assembly on "The Question of Aging and the Aged" (1971), the following statements appeared:

---

*Deputy Director, Center for Geriatrics and Gerontology Faculty of Medicine, Columbia University; Associate Professor of Clinical Psychiatry, Columbia University; Adjunct Professor, Teachers College, Columbia University.

Social and psychological factors seem to contribute to some of the deterioration observed to accompany aging. There is some evidence in developed countries attesting to the negative impact of "role loss" and social isolation. Apparently, progressive losses of resources tend to arouse feelings of helplessness These feelings in turn, serve to create anxieties. (p. 5)

Loneliness, desolation and isolation characterize the social lives of many of the aged, particularly in many developed countries. Loneliness is reported with great frequency by older women surveyed in some of these countries. In these surveys, desolation is the sense of loss that occurs when bereaved by death of spouse. Social isolation refers to the objective situation in which the aged find themselves as a result of mandatory retirement policies which cut them off from work relationships, mobility of children, deaths of spouse, relatives and friends, and losses of organizational memberships. Very little is available to compensate for role losses both within and outside the family. However, recent research indicates that the presence of a friend may make the difference between independent living in the community and institutionalization. (p. 12)

In 1978, at a World Experts on Aging Conference held at the United Nations and co-sponsored by United Nations Fund for Population Activities (UNFPA) and Institut de la Vie, the following statement appeared in the proceedings:

The Expert Group identified aging as a problem to the individual, the family, and the society. For the individual there is the potential problem of personal and social isolation. For those of advanced age, with a reduction in energy and life-force, there is a withdrawal from those central activities which require such capacities. For others, because of the application of chronological age definitions, the right to work may be destroyed. The older person may not be permitted or able to work. For many older persons, probably the majority, there is the question of their exhausting material resources and their ability to survive. (p. 9)

It was stressed at the conference that the concept of isolation—the deprivation of social contact and content—must be distinguished from the concept of loneliness, which is a psychological state.

The consequences of social isolation for the individual and the society require examination. Studies suggest that isolation and loneliness is a problem of only a small minority of the elderly There is a need to revive, where they previously existed, or to establish cultural norms and approaches that promote social interaction between older individuals and society. For those aged who are isolated there is a need for resocialization, which is particularly important to older persons at points of death and/or institutionalization. The participants at the conference agreed that the questions related to the extended family, social isolation and loneliness have been confused. In the developed countries, where the aged have economic resources, the evidence points to their not wanting to live in the households of younger family members. In Sweden, for example, those older persons who live alone favor social contacts in the following rank order: family, old friends, neighbors. Also, in Sweden it was found that socially isolated elders use more health services and resources. Living alone, it was suggested, does not necessarily mean that the older individual is either lonely or isolated. It may relate to the individual's desire to retain the right of decision making and mastery over himself and his environment. There is also a need to understand cultural differences in regard to isolation and loneliness. The issue of age segregation was identified at the conference as one requiring careful analysis and study. In many of the developed countries there are concentrations of the elderly in urban and rural areas, with housing, environmental and service programs based on age-segregated policies and practices. The question of social contacts and relationships between the young and the old was raised. Often the young are not aware of the aged, or of their own prospects for aging. The need for primary school education about aging and structured opportunities for the young and old to relate was underscored. The emphasis should be on intergenerational and age-integrated approaches to policies, practices and services for the aging. At the same time there was recognition of the special characteristics and needs of older persons, particularly the very old.

One of the concerns expressed by the participants at the conference was our lack of knowledge about the present and potential roles and characteristics of the aging in the societies of the world. If older persons are not to be viewed as problems, there is a need to identify and recognize their present and potential capacities and contributions to themselves, their families and society.

Isolation was regarded at the World Experts Conference as bad in and of itself and not necessarily because of its consequences for either individuals or society, which are not well known. Like illness, it is regarded by experts as a problem that must be solved, or perhaps as a social defect.

As far back as 1968, isolation was viewed as a major theme in the study of aging. Shanas et al. (1968) wrote that:

The basic preoccupation of social gerontology as it has emerged within the last two decades may be categorized as being concerned with integration versus segregation. Are old people integrated into society or are they separated from it? This is perhaps not only the most important theoretical question affecting all policies concerning the aged. Specifically, should old people be integrated into society by new forms of employment and social activities, or should they be removed from the main streams and the cross-currents of ordinary life? Do they prefer to live in the midst of the larger society or in retirement communities (such as groups of bungalows and residential institutions)? The answers given to these questions and others like them could make a very great difference in how governments interpret the needs of old people and go about meeting them. (p. 3)

A United Nations (1973) General Assembly report devoted an entire section to "Isolation" which noted that: "Increasing isolation and solitude among the aged is underlined in the report on Western Europe. In France for example, more than 50 percent of the elderly live alone or with an elderly spouse . . . . In most countries in Western Europe, it was reported, geographic or familial isolation increased with age, together with physical incapacity and dependence. All surveys of different countries in Europe come to the same conclusion: the present situation of many aged people is critical" (p. 30).

Differences in the United States and the United Kingdom in the social status of the elderly were reported in the literature in the 1950s. Townsend (1957) found that in England 52% of those over 60 lived with children or within a mile of them. In the United States, fewer older people lived with children. Several years later, Shanas et al. (1968) found that nearly half of the elderly population in the United States and just over half in Britain were single or widowed. By and large they found a "broad similarity in pattern of family contacts" (p. 174) in the United States and the United Kingdom. The overall difference between the elderly populations in patterns of contact with children was relatively small. Over three-fifths in both the United States and the United Kingdom had seen a child the same or the previous day and another fifth within the previous week, indicating that despite structural variations the overall visiting patterns were similar.

There was also great similarity in the United States and the United Kingdom in degree of isolation. "Only a small minority (4 percent or fewer) of old people were found to be living in extreme isolation in the sense that a week or even a day could pass without human contact" (p. 285). However, "a larger proportion (a quarter in each country) said they were often alone. Relatively more women than men were often alone, and this tended to correspond with the larger proportion of women who were found to be widowed and living alone" (p. 285).

Special note was made by Shanas et al. (1968) of the need to develop a complex measure of isolation: "Those who were isolated were generally persons who were living alone, older than average, single or widowed, lacking children and other relatives living nearby, retired and infirm. Three or more of these factors acting together were more likely to produce social isolation than was any single factor" (p. 285).

It is precisely this multifaceted aspect of isolation with which we have been concerned in over 20 years of research on isolation.

Of major concern in our research have been and are: (1) how to detect an isolate; (2) how to identify different types of isolates; (3) what the consequences of isolation are; (4) how to determine which types of isolates need help and can benefit from help; and (5) what sorts of help they need.

Chapter 2 contains a discussion of the concept and measurement of social isolation and the methods developed to detect an isolate, as well as descriptions of different types of isolates. These were first described by Bennett [Granick] and Nahemow in 1961 and 1965.

An isolate is an individual with a low social contact score based on assessing number of roles that require activation. For the most part, findings presented in this book are based on the measures described in Chapter 2 and developed over the past 22 years. These two measures are: the Past Month Isolation Index (PMI) and the Adulthood Isolation Index (AI). Based on these two measures, four isolation patterns have been differentiated by taking median breaks and grouping people according to whether they were above or below median on each of the two isolation measures. We have classified these people as voluntary or lifelong isolates, involuntary or recent isolates, early isolates, and nonisolates. This typology will be discussed in greater detail in Chapter 2.

Chapter 3 contains results of our early studies of social isolation, adjustment and mental health. In these studies we found that isolation had a negative impact on the aged: In the first published paper of our work (Tec and Bennett [Granick] 1959–60) we speculated that isolation resulted in desocialization, a process by which older people lose their social skills through disuse. Although desocialization may not handicap them in their solitary existence in the community, it may hamper social adjustment to settings in which they are forced to interact with others (e.g., institutions and senior centers).

The study of the relationship between isolation and adjustment was conducted first in a home for the aged, and then was extended into four other settings ordered by degree of totality. A mental hospital was seen as the most totalistic institution; an apartment project for senior citizens was seen as the least totalistic. The findings described in Chapter 3, indicate that the experience of pre-entry isolation has a negative effect on socialization to norms of the setting in all but one residential institution—the mental hospital. Aspects of adjustment other than socialization were differently affected in the different types of institutions. Some findings of our current studies of the community-based elderly in New York City are also described in Chapter 3.

Chapter 4 contains a description of research on the relationship between attitudinal dependence and social isolation. At one point, we thought that although isolation was related to poor socialization and adjustment, it might have some salutary social psychological effects. We thought that the isolate might be some sort of "rugged individualist," holding out against institutional constraints and restraints. We found the opposite to be the case; isolates were quite docile and acquiescent, whereas socially integrated individuals were willing to defend their own point of view against strong opposition. From this series of studies, we became convinced that the best thing to do about isolation was to prevent or reduce it.

In order to try to reduce social isolation, we began, on an experimental basis, the Friendly Visitor Program in the Morningside Health Catchment Area, from which residents of some of the institutions studied in earlier work were drawn. This friendly visiting program is described in Chapter 5. Findings from an evaluation of the program, also described in Chapter 5, showed observable differences in communicativeness, sociability, the condition of the apartment, and personal grooming between the first and the succeeding visits. Differences between experimental subjects who were visited and controls who were not, also were found.

We believed it was important to reduce isolation in any setting in which the aged were found. Thus, in a medical clinic at Coney Island Hospital, elderly patients were grouped and placed experimentally in a resocialization group, which is described in Chapter 6. Those who were in such a group improved on a variety of measures of socialization and adjustment.

Although isolation may not necessarily predispose one to poor adjustment in a community in which one is already settled, it may have negative consequences if one is moved into an institution. Therefore, several resocialization experiements were undertaken with residents of institutions in order both to develop ways of combatting isolation or its effects in institutional residents and to determine if some patterns of isolation were found to be more amenable to treatment than others.

As is seen in Chapter 7, remotivation turned out to be very successful as a group resocialization form with the elderly.

In Chapter 8, type of group leadership is described in relation to the process of resocialization. Professional group leaders were more effective than elderly persons in resocialization efforts in DIPHA homes.

In an experiment utilizing time-limited group therapy methods described in Chapter 9, it was found that some patterns of isolation were more treatable than others. It was found that involuntary isolates were most responsive to group resocialization efforts. It was thought that it might be effective to target involuntary isolates for group resocialization efforts, as they seemed to benefit the most.

Chapter 10 contains a summary, a description of some work in progress and some concluding remarks.

This book should prove of interest to geriatricians and gerontologists who are concerned with assessment of isolation as well as with the delivery of services to the isolated elderly. The problems of measurement seem to be of general interest to students, researchers and practitioners. The development of services that are based on theory should also prove of general interest.

REFERENCES

Bennett [Granick] R., and Nahemow, L. Preadmission isolation as a factor in adjustment to an old age home. In P. Hoch and J. Zubin (Eds.), *Psychopathology of Aging*. New York: Grune and Stratton, 1961, 285–302.

Bennett, R., and Nahemow, L. The relations between social isolation, socialization and adjustment in residents of a home for aged. In M. Powell Lawton and Fay Lawton (Eds.), *Proceedings of Institute on the Mentally Impaired Aged*. Philadelphia: Maurice Jacob Press, 1965, 90–108.

Shanas, E., et al. *Old People in Three Industrial Societies*. New York: Atherton Press, 1968.

Tec, N., and Bennett [Granick], R. Social isolation and difficulties in social interaction in residents of a home for the aged. *Social Problems*, 1959–60, 7, No. 1, 226–232.

Townsend, P. *The Family Life of Old People*. London: Routledge and Kegan Paul, 1957.

U.N. General Assembly. The question of aging and the aged. Unpublished report presented by the Secretary General. United Nations, 1971.

U.N. General Assembly. More on the question of aging and the aged. Unpublished report presented by the Secretary General. United Nations, 1973.

UNFPA and Institut de la Vie. Proceedings of World Experts on Aging Conference. United Nations, 1978.

2
The Concept and Measurement of Social Isolation

Ruth Bennett, Ph.D.

Biologically, aging may be viewed as mental, physical and functional deterioration; in its various aspects, it may be thought of as either natural or pathological. Sociologically, aging may be viewed as a process accompanied by social isolation, voluntary and involuntary. As a voluntary process, the individual disengages himself from society as his energy level diminishes. As an involuntary process, isolation results from the simultaneous occurrence of physical deterioration, death of peers, stigma, enforced retirement and the predominance of the mobile, nuclear family. In our society the label "aged" is usually applied to persons 65 and over, irrespective of how they act or feel. This label implies anticipation of a range of behaviors in accordance with a predetermined role and status structure available to older persons. In some societies, the term aged implies *expansion* of roles, particularly those involving exercise of judgment and wisdom. Presumably, this is the case in traditionalist societies where age is honored because the aged are seen as the transmitters of cultural norms and knowledge. In other societies, particularly rapidly changing ones, the term aged is to be avoided because it brings with it role constriction and, therefore, isolation and segregation. It should be noted that isolation and segregation are usually reserved for all categories of social undesirables and public nuisances; for example, the mentally ill, people infected with serious contagious diseases, deviants and criminals. Isolation and segregation of the aged seem normative and acceptable to both young and old in our society, as is indicated by the fact that little has been done to alter the situation.

Moreover, various "myths" have developed to justify ways of treating those categorized as aged. Segregation and isolation of the aged are usually rationalized on practical, moral and medico-psychiatric grounds. The practical approach takes for granted the mobile, nuclear family, within which the aged are superfluous. The moral approach may result from an unconscious stigmatization of aging, possibly because of its nearness to death, and those assuming this point of view sometimes refer to the aged as morally bankrupt. The medico-psychiatric viewpoint, which has gained currency, regards aging as pathological. The terms care, treatment and rehabilitation are used to justify segregating old people into specialized institutions.

Constriction of roles forms the basis for the definition of isolation used in our studies. Before we describe the studies mentioned in Chapter 1, the conceptualization and measurement of isolation will be discussed and described.

Currently, few groups other than our own research group seem to be assessing isolation directly. Several groups other than our own are currently using the two measures of isolation developed in our research, but none has reported its results as yet. Oddly, there does not seem to be a great deal of activity in the study of social isolation at this time.

However, there was a time when discussion of and the study of isolation seemed to be burgeoning.

Before 1960, major sociologists wrote about aging as a process by which individuals become isolated from others through loss of major role relationships, especially within the familial and occupational spheres. According to Parsons (1942) the aged in our society experience extreme isolation because of three factors: the exclusiveness of the conjugal family that is prevalent in many segments of our population, the occupational structure and the functional interrelation between jobs and places of residence. Thus, exclusion from participation in the families of their adult children, inability to maintain jobs and the probability of having to live alone confront the aged with the prospect of social isolation.

Lundberg and Lawsing (1949) wrote that "the completely isolated individual would be one who was not chosen by anyone as an associate in any of the activities or relations of a community" (p. 277). Lundberg and Lawsing hypothesized that the isolated individual "could not be very sensitive to the behavioral standards of the community because he is cut off from the currents which constitute the pressures by which these standards become operative on the individual, and hence he is almost certain to be a social problem" (p. 277). The relationship between isolation and psychopathology was investigated in younger age groups, but findings were not generalized to the older group.

Clausen and Kohn (1954) conceptualized isolation as the "attenuation of interpersonal relationships." They pointed out that it is difficult to ascertain what constitutes sufficient attenuation of interpersonal relationships to warrant being called isolation.

Kutner (1956) found that willingness to use health services was affected by marital status and having living friends. The keeping of social contacts by the widowed seemed to dispose them toward a favorable reception of health services. Activity level had no bearing on use of health services. It cannot be assumed that healthy, active people will seek out their own health care. Kutner postulated that rather then activity itself, social activity is the catalyst toward using health services.

Townsend (1957) defined isolation operationally. According to him, an "isolate" is an elderly individual with a social contact score of 21 contacts per week or less. In addition, he distinguished "isolates" from "desolates," defining the latter as those who have experienced recent bereavement. Another often used operational indicator of isolation was that of "living alone" or living in a "single person household." It was used similarly by Tunstall (1966) and in the above-mentioned study conducted by Shanas et al. (1968).

A number of sociologists were concerned with the consequences of social isolation. Blau (1957) found that loss of contact among the aged negatively affects their self-image. Williams and Jaco (1958) found that "reduced social interaction or social disarticulation was implicated as an etiological or contributing factor in mental illness in old age," and that "significant improvement in overt behavior in so-called psychotics could be brought about by increased social activities in a mental hospital." Bellin and Hardt (1958) found that widowed aged, who were considered isolated only compared with those who were married, tend to have poorer mental health than their counterparts with living spouses. Wanklin et al. (1958), who studied admissions to mental hospitals in Canada, found that fewer of the aged who are admitted to mental hospitals tend to have histories of isolation than do residents of homes for the aged. This result was similar to findings of Nahemow and Bennett (1968), who speculated that this was so because at least one family member is needed to commit a person to a mental hospital, whereas an isolated older person can voluntarily enter a home for the aged or a nursing home.

After 1960, the concept of isolation seems to have been upstaged by the concept of disengagement (Cumming and Henry, 1961), but relatively little research has been conducted in which the two concepts were measured simultaneously or directly. It does not seem possible that the two concepts are mutually exclusive, and it would be worthwhile to collect data to test this notion in the future. It is important to know to what extent and in whom isolation is involuntary, and to what extent and in whom it is more or less voluntary, a voluntary situation being what the term disengagement implies. Aside from that, it would be interesting to determine the social and psychological causes and consequences of both voluntary and involuntary isolation.

In recent years, at least six other research workers have worked with concepts of isolation similar to those we have used: Marjorie F. Lowenthal (1964), Martin Hyman (1972), Burton Dunlop (1973), T. J. Curry and B. W. Ratliff (1973), and E. Rathbone-McCuan (1975).

Lowenthal (1964) found that:

lifelong extreme isolation (or alienation) is not necessarily conducive to the development of the kinds of mental disorder that bring persons to the psychiatric ward in their old age; lifelong marginal social adjustment may be conducive to the development of such disorders; late-developing isolation is apparently linked with mental disorder but it is of no greater significance among those with psychogenic disorders than among those with organic disorders, and may be more of a consequence than a cause of mental illness in the elderly; finally, physical illness may be the critical antecedent to both the isolation and the mental illness. (p. 70)

Hyman (1972) found adverse effects of social isolation on stroke rehabilitation. Apparently isolation rendered patients less malleable to the influence of a rehabilitation program.

Dunlop (1973) discussed the importance of knowing or being able to estimate the incidence of social isolation in order to be able to direct programs of isolation reduction at the population at risk.

Curry and Ratliff (1973) found that significantly more residents in large-size homes were isolated from friends and relatives than was true of those in smaller homes.

Rathbone-McCuan (1975) found improved social interaction after participation in a day care program.

The need for continued efforts at research in this area simply cries out at us. Certainly assessment of isolation is needed to determine who can profit most from much-needed isolation-reduction programs. By virtue of the fact that isolation has not been dealt with in any programmatic way, a review of the studies of the late 1970s is like a replay of the studies conducted 20 years ago.

Twenty years ago we pulled 100 case records of residents who were transferred to a mental hospital from the Jewish Home and Hospital for the Aged* (JHHA) and those who were not. Fifty residents of the Home who were transferred were compared to controls matched for age, sex and length of residence who remained in the Home. The findings showed social isolation experienced prior to entering the Home was related to inability to get along with staff members and other residents, a sign of maladjustment that often resulted in transfer to a mental hospital. The other factors that predicted to transfer were low socioeconomic status in childhood, negative attitudes toward the Home on initial admission and being labeled a management problem. Neither psychiatric diagnosis nor psychiatric history was related to transfer to a mental hospital, probably because at that time the Home made it a point to screen out persons with a psychiatric history or a known diagnosis. Only those who were mildly disordered or demented turned up in the study, and many of them seemed to adjust well so that they did not need to be transferred to a mental hospital (Tec and Bennett [Granick], 1959).

Nearly 20 years after we conducted our study, a similar study of case records of 100 persons was conducted at the Jewish Home and Hospital for the Aged by Rodstein et al. (1976) who found that:

The aged persons most likely to have initial adjustment difficulties usually had poor capacity for interpersonal relationships, were socially isolated, were either single or divorced, had a dependent personality, had severe chronic brain syndrome, had a negative or ambivalent attitude toward admission and often had been referred for psychiatric evaluation before admission. (p. 65)

Both the similarities and the differences in the findings of the two studies conducted 20 years apart are of interest. First, the similar-

---

*Then known as the Home for Aged and Infirm Hebrews. This study was made possible by Research Grants M586 and M1440 from the National Institute of Mental Health, HEW. The grants were awarded to Dr. Joseph Zubin, Chief of Biometrics Research of the New York State Department of Mental Hygiene in 1956.

ities: Isolation and negative attitudes on admission continue to predict to poor adjustment initially. Second, the differences: These findings probably can be accounted for by the change in the average age on admission (from midseventies to mideighties in 20 years, which probably accounts for the admission of more severely mentally ill persons), the change in the Home's policy to admit and retain those with psychiatric disorders and histories and the change in the Home's psychiatric capabilities, a circumstance that makes it possible for the Home to retain the mentally disordered and not require that they be transferred to a mental hospital.

Presumably the increased capacity to diagnose and treat the mentally ill who become maladjusted accounts in part for the findings of Rodstein et al. that over half of the 50 patients with initial adjustment difficulties reached a satisfactory level of adaptation during the first six months after admission.

The findings of Rodstein et al. cited above may reflect the accumulation of research results that now make it possible to differentiate mental illnesses, separate illness from maladjustment and introduce appropriate interventions. This idea is implicit, not explicit, in their paper.

Another indication of the 20-year failure to do much about isolation follows.

With a study by Ross and Kedward (1976), the study of the relationship between isolation and institutionalization in the elderly in Canada returns full circle to the Canadian study by Wanklin et al. (1958), which caused our group to look into the concept of social isolation 20 years ago. Thus, about 20 years after the Wanklin et al. (1958) study, Ross and Kedward (1976) reported that a comparison of psychogeriatric admissions to three hospitals to the population aged 65 and over in the catchment area from which the patients were drawn showed that these high-risk groups include separated and widowed men, elderly persons living alone, residents of nursing homes and women with smaller-than-average families. The authors concluded that social isolation tends to lead to institutional admission and emphasized the need for primary and secondary prevention in planning health care services.

Ross and Kedward's results coupled with the above-cited findings of Rodstein et al. (1976) indicate that nothing much is being done about isolation or isolates. Isolation predisposes to institutionalization; isolates have had trouble adjusting to institutions in the 1970s as in the 1950s; and no programmatic efforts have been undertaken either to: (a) prevent isolation in the community-dwelling elderly, or (b) assist the isolated elderly to adjust.

MEASUREMENT OF SOCIAL ISOLATION

While the isolation measures used by some of the authors mentioned above are similar to those used by our group, we have consistently used variants of the same two measures of isolation over many years in a wide variety of settings (Bennett, 1973a; 1973b). Despite the apparent importance of isolation in studies, no direct, complex measurement of it appears in large-scale surveys. Usually it is measured in an ad hoc way—for example, some count of participation in whatever activities the surveyor chooses to include or a frequency-of-visits count. Tables 2.1 and 2.2 show the two measures we have been using over the years. (Bennett [Granick] and Nahemow; 1961; 1965). These measures are: (1) the Past Month Isolation Index, which takes into account the number of role contacts that the individual has had in the past month; and (2) the Adulthood Isolation Index, which takes into account the number of role contacts that the individual has had during all of his adult years.

These indexes have been used more or less in the same manner in all the studies we have conducted in the past 20 years.

The measurements of isolation we have used follow directly from our definition of isolation: Social isolation is defined as the absence of specific role relationships which are generally activated and sustained through direct personal face-to-face interaction.

PAST MONTH ISOLATION INDEX

The Past Month Isolation Index* shown in Table 2.1, measures the number of role relationships in which an individual was involved in

---

*This was called Pre-Entry Isolation Index in some of our earlier studies conducted in institutions because we interviewed people on admission to a home. Admission was viewed as a milestone in the lives of the aged. Therefore, we thought it was easier to remember events in terms of whether they occurred before, after or on admission. When we directed the identical questions to community-residing elderly who had not been admitted anywhere, we had to change the questions slightly so that we asked them about the past month rather than events occurring before admission.

Table 2.1. Past Month Isolation Index

Category	Number of Role Contacts	Score
Organization	A. Individual did not report membership in any organization such as church, social club or political club during the past month.	0
	B. Individual reported membership in one organization during the past month.	1
	C. Individual reported membership in two or more organizations in the past month.	2
Children	A. Individual did not report any contact with children during the past month.	0
	B. Individual reported contact with one child during the past month.	1
	C. Individual reported contact with two or more children during the past month.	2
Siblings	A. Individual did not report any contact with siblings during the past month.	0
	B. Individual reported contact with one sibling during the past month.	1
	C. Individual reported contact with two or more siblings during the past month.	2
Friends	A. Individual did not report any contact with friends during the past month.	0
	B. Individual reported contact with one friend during the past month.	1
	C. Individual reported contact with two or more friends during the past month.	2
Relatives	A. Individual did not report contact with any relatives other than children or siblings during the past month.	0
	B. Individual reported contact with one such relative during the past month.	1
	C. Individual reported contact with two or more relatives during the past month.	2

the preceding month. When a respondent could not specify that a relationship occurred in the past month, a statement such as "just before being interviewed" was regarded as equivalent. Most of the aged individuals we saw were involved in so few relationships (e.g., only a small proportion had seen even two friends in the past month) that for purposes of comparison an individual with two friends was considered a nonisolate with respect to the friendship item on the index.

The Past Month Isolation Index was constructed with possible scores ranging from 0 to 10. The following five types of role relationships comprise the Index: relationships with children, siblings, friends, relatives and active membership in organizations. Because of

Table 2.2. Adulthood Isolation Index

Category	Number of Role Contacts	Score
Organization	A. Individual did not report membership in any organization during adulthood.	0
	B. Individual reported membership in one organization.	1
	C. Individual reported membership in two organizations.	2
	D. Individual reported membership in three organizations.	3
	E. Individual reported membership in four or more organizations.	4
Children	A. Individual did not report direct contact with any children at all or with children beyond their infancy.	0
	B. Individual reported direct contact with one child.	1
	C. Individual reported direct contact with two children.	2
	D. Individual reported direct contact with three children.	3
	E. Individual reported direct contact with four or more children.	4
Siblings	A. Individual did not report direct contact with any siblings at all or with siblings beyond their infancy.	0
	B. Individual reported direct contact with one sibling.	1
	C. Individual reported direct contact with two siblings.	2
	D. Individual reported direct contact with three siblings.	3
	E. Individual reported direct contact with four or more siblings.	4
Relatives	A. Individual did not report direct contact with any relatives in adulthood.	0
	B. Individual reported direct contact with one relative.	1
	C. Individual reported direct contact with two relatives.	2
	D. Individual reported direct contact with three relatives.	3
	E. Individual reported direct contact with four or more relatives.	4
Friends	A. Individual did not report any friends in adulthood.	0
	B. Individual reported direct contact with one friend.	1
	C. Individual reported direct contact with two friends.	2
	D. Individual reported direct contact with three friends.	3
	E. Individual reported direct contact with four or more friends.	4
Mother	A. The individual reported he maintained no contact with his mother during adulthood.	0
	B. Individual reported that he either maintained some contact with his mother over a period of 15 years, or that he saw her frequently for a period of less than 15 years.	1
	C. The individual reported that he maintained frequent contact with his mother; i.e., he saw her at least once a month, for a minimum of 15 years in adulthood.	2

Table 2.2. Adulthood Isolation Index (con't)

Category	Number of Role Contacts	Score
Father	A. The individual reported that he maintained no contact with his father during adulthood.	0
	B. The individual reported that he either maintained some contact with his father over a period of 15 years or that he saw him frequently for a period of less than 15 years.	1
	C. The individual reported that he maintained frequent contact with his father; i.e., he saw him at least once a month, for a minimum of 15 years in adulthood.	2
Spouse	A. Never married.	0
	B. Married less than 15 years.	2
	C. Daily contact with spouse for a period of at least 15 years.	4
Job	A. Individual never worked in adulthood.	0
	B. Individual held any job.	1
	C. Individual worked at least 10 years.	2
	D. Individual held several types of jobs and worked during his entire adult life.	3
	E. Individual maintained one job or worked in the same field during most of his adult life.	4

the limited range of relationships in which an elderly individual has been involved in the past month, a maximum number of two points is allotted for each relationship. Thus, if an individual has contact with only one child during that period, he is given one point; if he has contact with two or more children, two points are assigned.

Individuals are compared to each other on the dimension of social isolation. Thus, they are designated as isolates and nonisolates, bearing in mind that these terms are used as relative ones within a comparatively isolated population.

ADULTHOOD ISOLATION INDEX

The Adulthood Isolation Index is shown in Table 2.2. It was constructed to take into account the number of interpersonal relationships experienced by the individual during his adulthood. The possible scores range from 0 to 32. When specific information is available, the age of 17, or marriage if it occurred prior to or at 21, have been arbitrarily selected to mark the onset of adulthood. Sometimes the respondent cannot pinpoint the exact time at which specific relationships occurred, and the investigator is forced to estimate it within the limits of the above-mentioned criteria.

For the Adulthood Isolation Index, three dimensions of role relationships are assessed, depending upon the relationship under consideration. These dimensions are: number of role relationships, frequency of activation of the relationship and duration of the relationship. The following five relationships were assessed simply in terms of number: relationships with children, siblings, friends, relatives and active memberships in organizations. A maximum number of four points is allotted for each relationship. Thus, if an individual has contact with any one child at any time during his adult life, he is given one point; if he has contact with two children, he is given two points; if he has contact with four or more children, he is given four points.

In order to score relationships with mother, father, spouse and work associates, a combination of frequency and duration of contact was used as a criterion. For example, if an individual maintained no contact with his mother in adulthood, he received a score of 0. If he reported that he either maintained infrequent contact with his mother over a period of 15 years in adulthood or that he saw her frequently but for a period of less than 15 years, he received a score of 1. If he reported that he maintained frequent contact (i.e., saw his mother at least once a month for a period of 15 years), he received a score of 2. The same scoring procedure was used to analyze his relationship with his father. Thus, if he saw both parents frequently during a 15-year period in adulthood, he received a total score of 4.

The marital relationship was scored in a similar manner. If an individual never married, he received a score of 0; if he was married for a period of less than 15 years, he received a score of 2; and if he was married for a period of more than 15 years, he received a score of 4. Thus, a relationship with two parents that was frequent and sustained for 15 years was equated in weight to a relationship with a spouse for the same length of time.

The work relationship was scored in the following manner: An individual who never worked received a score of 0; one who had held any job at all was given a score of 1; one who worked at least 10 years in his adulthood was given a score of 2; one who held several jobs but who worked all his life was given a score of 3; and one who maintained one job or worked in the same field during most of his life was given a score of 4. The last category included people who had made a "career" as housekeepers as well as those who were registered nurses.

Needless to say, these weights are arbitrary. For the latter four relationships, it is not meaningful simply to count noses. Typically one has only one mother or father; four spouses obviously do not reflect four times the social contact at one time period that one spouse does; and similarly having had four jobs does not imply four times the social contacts of one job. Thus, these relationships, which are important ones in an individual's lifetime but which are limited in number by their nature, were weighted in terms of duration and frequency of contact.

RELIABILITY AND VALIDITY ISSUES

It was not possible to get any corroborative data regarding the subject's past life outside of the Home in our early studies. It was necessary, therefore, to rely exclusively upon the resident's own report of his life. There are difficulties inherent in every measure that relies on a self report. These difficulties are exaggerated when one asks questions about events that occurred in the past. For old people some of the relationships about which they were questioned had occurred as many as 60 or 70 years in the past.

However, since 1976 we have been investigating the phenomenon of social isolation cross-nationally. B. Gurland, R. Bennett and D. Wilder (in press) have collaborated in a United States–United Kingdom study of the community-based elderly with a research team based at Maudsley Hospital in London. This study of the health, mental health and social problems in the community-based elderly and a one-year follow-up have given us, among other things, the opportunity for the first time to look at how isolation is distributed in random samples of the elderly in New York and London, and how it correlates with mental health, physical health and social problems.

In their report, Gurland et al. (1980) report face vailidity in the relationship between AI and PMI, as is indicated by the moderately high correlations in the .5–.6 range, between the two over time and in different populations. Only the Brooklyn State Hospital patients, a mental hospital group, differed in that the correlation between the two measures was low. We would expect unpredictability in mental patients of any age. The correlation obtained in the New York City sample recently is consistent with correlations obtained in elderly community samples studied earlier, as may be seen in Chapter 3.

Measures of central tendency on the Adulthood Isolation Index (AI) and the Past Month Isolation Index (PMI) as well as correlations of the two indexes obtained in seven samples studied in different New York City settings from 1957 to the present are similar, as may be seen in Chapter 3, Table 3.14. The mean PMI and AI vary across settings, but in a predictable fashion.

The most isolated individuals are those who were chosen for this purpose. They were individuals selected for participation in a friendly visiting program precisely because they were isolated (Mulligan and Bennett, 1978).

The least isolated are the community aged, with a variety of institutional groups obtaining scores between the most and least extreme values.

There is face validity to the PMI as indicated by measures of central tendency. The groups expected to be most isolated are most isolated (e.g., those selected for friendly visiting). There is test–retest reliability in AI, which contains background information that should not vary at two points in time. Initially, this reliability was found by retesting half of the first group of 100 studied at JHHA about two years later and obtaining a correlation coefficient of .62. Reliability testing of the entire Comprehensive Assessment and Referral Evaluation (CARE) instrument containing these measures has subsequently been repeated, and the entire measure is highly reliable, as is reported in Gurland et al. (in press).

ISOLATION PATTERNS

Patterns of isolation were obtained by taking median breaks on both measures of isolation and considering those above the median as integrated, meaning having many contacts, and those below the median as isolated, meaning having few contacts. These groups broken at the median were combined to produce four types: (1) those integrated over a lifetime; (2) the early isolate, who was isolated as an adult but is comparatively active in old age; (3) the involuntary or recent isolate, active early in life but not in old age; and (4) the lifelong or voluntary isolate, for whom isolation was a lifestyle.

When we compared the distributions of isolation types for the New York City elderly studied in connection with the United States–United Kingdom study and an institutionalized group studied earlier, we found some interesting differences (Gurland et al., in press). There are more lifelong isolates in the institution (45%) than in the community (32%), suggesting that those who have accumulated few social supports over a lifetime end up in institutions, whereas other, perhaps comparably frail but better supported, elderly remain in the community.

Some cases illustrative of the four types of isolates are cited below to give concrete examples that indicate the recognizability of the patterns described.

CASE STUDIES ILLUSTRATING ISOLATION PATTERNS

The following hypothetical, composite case studies taken from Gurland et al. (1980) indicate the types of people thought to fit the isolation patterns listed above.

Lifelong Isolate (Isolated All of Adult Life)

Case #1. Mr. S., 67 Years Old, Living with Wife. Mr. S. is a 67-year-old man who lives with his wife in an apartment house. He came to the United States from abroad at age 21. He speaks English well, though he is a little hard to understand. He was first very resistant to being interviewed and skeptical, and wanted to know how this could help him and could he call us if he needed help. He especially emphasized this when he was asked what he would do in an emergency. He said he doesn't have anyone to call. He has a "family doctor" but hasn't been there in years and doesn't want to go because it costs too much. As a result he goes to a clinic because he just shows his Medicare card and pays nothing. He went there for a cold one year before being interviewed, and had a full check-up. He figures if he had an emergency he'd call the private doctor.

He reports that his health is fine and he has no problems, but then spontaneously offers the information that he drinks a lot. He drinks about a quart a week of scotch, and has been drinking heavily since World War II. He says he used to drink much more when he was younger. He drinks whenever he feels the urge. He also reports that he is overweight and feels that it may be the drinking that affects that and makes him eat more. He has no obvious impairments, no memory loss, a bit of arthritis in his fingers. He also spontaneously reports that he has trouble sleeping. He says he goes to bed when he feels tired—about 10 P.M. or so but can only sleep for four hours and then gets up and can't get back to sleep. He claims it's normal for older people not to need more.

He says he has enough energy and is not slowed down. He's upset he had to retire two years ago, because of a company rule. He's also upset that his income has dropped. His son contributes to the house, and his wife works five days a week.

He admits that he has been very irritable, and that he is always yelling. He says he has a very hot temper and yells all the time. He says he is not depressed, but says he is an unhappy person and that "you can't get anything you want in this life." He has friends but says he is not close to anyone and can't talk to them about his troubles. He has a brother in another state and other relatives abroad. He admits that he worries about his family but is not in contact with them.

He says that in the many years he's been living there, the neighborhood has changed and has gotten a little rougher. There's not a lot of crime, but people have been attacked. Nothing's happened to him, and he's not afraid, but he doesn't go out at night.

Involuntary Isolate (Isolated in Conjunction with Aging)

Case #2. Mr. W., Age 89, Lives with his Wife in New York City. Mr. W. is a slightly built, bearded man of 89, who came to New York from abroad in 1920 and worked as a peddler (he was 35 when he arrived in the United States). After spending two or three years in Harlem, he moved to his present neighborhood in 1923 or 1924.

He expressed financial difficulties living only on social security, which is not enough for all his needs, and he economizes on food, not buying meat, chicken, fish or milk.

Physically he complains of arthritis and pain in his joints, arms and legs, which limits his activities. He denied any other physical ailments.

His wife is bedridden and has been for 12 years. She is said by a home health aide to have parkinsonism, and there are some signs of tremor on the left side. The entire right side of her body is paralyzed.

Socially he appears isolated because of time spent caring for his wife. He does not appear to have friends. He claims (and the health aide agrees) that there is no contact between himself and the neighbors in the building.

He has some contact with his sons but none with his daughters-in-law and grandchildren.

Early Isolate (Isolated Early in Life but Not in Old Age)

Case #3. Miss L., 70, Lives with Sister. Miss L. and her sister never married. They are the types of people one might regard as "eccentric loners." Often such people become of interest to younger relatives and acquaintances as they age because they have led unusual, though isolated lives.

She says her health has been excellent. She went to a doctor for a checkup a month before being interviewed. He checked her heart, pulse and blood pressure, and her health is good.

She has friends at church, which she attends regularly, and belongs to a club at the company where she had worked since after World War II. She attends luncheons, outings and excursions. She also enjoys frequent visits with nephews and cousins, who come to take her out to their homes.

She is financially secure and gets Social Security, has a private pension and has held stock in her company since beginning to work there. She also owns her own house.

Integrated over Lifetime (One Who Is Socially Active throughout Life into Old Age)

Case #4. Mr. L., Age 69, Living with Wife. Mr. L. is a very busy lawyer who is working part-time. Before the interview, Mr. L. had a mild heart attack and spent a couple of months recuperating. He slowly returned to work. He continues to take medication for this condition.

He moved to his current house many years ago, and he owns it outright.

He is extremely active, both physically and socially.

He lives at home with his wife, who is somewhat younger than he is and who also has a part-time job. They lead a fairly active life socially. They belong to clubs, have many friends and have traveled a great deal all over the world. They have been married a long time. He has married children with grandchildren living nearby with whom he exchanges frequent visits.

He is close to his children, grandchildren, siblings and other relatives. He has a large number of friends from his entire life, and they are in regular contact with each other by telephone, letter and face-to-face contact. At least twice a week he and his wife dine out with close friends.

He has no financial problems.

Correlates of Isolation Patterns

In their report, Gurland et al. (1980) examine isolation patterns and current condition, service use and other factors; and to some extent their findings are discussed in Chapter 3. There are very few significant differences among the four groups, but those that do exist are telling, and there are definite trends. Lifelong or voluntary isolates are more likely to be nonwhite, blue-collar, and low on income and other socioeconomic status indicators. These characteristics do not significantly set them off from the other isolates. All isolates are significantly poorer than those who have been socially integrated over their lifespan. Voluntary or lifelong isolates are more likely to remain in need, whereas involuntary or recent isolates make greater use of the formal service delivery system, such as meal delivery programs.

More lifelong (voluntary) and recent (involuntary) isolates will remain in need as compared with the others. However, more involuntary isolates seem to make use of the formal service system. This is consistent with the findings of the study of Powell in Chapter 9, which first suggested to us that involuntary isolates are a good target group for assistance, especially if resources are limited. Of course, one might want to assist other groups as well, especially if they run the risk of losing their supports; this aid should be given in order to prevent any crises from having serious deleterious effects.

REFERENCES

Bellin, S., and Hardt, R. H. Marital status and mental disorders among the aged. *Am. Soc. Rev.*, 1958, *23*, 155-162.

Bennett, R. Living conditions and everyday needs of the aged with specific reference to social isolation. *J. Aging Hum. Dev.*, 1973a, *IV, 3*, 179-198.

Bennett, R. Isolation and isolation-reducing programs. *Bull. N.Y. Acad. Med.*, 2nd Ser. Dec. 1973b, *49, 12*, 1143-1163.

Bennett [Granick], R., and Nahemow, L. Preadmission isolation as a factor in adjustment to an old age home. In P. Hoch and J. Zubin (Eds.), *Psychopathology of Aging*. New York: Grune and Stratton, 1961, 285-302.

Bennett, R., and Nahemow, L. The relations between social isolation, socialization and adjustment in residents of a home for aged. In M. P. Lawton and F. Lawton (Eds.), *Proceedings of Institute on the Mentally Impaired Aged*. Philadelphia: Maurice Jacob Press, 1965, 90-108.

Blau, Z. S. Old age: A study of change in status. Unpublished Ph.D. dissertation, Columbia University, 1957.

Clausen, J., and Kohn, M. The ecological approach in social psychiatry. *Am. J. Soc.*, 1954, *60*, 140-151.

Cumming, M. E., and Henry, W. *Growing Old*. New York: Basic Books, 1961.

Curry, T. J., and Ratliff, B. W. The effects of nursing home size on resident isolation and life satisfaction. *Gerontologist*, 1973, *13, 3*, 295-298.

Dunlop, B. Isolation among the elderly. Unpublished paper circulated by Urban Research Associates, Washington, D. C. Ca. 1973.

Gurland, B., Bennett, R., and Wilder, D. Planning for the elderly in New York City: An assessment of depression, dementia and isolation. *Proceedings of Research Utilization Workshop*. Community Council of Greater N. Y. (March, 1980).

Hyman, M. D. Social isolation and performance in rehabilitation. *J. Chron. Dis.*, 1972, *25*, 85-97.

Kutner, Bernard, Fanshel, David, Togo, Alice M., and Langner, Thomas S. *Five Hundred Over Sixty*, New York: Russell Sage Foundation, 1956.

Lowenthal, M. F. Social isolation and mental illness in old age. *Am. Soc. Rev.*, 1964, *29*, 54-70.

Lundberg, G. A., and Lawsing, M. The Sociography of some community relations. In Logan Wilson and William L. Kolb (Eds.), *Sociological Analysis*, New York: Harcourt, Brace, 1949, 271–286.

Mulligan, Sister Mary Anne, and Bennett, R. Assessment of mental health and social problems during multiple friendly visits: The development and evaluation of a friendly visiting program for the isolated elderly. *J. Aging Hum. Dev.*, 1978, *8, 1*, 43–65.

Nahemow, L., and Bennett, R. Attitude change in the aged with institutionalization. Unpublished NIMH final report (mimeo), 1968, 53 pp. and appendices.

Parsons, T. Age and sex in the social structure of the United States. *Am. Soc. Rev.*, 1942, *7*, 604–616.

Rathbone-McCuan, E. Impact of socialization therapy in a geriatric day-care setting. *Gerontologist*, 1975, *15*, 338–342.

Rodstein, M., Savitsky, E., and Starkman, R. Initial adjustment to a long term care institution: Behavioral aspects. *J. Am. Geriatr. Soc.*, 1976, *XXIV, 2*, 65–71.

Ross, H. E., and Kedward, H. B. Demographic and social correlates of psychogeriatric hospitalization. *Soc. Psychiat.*, July 1976, *11*, 3, 121–126.

Shanas, E., et al. *Old People in Three Industrial Societies*. New York: Atherton Press, 1968.

Tec, N., and Bennett [Granick], R. Social isolation and difficulties in social interaction in residents of a home for the aged. *Social Problems*, 1959–60, 226–232.

Townsend, P. *The Family Life of Old People*. London: Routledge and Kegan Paul, 1957.

Tunstall, Jeremy. *Old and Alone*. London: Routledge and Kegan Paul, Ltd., 1966.

Wanklin, J. M., et al. A comparative study of elderly mental patients hospital and resident of homes for the aged. *J. Gerontol.*, 1958, *13*, 60–69.

Williams, Warren S., and Jaco, E. Gartly. An evaluation of functional psychoses in old age. *Am. J. Psychiat.*, 1958, *114*, 910–916.

3
Isolation, Social Adjustment and Mental Disorder in the Institutionalized and Community-Based Aged*
Ruth Bennett, Ph.D.

This chapter contains a review of research on social isolation, social adjustment and mental disorders conducted by myself, colleagues and students during the past 22 years. Some of this work has already appeared in review articles in published form (Bennett, 1973 a, b).

Research on social isolation was begun by our group in 1956 with a study of prognosis in mental disorders of the senium in which the records of 100 residents of a Jewish voluntary old age home were used. The purpose was to identify the characteristics that would differentiate those transferred to a mental hospital from those who were not. Five pre-entry characteristics of the aged that were found to be predictive of their transfer from the home to a mental hospital were: (1) their initially negative attitudes upon entering the Home; (2) their negative evaluations of themselves; (3) their low childhood socioeconomic level; (4) the fact that they had been socially isolated prior to entry; and (5) their being labeled a management problem in the Home.

In a paper based on some of these results (Tec and Bennett [Granick], 1959), the following findings concerning the relationship between pre-entry isolation and subsequent social adjustment were discussed: (1) Residents who were isolated prior to entry encountered difficulties in interacting with their peers. (2) Residents who were isolated prior to entry encountered difficulties in interacting with staff members. (3) Residents who were isolated prior to entry appeared

*Some of this research was part of a dissertation presented by the author at Columbia University in candidacy for the degree of doctor of philosophy. The author was advised by Frederic Zeman, M. D., Alvin Goldfarb, M. D. and other personnel of the Jewish Home and Hospital for the Aged, New York City. The author was also advised by Professors J. Zubin and H. Hyman of Columbia University. The author was also assisted by Lucille Nahemow, Ph.D. and by Henry J. Walton, M. D., D. P. M. of the University of Edinburgh, who conducted psychiatric examinations under a United States Public Health Service research fellowship. This study was supported by research grants M2775, awarded by the National Institute of Mental Health, 1957 and Continuation Grants, MH2775 and MH02775.

to be more likely to be transferred out of the home to a mental hospital, but this relationship was not significant.

In this study we discovered the isolation factor. At that time we suspected that there were possibly two or more syndromes related to similarly disruptive behavior found in the institutionalized aged: one was mental disorder, which probably led to the hospital; the other was what might be called the *isolation syndrome*, a semivoluntary or involuntary process that coincides with aging and results in desocialization or the loss of sensitivity to social cues necessary for adequate social functioning. Presumably, this deficit, if we may call it that, can be remedied or treated, whereas old-age mental disorders are more difficult to treat.

Given limitations of case record studies, a direct study of 100 elderly residents of a home was undertaken. The relations between adjustment and social isolation experienced prior to entry as well as during adulthood in new admissions to a home for the aged were investigated. One hundred consecutive admissions to a home for the aged were interviewed three times, once on admission and again at one- and two-month intervals. Data on six-month adjustment were collected from social work case records, and from interviews with recreation workers in the Home. The methods of participant observation, sociological analysis, interviews and content analysis were used to study the normative structure of the Home in order to construct socialization and social adjustment indices. Social adjustment was measured in terms of three indices called conformity, integration and evaluation. Socialization referred to the learning of social norms and was thought to precede social adjustment.

Socialization

Socialization generally refers to the process by which individuals learn about, and orient themselves to, the social norms of a group into which they enter. For the most part, the literature on socialization concentrates on the training of the young. Parsons (1951) wrote:

The acquisition of the requisite orientations for satisfactory functioning in a role is a learning process, but it is not learning in general, but a particular part of learning. This process will be called the process of *socialization* . . . . (p. 205)

He went on to say:

The term socialization in its current usage in the literature refers primarily to the process of child development . . . but it should be made clear that the term is here used in a broader sense than the current one to designate the learning of *any* orientations of functional significance to the operation of a system of complementary role-expectations. In this sense, socialization, like learning, goes on throughout life. (p. 207)

Parsons used the concept of socialization to refer primarily to orientations to a system of interaction. It was used in our research on isolation and adjustment in this way, and referred to the ability on the part of individuals to perceive social norms and to show awareness of affairs pertaining to the group. In short, it refers to the ability of the new admission to "learn the ropes" of the Home. Operationally, an accurate social cognition refers to the ability to see things as a majority of others do. Newcomb (1959) wrote that perceiving things as others do, does not imply conformity with what is done.

The factor of socialization as used in this study had not been studied directly before this research. It had been used as an intervening variable within the framework of communication theory. For example, Gibb (1954) reported that one of the characteristics of a leader is that he "shows awareness of affairs pertaining to the group." It has always been assumed by sociologists that social systems must socialize new members or risk the possibility of system disequilibration or disintegration.

Once norms are investigated, people may be compared on their ability to perceive them, and an individual's rate of learning the framework of his social milieu may be assessed.

Social Adjustment

Social scientists assume that in order for new recruits to adjust to a group into which they enter, they must first be socialized (i.e., learn its norms). At the time this study was conducted, there was no clear-cut definition of the concept of social adjustment in the literature except that it appeared to be distinguishable from the concept of personal adjustment. Personal adjustment usually refers to such phenomena as "need satisfaction," feelings of satisfaction and good morale—in sum, subjective states of contentment.

Social adjustment was seen to differ conceptually from personal adjustment in that it contains within it the notion of living up to the expectations of others. Pollak (1948) gave the following definition of social adjustment:

Patterns of adjustment in their broadest range can be conveniently covered by the term social adjustment which in its common-sense meaning refers to all efforts of human beings to find more satisfactory ways of getting along with one another. In this sense, it includes the efforts of an individual to satisfy his personal needs as well as to live up to the expectations of others . . . . (p. 6)

Barrabee et al. (1955) wrote that the "term social adjustment can be considered as either a 'process' or an 'evaluation'. As a process, social adjustment is a dynamic concept that includes both doing and feeling . . . " (p. 252). For construction of a scale to measure adjustment to the community in individuals released from mental hospitals, they defined social adjustment as follows: "The degree to which a person fulfills the normative social expectations of behavior that constitute his roles."

Oberleder (1957, pp. 60–61), who had staff members select a group of "troublesome" and a group of "adjusted" residents of the Home we studied, set up criteria of being troublesome and being adjusted. The "troublesome" resident is "the resident who you feel could be classed as a 'management problem' on the basis of behavior difficulties which have arisen or have become exaggerated in the home."

In the study described here social adjustment was defined as being composed of three components: (1) social integration, (2) social evaluation and (3) conformity to social norms relevant to the Home as a whole. A well-adjusted individual is one who is integrated, thinks highly of the Home and conforms to its norms. It should be noted that adjustment to the Home as a whole was being observed rather than adjustment to any particular cliques or subgroups.

Integration was defined as participating in many activities in the Home and is the opposite of isolation, which refers to having relatively few contacts.

The term positive social evaluations refers to having a relatively high opinion of various facets of the Home of which one is a member. This implies that the individual is using this organization as a positive reference group and feels highly invested in its affairs.

Conformity refers to behavior that is enacted in accord with social norms and expectations; it is the opposite of deviance, which is defined by Parsons (1951) as:

Tendencies . . . to depart from conformity with the normative standards which have come to be set up as the common culture. A tendency to deviance in this sense is a process of motivated action on the part of an actor who has unquestionably had a full opportunity to learn the requisite orientations, tending to deviate from the complementary expectations of conformity with common standards so far as these are relevant to the definitions of his role. (p. 206)

Insofar as was possible, indices used in this study reflect the theoretical definitions of concepts listed above.

THE FIRST STUDY

The general hypothesis of this study was that isolation of aged individuals prior to admission renders them less able to adapt to a new social milieu into which they move.
The specific hypotheses were:

1. Socially isolated individuals are more poorly socialized to their new environment.
2. Lifelong isolates are most poorly socialized.
3. Those who are involuntarily isolated in old age are more poorly socialized than those who have never been isolated.
4. Socially isolated individuals of all types are poorly adjusted to their environment.
5. Lifelong isolates will be most poorly adjusted.
6. Those who are involuntarily isolated in old age will adjust more poorly than those who have never been isolated.

The home for aged was conceptualized as a factor that disrupts a characteristic mode of adaptation found among the aged in the community. In its place, the home resocializes the aged to the new way of life of a total institution.
Two additional specific hypotheses tested in line with the theoretical position stated above were as follows:

1. Socialization to the home is an intervening factor which mediates between isolation experienced prior to entry and social adjustment to a home for aged. Thus, those individuals who adapt to the home will be those who become socialized to the way in which the home functions.

2. There is a positive relation between three dimensions of adjust-
    ment: integration, evaluation and conformity. These behaviors
    are expected to relate to each other with increased strength as
    the home takes a greater hold upon individuals over time. The
    relation between isolation experienced prior to entry and adap-
    tation is not expected to increase over time.

Method

One hundred residents of a home for aged were interviewed once
on admission, and again at intervals of both one and two months after
admission. Initial interviews were focused on obtaining background
information and, specifically, information concerning the amount of
social isolation experienced immediately prior to entry and in the
course of adulthood. The one- and two-month postadmission interviews were designed to assess the degree of socialization, integration
and conformity and the quality of evaluations of the Home after one
and two months of residence.

Six indices were constructed to facilitate analysis of the data: (1)
the Pre-Entry (Past Month) Isolation Index, described in Chapter 2;
(2) the Adulthood Isolation Index, described in Chapter 2; (3) the
one- and two-month socialization index; (4) the one- and two-month
integration index; (5) the one- and two-month evaluation index; (6)
the one- and two-month conformity index.

The socialization and conformity indices were based upon a measure of social norms that was obtained through assessment of consensus on how things get done among new residents. Consensus
refers to agreement among 50% or more of those who gave any response at all.

Because the background factors of age and physical status were
associated with the socialization and adjustment variables, an attempt
was made to control for their effects by holding them constant when
analyzing the relations between any two sets of variables. The factors
of sex and amount of education were associated with evaluation and
conformity so that an attempt was made to control for them when
relating evaluations to conformity.

In order to obtain some indication of the validity of the adjustment
measures as well as follow-up information, social work records were
used, and a social work index of adjustment was constructed.

Findings

The scores obtained on the Pre-Entry Isolation Index ranged from 1 to 9; the median score was 4.47. Table 3.1 shows that 59 of the respondents reported contact with fewer than five people in the month prior to admission to the Home and were, therefore, considered to be isolated in old age. The other 41 reported that they had seen at least five different people (or three people, and had attended at least one organization meeting) and were regarded as nonisolates in old age.

Scores on the Adulthood Isolation Index ranged from 5 to 24 points; the median score was 16.50. On this index, as on the former, a score below median indicates relative isolation. Table 3.2 shows the distribution of scores on the Adulthood Isolation Index.

Isolation and Adjustment Over Time

Table 3.3 contains a correlation matrix indicating the relations between all of the indices used at three points in time. Isolates tended to be poorly integrated after both one month and two months of residence. However, at two months when age and physical status were held constant, this relationship between isolation and integration disappeared.

The interrelations between the various components of adjustment increased over time. That is, with the passage of time, individuals who became integrated were likely to conform and make positive evaluations of the Home. Similarly, individuals who conformed were likely to be integrated and made positive evaluations of the Home. The relations between isolation and socialization and between isolation and integration were lower at all times than were the interrelations between the various components of adjustment. Moreover, the relations between isolation and socialization and between isolation and integration did not increase with time. Thus, processes internal to the Home were thought to be more significant determinants of behavior over time in the organization than was the position occupied by the resident prior to entry. Although the interrelations between adjustment factors increased with time, the relations between socialization and these adjustment factors tended to decrease with time. Thus, socialization may be seen as a process that differs from adjustment. In the home studied, adjustment generally improved with time (Bennett and Nahemow, 1965), as is reported on page 36.

Table 3.1. Frequency Distribution of Pre-Entry Isolation Scores

Pre-entry isolation scores	Frequency
0	0
1	9
2	15
3	18
4	17
5	10
6	14
7	11
8	4
9	2
10	0
N 100	
Median 4.47	

Table 3.2. Frequency Distributions of Adulthood Isolation Scores

Adulthood isolation scores	Frequency
0	
1	
2	
3	
4	
5	2
6	
7	2
8	
9	4
10	2
11	5
12	7
13	7
14	9
15	7
16	10
17	11
18	9
19	8
20	7
21	6
22	
23	3
24	1
25	
26	
27	N 100
28	Median 16.5
29	
31	
32	

Table 3.3. Spearman Rho Correlations between Social Isolation and Social Adjustment at Selected Time Intervals after Admission and during the First Year of Residence

Factors	Adulthood Isolation	Past Month Isolation	1-Month Socialization	2-Month Socialization	1-month Integration	2-month Integration	1-Month Evaluation	2-Month Evaluation	1-Month Conformity	2-Month Conformity	1-6-Month Adjustment	1-12-Month Adjustment
Adulthood Isolation												
Past month isolation	.55**											
1-Month socialization	.23*	.27**										
2-Month socialization	.22*	.27**	.79***									
1-Month integration	.21*	.16	.51***	.53***								
2-Month integration	.23*	.22*	.50***	.48***	.67***							
1-Month evaluation	-.02	.07	.26**	.26**	.32**	.46***						
2-Month evaluation	-.04	.08	.12	.10	.17	.41***	.19*					
1-Month conformity	-.00	-.02	.08	.00	.17	.17	.37**	.35**				
2-Month conformity	.11	.13	.02	-.04	.05	.14	.18	.41***	.58***			
1-6 Month adjustment	.09	.17	.32**	.26**	.28**	.36**	.47***	.40*	.34**	.43***		
6-12 Month adjustment	.24*	.11	.07	.11	.22*	.26**	.25**	.27**	.21*	.36**	.48***	

*Significant at .05 level.
**Significant at .01 level.
***Significant at .001 level.

TWO-YEAR FOLLOW-UP OF ISOLATION AND ADJUSTMENT

Forty-five survivors of the sample were interviewed again after two years, and an additional 51 residents who had entered the Home consecutively just before and just after the original group were also obtained, in all totaling 96 residents who had been in the Home between one and three years. About two-thirds of the sample were women. All were of the Jewish faith; about two-thirds of the sample were born in Europe. Some had no schooling, and some were college graduates; the average resident had completed elementary school. Every resident had some physical disability, though none was bedridden. It was the policy of the Home at the time of the original study to exclude applicants with a history of psychiatric disorder.

Procedure

Each resident was interviewed three times after entry: once within a week, once one month later and once two months later. Forty-five were seen after two years.

Findings

As noted above, adjustment improved with time—after one month, two months and two years of residence. After one month in the Home, 15 residents did not participate in a single activity, by two months this number was reduced to 12, and after two years of residence there were only 2 residents who did not participate in any activity. The average resident began the process of becoming integrated into the Home soon after entrance. After one month's stay most of the residents had attended at least one activity or associated themselves with one informal friendship group. The median integration score after one month indicated that the average number of activities attended was between two and three. By two months the median integration score had risen to about three. After two years of residence the average resident attended between four and five activities in the Home, though he may not have been active in clubs or held jobs or written articles for the Home's newspaper.

Changes also occurred in the residents' evaluations of the Home with increased tenure. When residents first entered, they were asked what they thought of various aspects of life in the Home. Many gave unqualified responses, which in most cases were positive. At two months, there were fewer unqualified positive responses, and after two years of residence, there were even fewer. Unqualified positive responses showed a progressive decline on two-thirds of the items. Unqualified negative responses showed no pattern. Rather, the major source of change was in the proportions of mixed responses.

The proportions of mixed responses increased with increased stay in the Home. After having been in the Home for two years, nearly one-third of the residents gave a mixed response to the question, "How do you feel about the neighbors on your floor?" An example of a mixed response is "I like some but not others." After one month, only 8% of the residents gave such responses. The percent of residents giving mixed responses increased for every question asked. Conforming behavior was exhibited early. At one month 72% of the residents reported no overt conflict with their roommates, 88% of the residents reported no conflict with tablemates, 58% said they would not ask staff members to have their room changed, and 74% said they tipped the help. The norm of tipping is rather interesting. A large proportion of the residents gave tips to the help as soon as they entered despite the fact that they were violating a policy of the Home. It was one of the few subgroup norms found among residents that did not parallel staff norms.

The findings indicated that there were characteristic patterns of adjustment, and that over a two-year period changes occurred that were different for each component of adjustment, suggesting that components are independent. The findings also suggested that the phases of adjustment are independent, and that one may conceive of an early phase and a late phase. A further indication of the independence of adjustment phases came from the manner in which the adjustment components related to one another at the three time periods.

Table 3.4 shows the correlations between components of adjustment at one month, two months and two years.

Generally the size of the correlations decreased with time. At one month, all three adjustment components intercorrelated positively and significantly. At two months, this was even more marked. By two years these correlations had decreased. Thus, there was evidence that adjustment became less unitary over time and that it may make little sense to use a global concept of long-range adjustment.

The fact that adjustment became less unitary with time had implications for the observability of residents' behavior by social workers.

Table 3.4. Correlations between Components of Adjustment at One Month, Two Months and Two Years

	One Month	Two Months	Two Years
Integration and evaluation	+.32***	+.41***	+.21**
Evaluation and conformity	+.37***	+.41***	+.37***
Integration and conformity	+.17*	+.14	−.03

***$p < .001$.
**$p < .01$.
*$p < .05$.

Table 3.5. Correlations between Adjustment Indices and Social Workers' Estimates of Adjustment

Adjustment Indices	Social Workers' Estimates	
One Month		
Integration	+.24	$p < .01$
Conformity	+.34	$p < .001$
Evaluations	+.42	$p < .001$
Two Months		
Integration	+.36	$p < .001$
Conformity	+.43	$p < .001$
Evaluations	+.40	$p < .001$
Two Years		
Integration	−.23	$p < .05$
Conformity	+.05	NS
Evaluations	−.10	NS

Table 3.5 shows the correlation coefficients between adjustment components measured at one month, two months and two years and social workers' early and late estimates of residents' adjustment. Social workers generally evaluated residents' early adjustment at about six months and from then on wrote annual summaries.

In order to obtain the maximum amount of information on social workers' estimates of adjustment, a composite adjustment measure was obtained from case records. Data were collected on the following items: (1) general adjustment, (2) relationship with roommates, and (3) complaints about various aspects of life in the Home. A scoring system was devised, and a positive report on an item was scored as 2, no information as 1 and a negative report as 0. There was no information in the records on at least one item for about half the sample.

Table 3.5 shows that all of the one- and two-month adjustment components correlated significantly with social workers' estimates, and that the size of the correlations had increased by two months. The two-month interval was closer to the point at which the social workers made their estimates, which makes the increased size of the correlations understandable. However, at two years there was no positive relation between adjustment measures and social workers' estimates.

There were no significant relationships between isolation experienced prior to entry and the adjustment components of conformity, evaluation and integration at two years.

The findings indicated that the adjustment factors of integration, evaluation and conformity were independent processes. They also indicated that adjustment phases in a home for the aged were independent and at least two phases, an early and a late one, emerged; these phases correspond, perhaps, to the role labels of "newcomer" and "oldtimer." The evidence lends support to a theoretical note written by Tréanton (1962). He wrote that the concept of social adjustment was inherited from the nineteenth-century intellectual tradition but was becoming less frequently used in the social sciences because, like the concepts of personality or morale, it had an ambiguous meaning even if personal was distinguished from social adjustment. Tréanton also thought that when studying older people, it was important to keep clearly separated: (1) the subject's verbal expression of satisfaction; and (2) the subject's *behavior* in social areas of life. The findings also lend support to an implication that the phases of adjustment are independent that comes from Rosen (1964), who wrote that "to understand what happens to an elderly person who enters a home for aged, one must view residence in the home as a process that has a beginning, a middle, and an end." (p. 130)

The implication of these findings is that to understand adjustment of any one individual at each adjustment phase, the pattern of the group must be understood. If the pattern is one of growing more discriminating in one's evaluations at two years, then an individual who complains is not deviant even if he was a well known "eager beaver" on entry. Also, the group must be considered in trying to change a norm (e.g., the practice of tipping).

Socialization Effects

Socialization to the Home acted as an intervening process. Both isolates and nonisolates who were poorly socialized tended to be poorly integrated and had negative evaluations of the Home at both one and two months. Those who were poorly socialized were poorly adjusted— over time, that is—as was indicated in the social workers' charts at six months.

The relation between socialization and isolation was greater than the relation between isolation and any of the three components of adjustment, thus supporting a hypothesis that desocialization or the inability to perceive correct social cues was an intervening factor that mediated between isolation experienced prior to entry and subsequent poor adjustment. Early or rapid socialization, rather than socialization per se, related best to adjustment; that is, those who learned the norms in the first month adjusted better than those who subsequently learned them.

Isolation Patterns and Socialization

Contrary to expectation, socialization was not affected by duration of social isolation alone (Bennett and Nahemow, 1965). Table 3.6 shows that it was the pattern of isolation that was most relevant. Individuals who were relatively isolated in adulthood but not in old age were compared with those who were isolated for the first time as a concomitant of aging. The latter had greater difficulty becoming socialized, which suggested that there may be critical periods for desocialization, as well as resocialization. We also found that all isolation was bad as far as its effects on socialization go. The score differences between nonisolates and the group next in line were greater than between any other two groups. Although the voluntary or lifelong isolates (perhaps they were mentally disordered) did worst of all, they were not much worse than involuntary isolates. However, the gap widens between involuntary isolation and early isolation and widens most between early isolation and no isolation at all.

ISOLATION, SOCIALIZATION AND COGNITIVE PERFORMANCE

At one point, we asked the question: Can we explain the low scores in socialization found in isolates simply as indicative of either decline

Table 3.6. Relation between Pattern of Isolation and Socialization at Two Months

Isolation Pattern	Adulthood	Pre-Entry	N	Socialization At Two Months % Above Median
Integrated over the lifetime	Not isolated	Not isolated	31	77
Early isolate	Isolated	Not isolated	10	50
Involuntary isolate	Not isolated	Isolated	14	36
Lifelong or voluntary isolate	Isolated	Isolated	45	29

in cognitive ability associated with aging or with low education level found among the aged? In other words, is socialization just another measure of intelligence or intelligence-related abilities?

Two studies reported below were conducted in Jewish Home and Hospital for the Aged samples to determine if some types of social involvement were related to the maintenance of a high level of cognitive functioning in the aged. In the first investigation, attention was given to the relations between cognitive performance and social cognition, social isolation, age and mental status in three populations: "newcomers" and "oldtimers" residing in the home for the aged, and a "waiting-list" group residing in the community. The major hypothesis was that aged persons within a stimulating social environment can perform at relatively high levels on tests of cognitive ability as compared with their socially deprived counterparts. Age, per se, was not thought to be the factor accounting for poor cognitive functioning. The second study is a follow-up and will be reported separately.

INITIAL STUDY OF THE RELATIONSHIP BETWEEN ISOLATION, SOCIALIZATION AND TESTS OF COGNITIVE PERFORMANCE*

Sample

Sixty persons, over 65 years of age, comparable on background characteristics such as age, sex, education, religion and place of birth, and differing only as to place and length of residence, were interviewed. Two-thirds were female, one-third male. More than half of the total sample was in the 80–89-year-old range. Oldtimers had a mean age of 83.7, waiting-list subjects, 79.8, and newcomers, 79.3. Forty percent of the total sample had had at least some high school education. Over 40% of the total sample were native-born Americans. The newcomers had the highest proportion of foreign-born subjects. The sample was divided for place and length of residence as follows: 20 subjects on the Jewish Home and Hospital waiting list residing in the community, 20 newcomers to the Home and 20 oldtimers whose length of residence in the Home was more than one year. Newcomers who were selected included 20 consecutive new admissions to the Home who were English-speaking and could complete the interview. Oldtimers and waiting-list subjects were selected by staff members of the Home's social service department according to their estimate of the subjects' fluency in English and intactness.

Method

A standard interview lasting approximately one hour was administered. It contained the following indices:

1. The Adulthood Isolation Index, which is a measure of the extent of lifetime social contacts with family, friends, work and organizations (described in Chapter 2).

*The first of the two studies reported here is based in part on data from a 1968 Ed.D. thesis from the Department of Developmental Psychology, Teachers College, Columbia University, supported in part by a predoctoral fellowship from the New York State Department of Education. An earlier version of the paper was presented at the annual meetings of the Gerontological Society, in Denver, 1968. The second study was reported at the International Congress of Gerontology, Washington, D.C., in 1969 and published as "From 'Waiting on the List' to becoming a 'Newcomer' and an 'Oldtimer' in a Home for the Aged: Two Studies of Socialization and its impact upon Cognitive Functioning" by Comilda Weinstock, Ed.D., and Ruth Bennett, Ph.D., in *Aging and Human Development*, 1971, *2*, 46–58.

2. Past Month Isolation Index, which is a measure of number of social contacts outside of the institutions in the month prior to the interview (described in Chapter 2).
3. Three Wechsler Adult Intelligence Scale (WAIS) subtests, developed by Wechsler (1961): Information, containing 20 questions measuring basic knowledge of topics ranging from names of composers to the colors in the flag; Comprehension, containing 14 items designed to measure the ability to combine information into new forms; and Similarities, which is a measure of conceptualization with 13 items of paired association.
4. Socialization Index, which is a measure of the amount of information learned about life in the Home, consisting of 15 questions about formal procedures and norms in the Home such as "What kinds of activities are available during the day?" (described above).

Means and standard deviations of total scores were obtained for all indices. Pearson correlation coefficients were computed to demonstrate correlations between major independent and dependent variables.

Findings

The correlations between scores on all WAIS subtests and scores on the Socialization Index are shown in Table 3.7. For newcomers, correlation coefficients for the relations between all WAIS subtests and the Socialization Index were significantly higher than for those of the other two groups. The correlation coefficients were as follows: .77 for information and socialization, .51 for similarities and socialization, .78 for comprehension and socialization and .74 for WAIS total and socialization. Newcomers appeared to be so highly involved in a salient learning experience that they performed better on all measures of cognitive skills. The awareness brought about by involvement in the socialization process seemed to "spill over" to performance on the other tests. Level of education did not correlate with either WAIS subtests or the Socialization measure.

The data also showed that in residents as a group, socialization related most to the measure most like it, comprehension. This was most evident in the newcomer group. Thus, it appeared that residents who were stimulated by involvement in the socialization process were

Table 3.7. Correlation Coefficients between WAIS Subtests and Socialization Index for the Waiting List, Newcomer and Oldtimer Groups

WAIS Tests	Socialization Index		
	Waiting List Group	Newcomers	Oldtimers
Information	.45*	.77**	.60**
Similarities	.51*	.51*	.18
Comprehension	.57**	.78**	.65**
WAIS Total	.56**	.74**	.58**

* $p < .05$.
** $p < .01$.

more likely to demonstrate this stimulation by a high level of general comprehension and information, not just about life in the Home but also about the world outside.

Another factor thought to affect cognitive performance was that of social isolation. We expected the waiting-list group to be significantly more socially isolated than the resident groups, and thought social isolation might have explained the obtained results. However, this was not the case. There were no significant correlations between isolation and WAIS subtests. Furthermore, the waiting-list subjects were not significantly more isolated than the other two groups. Because no significant differences were found among groups with regard to either adulthood or present isolation, further analysis attempted to use the patterns of isolation described above. The four categories of isolation were as follows: (a) lifelong isolates—those subjects who had below-median scores on both the Adulthood and Past Month Isolation indices; (b) old age isolates (involuntary isolates)—those subjects who had above-median scores on the Adulthood Isolation Index but below-median scores on the Past Month Isolation Index; (c) old age non isolates—those subjects who scored below the median on the Adulthood Isolation Index but above the median on Past Month Isolation; (d) lifelong non isolates—those subjects who scored above the median on both the Adulthood Isolation and Past Month Isolation indices.

When subjects were divided according to these patterns of isolation, there were some interesting differences. Table 3.8 shows the relationship between patterns of isolation and cognitive performance in the

Table 3.8. Mean Test Scores According to Patterns of Isolation for Waiting List, Newcomer and Oldtimer Groups

WAIS Tests	Waiting-List Group				Newcomers				Oldtimers			
	Life-Long Isol.	Old Age Isol.	Old Age Non-Isol.*	Life-Long Non-Isol.	Life-Long Isol.	Old Age Isol.	Old Age Non-Isol.	Life-Long Non-Isol.	Life-Long Isol.	Old Age Isol.	Old Age Non-Isol.	Life-Long Non-Isol.
Information	13.6	8.8		15.0	8.3	18.5	17.5	14.5	12.0	11.0	17.0	16.2
Similarities	4.3	3.8		7.9	1.5	7.3	9.3	10.2	5.9	5.2	11.0	5.4
Comprehension	13.1	9.8		16.1	9.8	17.8	17.0	16.5	15.3	13.0	23.0	19.6
WAIS total	32.1	22.3		39.0	19.5	43.5	43.8	41.2	34.6	29.2	51.0	39.2
Socialization Index	9.8	8.5		10.9	15.0	21.0	18.5	18.3	19.1	18.8	21.3	27.0
Total number	9	4		7	4	6	4	6	7	5	3	5

*None found in this group.

newcomer, oldtimer and waiting-list groups. Cognitive functioning was affected by pattern of isolation but not in the same manner for all groups. Old age or involuntary isolates were found to have the lowest scores on WAIS subtests within the waiting-list and oldtimer groups. These subjects seemed to suffer those effects of social isolation that are concomitant with aging. However, in the newcomer group those who had been involuntarily isolated performed very well on WAIS tests. Among newcomers, the involuntary isolates actually performed better on most cognitive and socialization measures than did the lifelong nonisolates in the other groups. This indicates that involuntary isolates benefit most from renewed contacts.

In the oldtimer group, involuntary isolates performed significantly worse on all tests than did any others in their group. However, even involuntarily isolated oldtimers performed better than involuntarily isolated waiting-list persons. Prolonged institutionalization seems to have had a positive effect on lifelong isolates. Of all lifelong isolates, those in the oldtimer group did best. This finding is encouraging in that it indicates that lifelong isolates may benefit from social contacts just as involuntary isolates do, though it may take them longer to do so.

These findings are highly suggestive of the need to consider the reversal of what appears to be desocialization among the aged.

FOLLOW-UP STUDY OF THE RELATIONS BETWEEN SOCIAL ISOLATION, SOCIALIZATION AND TESTS OF COGNITIVE PERFORMANCE

One year after the initial study, a follow-up was conducted at the same institution. The longitudinal extension tested the general hypothesis that the socialization process is a salient, highly stimulating learning experience that positively affects other cognitive processes. Therefore, we expected to find that a former waiting-list person when interviewed in his new status as a newcomer resident of the Home would not show signs of decline. We did not know what to predict for oldtimers grown even older.

Sample

The original sample had been divided for place and length of residence as follows: 20 waiting-list subjects who resided in the community, 20 newcomers to the Home whose length of residence was under two months (with an average of less than two weeks) and 20 oldtimers whose length of residence in the Home ranged from one to 18 years with an average of two years. The newcomer group consisted of 20 consecutive new admissions to the Home who were English-speaking and could complete the interview. Oldtimers and waiting-list subjects in the original sample were selected by members of the Home's social service department staff according to their estimate of the subjects' fluency in English and their intactness. The follow-up sample included all surviving subjects from the original sample whose physical and mental condition permitted their participating in an hour-long interview. The survivors constituted a group of 28 females and 12 males (the original sample of 60 had 41 females and 19 males). There were twelve surviving former waiting-list persons who became newcomers at the time of the second study. (Seven persons from the original 20 waiting-list persons were deceased and one had a serious heart condition that prevented her from being tested.) There were 14 former newcomers surviving as oldtimers in the duration of the second study. Four of the original 20 newcomers were deceased, and two had become senile and could not be retested. There were 14 former oldtimers who were given second interviews, and these old-timers were "older oldtimers" at the time of the second study. Three of the original sample of 20 were deceased, and three were senile and noninterviewable. Mean chronological ages of the groups were 79 years for former waiting-list persons, 80 for former newcomers and 85 for former oldtimers.

Method

A standard interview lasting approximately one hour was adminis-tered. It was identical to that given to the original sample in the first study. Means and standard deviations of total scores were obtained for all indices. Pearson correlation coefficients were computed to dem-onstrate correlations between major independent and dependent variables.

Results

The mean scores on the WAIS subtests for each group at each time are shown in Table 3.9. The former waiting-list group is the only group

Table 3.9.   Mean Scores on WAIS Subtests and Socialization Index for Studies 1 and 2 for Survivors Only (N = 40)

WAIS Subtest	Waiting-List Group		Newcomers		Oldtimers	
	Study 1	Study 2	Study 1	Study 2	Study 1	Study 2
Information	13.1	13.6	17.1	16.5	14.0	12.8
Similarities	6.6	8.1	8.6	9.4	6.9	4.8
Comprehension	13.9	14.9	17.1	16.5	17.0	14.1
WAIS total	33.7	36.6	42.8	42.5	37.9	31.6
Socialization Index	10.1	22.8	18.5	22.8	20.3	22.9

to show a gain in all WAIS measures. Former newcomers, who had been performing at the highest level of all groups on the first interview, continued to demonstrate their superiority on tests scores one year later, with only minor losses over time. Former oldtimers showed the most precipitous, general drop in scores on all WAIS subtests. However, the oldtimers continued to show some evidence of maintenance of cognitive functioning by their gain in socialization scores. Unlike the pattern of scores on the WAIS subtests, socialization scores appear to reflect increments in experience obtained with increased tenure in the Home. These scores show improvement through all groups, but the gains diminish, perhaps indicating that there is little more to be learned.

The factors of age, isolation and mental status were investigated to determine their effect on cognitive performance. Within groups, age per se did not relate to gains or losses on WAIS subtests. On retest oldtimers showed greatest losses, but this was evidently unrelated to chronological age because age cohorts in the waiting-list and newcomer groups did not show such losses.

Cognitive functioning was affected by patterns of isolation but not in the same manner for all groups (Table 3.10). All oldtimers demonstrated a drop in mean total WAIS score; involuntary or old age isolates showed the most precipitous drop. However, in the former waiting-list group, those who had been isolated performed very well on WAIS retesting. All isolates from the former waiting list actually performed better as newcomers on most cognitive measures. This had

Table 3.10.   Mean Total WAIS Scores According to Patterns of Isolation for Study 1 and Study 1 for All Groups

	Former Waiting-List Group		Former Newcomers		Former Oldtimers	
	Study 1	Study 2	Study 1	Study 2	Study 1	Study 2
Lifelong isolates	36.8	43.6	47.0	46.5	42.5	35.5
Old age isolates	10.0	16.0	32.3	29.3	49.0	33.0
Old age nonisolates	16.0	14.0	46.3	37.3	34.3	32.0
Lifelong nonisolates	38.8	38.4	48.3	50.3	35.0	29.7

been true of the newcomer group in the first study. At that time, in newcomers, the involuntary isolates actually performed better on cognitive and socialization measures than did the lifelong nonisolates in the other groups. The implication is that isolates benefited most from the environmental stimulation. Looking at the newcomer group, we can see that anyone with a history of isolation shows a drop in total WAIS score. Only the lifelong nonisolates continue to improve. Presumably, again, the Home seems to provide the initial force for maintenance, and/or improvement in intellectual functioning. However, with time this stimulation diminishes, and there is overall decline for all in the old-timer group.

It was concluded that socialization is not the same thing as cognitive ability in that it often improves with time and tenure in an organization, whereas scores on cognitive tests do not. Moreover, age alone does not account for declines in cognitive performance. Those individuals who appeared to be engaged in the socialization process in order to adapt to the role of newcomer showed gains in cognitive performance, despite their age. Former newcomers, who were beginning to settle into and accept oldtimer status, showed some signs of loss in performance on tests of cognitive abilities. Oldtimers showed the greatest percentage of loss in scores on all WAIS subtests of any of the three groups. Furthermore, they seemed most negatively affected by social isolation. Former waiting-list persons, stimulated by new experiences, were socially and cognitively alert.

Institutionalization affects people differently. After about one year of residence, the transition from newcomer to oldtimer status is achieved, and the lack of challenge and new roles and relationships seems to be in evidence. Newcomer status provides residents with daily stimulation and tangible goals, whereas oldtimer status—although not without privileges—provides fewer incentives because the environment and the residents have stabilized to a great extent. Using a longitudinal design, the follow-up study confirmed earlier findings of the first cross-sectional study. The longitudinal design of this study enabled us to pinpoint in time the onset of negative effects of institutionalization, insofar as cognitive performance is concerned.

Is the improved performance of the former waiting-list group a function of the increased stimulation provided during the socialization process? Or is it a mark of their greater fitness for survival? In point of fact, more former waiting-list persons died between Time 1 and Time 2 than was true for the other two groups. However, if survivorship alone accounted for improved performance, then the former newcomers who supposedly represented the most "fit" at Time 1 should have continued to improve cognitively with continued institutionalization. This was clearly not the case; although more of them survived, more of them declined in cognitive performance.

Studies by Lieberman and Lakin (1963) noted the debilitating and deteriorative aspects of institutionalization of the aged. Programs in institutions seek to introduce worklike recreation activities to attempt to maintain some semblance of former life patterns. But our data seem to point to the need for some further thought about institutional programming. If meaningful learning experiences or positive milestones were provided throughout a resident's length of tenure in an institution, then oldtimers might show fewer cognitive decrements.

ISOLATION AND MENTAL DISORDER*

In the course of conducting our studies it was not clear whether the maladjusted behavior seen in the institutionalized aged was the result of isolation or of mental disorder. Nor did we know if both isolation and maladjustment resulted from mental disorder. Thus, we

---

*This section appeared in part in the following publications: H. Walton, R. Bennett, and L. Nahemow, Psychiatric illness and adjustment in a home for the aged, in J. Zubin (Ed.), *Can psychopathology be measured?*, *Annals of the New York Academy of Science*, 1964, *105*, 897-918; H. H. Walton, R. Bennett, and L. Nahemow, The significance of psychiatric symptomatology for social adaptation, *British Journal of Psychiatry*, 1964, *110*, 548-554.

conducted a study to determine if isolation, mental disorder and mal-adjustment were correlated.

We did not assume that mental disorder was an inevitable by-product of aging, nor was it confounded with maladjustment to the degree that this occurred in the past.

The separation of these concepts probably was facilitated by the pioneering work of Alvin Goldfarb and his associates (1961). From his and other studies it seemed clear that institutionalization was not an adequate indicator of presence of mental disorder in the aged. Often, institutionalization occurred for social or health reasons. Moreover, type of institution into which an individual was placed was not necessarily indicative of type of disorder suffered by the elderly.

Adjustment

Adjustment is something more than conformity. It is behaving according to social expectations because one knows what those expectations are and can believe in them and/or accept them. Presumably one does this with some degree of personal satisfaction and comfort.

Adjustment is not blind conformity, nor is it robotlike behavior.

Mental Disorder

It is possible to distinguish patients with organic brain syndrome from those with other kinds of pathology:

1. *Organic Disorders.* Often the organic disorders are grouped and labeled as dementia. According to Wang (1973) organic brain syndrome is a disorder resulting from a diffuse impairment of brain tissue, characterized by memory loss, disorientation, impairment of intellectual function and judgment and lability and shallowness of affect.

2. *Functional Disorders.* Depression and anxiety are very common clinical problems among old people. The depression experienced by many elderly persons differs in several respects from that commonly seen among younger adults. In old age depression is often due largely to low self-esteem, which Busse (1961) found was secondary to the many losses inevitably associated with old age and retirement. Both depression and anxiety can be easily overlooked, because in this

age group their affective manifestations are often overshadowed by somatic symptoms. Although the latter are sometimes related to the physiological changes concomitant with the emotional disturbances, they do have a clear physical basis in many cases. Elderly persons with depression and anxiety often become preoccupied with their somatic symptoms and then use them, consciously or unconsciously, as a means to avoid recognizing their unpleasant emotions.

Utilizing the concepts defined above, we undertook a study of the relations between psychiatric illness, adjustment and pre-entry isolation. Fifty successive admissions to a home for the aged who were already studied in earlier research were independently evaluated by a psychiatrist,* using a crude standard diagnostic instrument of geriatric mental state to gauge impairment of intellectual ability and presence of functional psychiatric illness.

Description of the Sample

The mental status of a group of 50 elderly people in the Home was ascertained by psychiatric examination. They were surviving members of 100 persons, already studied extensively and described above, who had been consecutively admitted to the Home between May 1958 and August 1959. The original sample consisted of 28 men and 72 women ranging in age from 61 to 95 years. (It was the policy of this Home to exclude known psychotic persons from admission, as was noted earlier.) Fifty subjects had died or were in the infirmary. The survivors formed the study sample: 11 men and 39 women ranging in age from 63 to 92 years. These remaining 50 individuals may have differed psychiatrically from the members of the original sample not surviving. All accompanying sociological data below were pertinent only to the 50 persons examined clinically for psychiatric impairment.

The Psychiatric Examination

Clinical assessment of each subject took about 45 minutes. The examination covered uniform ground for each subject, and a previously

---

*Dr. Henry Walton of the University of Edinburgh conducted this work as a postdoctoral fellow of the United States Public Health Service.

devised protocol form was used for recording interview data. A life history was obtained and the mental status ascertained. In addition to the interview seeking to diagnose in each subject the presence or absence of organic brain syndrome and functional psychiatric disorder, a number of (1) scales were administered, and (2) items checked:

1. *Scales.* The Mental Status Questionnaire (Kahn et al., 1960) was given to each subject. This questionnaire consists of ten questions, dealing with orientation in time and place and including information items (e.g., "Who is the president of the U.S.A.?"). It tests the subject's cognitive functioning.

2. *Items Checked.* The protocol form included specific queries about: (a) sleeping behavior—whether the subject reported sleeping well, fairly well or poorly; (b) mood—whether the subject reported feeling in good spirits most of the time or seldom; (c) tendency to worry—whether little or a fair amount.

Assessment of Social Adjustment

Interviews were conducted independently of the psychiatric examination to assess the degree to which each person was adjusted to the Home. A standard interview was used to measure the three components of social adjustment, which are integration, conformity and evaluations of the Home (described above).

Findings

The data on the 50 psychiatric evaluation protocols were punched on IBM cards, together with a number of social indices measured independently by a sociologist and a social psychologist. The findings (Walton et al., 1964a,b) showed no relation between isolation prior to entry and mental disorder. However, some forms of mental disorder did result in extreme maladjustment. Residents suffering from senile and arteriosclerotic dementia were differentiated from those with functional psychiatric disorder by their social adjustment patterns. Those with dementia adjusted to the institutional environment with a sense of subjective satisfaction, and in accordance with the institution's expectations. But those with functional psychiatric disorder were unhappy and, in addition to this personal discomfort, did not conform to social rules or live up to the expectations and requirements of other residents.

This supported our earlier suspicion that there were two or possibly more "syndromes" that were related to similarly maladjusted behavior found among the elderly: one of them mental disorder, the other what may be termed the "isolation–desocialization" syndrome, which is not unlike what has in mental patients been termed the "social breakdown syndrome" (Gruenberg et al., 1969). The isolation–desocialization syndrome is a process that may be described as follows: An old person in the community becomes first isolated, then desocialized; he enters a home for the aged or some other setting, misperceives the norms and blunders socially soon after entrance; others single him out, perhaps as a "troublemaker," and avoid him; he then becomes involved in overt conflict with staff members and/or other residents. Presumably, long experience with social isolation would not be as great a handicap to an old person who remained in the community as it is to one who is relocated and must adjust socially. Presumably, also, the effects of the latter syndrome are more easily reversible than are those of mental disorder.

EXTENSION OF STUDIES OF ISOLATION, SOCIAL ADJUSTMENT AND MENTAL DISORDERS TO FIVE SETTINGS FOR THE AGED*

Old people are called on to adjust to a wide variety of social situations for which they may or may not be prepared. Irrespective of their physical and psychological status, most people who live to old age are required to make many changes in their way of life. Social skills, like other skills, are learned, and, as the results of previous research suggest, may be lost through disuse.

The various institutional settings to which the aged may have to adjust include: hospitals, mental hospitals, homes for the aged, nursing homes and terminal-care hospitals. In each of these social situations, different criteria of adjustment are established and must be met.

---

*This research was supported under USPHS Grant CD 00029 of the U.S.P.H.S., the Effect of Residences for the Aged on Social Adjustment awarded to Ruth Bennett, Ph.D., Biometrics Research, N.Y. State Department of Mental Hygiene, April 1, 1962–June 1, 1964. The early part of this research was supported by MH2775 and continuation grant MH02775 awarded to Dr. Bennett by the National Institute of Mental Health.

Many aged individuals may be called on to adjust to several new institutional settings, any one of which may work against subsequent adjustment to another. For example, there is the kind of adjustment an old person is expected to make on a mental hospital ward, where one general criterion of adjustment is to show the desire to get well and leave. Often this adjustment may be accompanied by verbal complaints, which are considered by staff members as signs of improvement. The opposite is true of a home for aged, where adjustment means settling down permanently and coming to feel that the Home is a real home. In homes, complaining is usually taken as a sign of poor adjustment. In order to understand what makes for social adjustment across institutional settings for the aged, research is needed on the nature of the social environment and criteria of adjustment in each setting.

The study of the adjustment of the aged has been of interest to scientists in several fields. However, almost no notice has been taken of the fact that the aged are required to adjust to numerous residential settings with distinct differences in organizational structure and adjustment requirements. Many of the settings to which the aged are expected to adjust fall into the class of organizations known conceptually as "total institutions." Goffman (1960) noted that "total institutions . . . are social hybrids, part residential community, part formal organization and therein lies their special sociological interest. There are other reasons . . . for being interested in them too. These establishments are the forcing houses for changing persons in our society. Each is a natural experiment, typically harsh on what can be done to the self" (p. 453).

Somer and Osmond (1961) noted that despite the fact that total institutions are believed to be the "forcing houses for changing persons," almost no systematic research is available on their impact on inmates. When research on either personal or social adjustment is available, it rarely focuses on the relation between institutional structure and adjustment.

The theory behind the research described below was that the organizational structure of an institution for the aged has an effect on the adjustment of new admissions. The general hypothesis tested was this: The greater the degree of totality of the institution is, the easier old people who had been isolated prior to entry find the adjustment process. This hypothesis was based, in part, on the notion that highly totalistic institutions have clearly enunciated norms and rules. This hypothesis was also based in part on the findings of previous research, described above, conducted on the relation between social isolation and adjustment in residents of a home for aged. In this study the findings substantiated the prediction that social adjustment to a home for aged is dependent, in part, on the degree to which individuals were socially isolated prior to entry. The findings showed that isolates had great difficulty becoming socialized to a home and that this difficulty, rather than isolation per se, resulted in poor adjustment. The findings also showed that it was the speed of, rather than the fact of, socialization that facilitated adjustment. It was concluded that a formal orientation process, early in their stay, may be particularly useful for those who have experienced isolation prior to entering an institution. It was assumed that highly totalistic institutions make orientation programs available to inmates.

There are many types of institutions that house the aged, of which the total institution is one type. The following residential settings were selected for study: (1) a geriatric apartment residence, (2) a nursing home, (3) a geriatric division of a mental hospital, (4) an apartment house and (5) a home for aged. These settings are structurally differentiated along a hypothetical continuum representing their degree of totality. An index constructed for measuring the degree of totality of institutions contained ten criteria according to which each residential setting for the aged could be given a score indicating high, medium or low totality. An institution that would receive a high score displays the following characteristics: (1) it is designed as a permanent residence; (2) all activities occur within the confines of the institution; (3) all activities are scheduled sequentially for the entire group of inmates; (4) provisions are made for formal "indoctrination" periods in order to teach the rules and standards of good and bad conduct; (5) provisions are made for continual observation by the staff of the inmate population; (6) standardized, objective rewards and punishments are used; (7) inmates are not allowed to make decisions regarding their time or property; (8) most personal property is removed from inmates; (9) inmates are recruited on an involuntary basis; and (10) congregate living is required as a residential pattern.

Sample

One hundred sixty-one new admissions to five settings for the elderly were studied.

Procedure

Interviews were conducted by two interviewers who used standard interview forms. At the beginning of the first interview, the resident was told that the interviewer was conducting research for an outside agency. Each resident was assured that everything he said would be kept confidential.

During the admission interview, information was obtained concerning the residents' previous interpersonal contacts. During the subsequent interviews, information concerning socialization and adjustment was obtained, which was used in the indices.

The admission interview used was similar for all settings. Isolation data were collected in this interview.

The adjustment interviews were constructed to contain some indices designed specifically for each institutional setting because the norms and criteria of adjustment varied markedly.

Findings

In order to determine where normative information was more accessible, that is, more clear-cut and explicit, preliminary research was undertaken in the form of participant observation and interviews with staff members and oldtimers in the five residential settings for the aged. The findings obtained showed a curvilinear relation between totality and clarity and complexity of social adjustment criteria. This came as a total surprise to us.

Residential settings with both extremely high and low totality ratings had in common the fact that adjustment criteria were vague. The criteria of adjustment in moderately total institutions such as the home and the apartment residence were clear and explicit, centering around participation in activities and other forms of social integration. The institutions at both extremes on the totality dimension, the state hospital, which was most total, and the housing project, which was the least total, had in common the fact that they were

Table 3.11. Mean MSQ Scores in Five Residential Settings for the Aged

	N	Mean MSQ
State hospital	11	7.33
Nursing home	20	6.20
Home for aged (institution)	52*	8.86
Home for aged (apartment)	10	9.00
Public housing development	20	8.75

*The MSQ was administered to only 52 persons in the JHHA.

not perceived by staff or by residents as being permanent residences (despite the fact that they usually were). It was tentatively concluded that normative information was best disseminated in residential settings that were communities and that served as permanent homes for all residents (Bennett and Nahemow, 1965).

Table 3.11 indicates the Mental Status Questionaire (MSQ) differences in the five settings for the aged. By and large, in all settings, residents were able to participate in interviews despite imperfect MSQ scores. It is interesting that average MSQ was lower in a nursing home than in a mental hospital.

Table 3.12 contains some of the data to test the hypothesis. The experience of pre-entry isolation appeared to have a negative effect on socialization in all but one setting, the apartment residence, where it would appear there was no relationship. The correlation was significant in a home for the aged where the 100 were studied ($r = .27$; $p < .05$), though it was higher in a public housing project where the sample was smaller ($r = .40; p = NS$). The experience of isolation immediately prior to entry was a better predictor of poor socialization than isolation experienced during adulthood. The correlations between pre-entry isolation and integration were positive but low except in a nursing home. There were no significant correlations between pre-entry isolation and other aspects of adjustment. However, this was thought to be a function of sample size. The correlations between both isolation and socialization and integration, although positive throughout, were generally higher in the moderately total institutions than in settings at both extremes of totality. Thus, a new admission to a nursing home, home for the aged or apartment residence who had

TABLE 3.12.   Correlations between Pre-Entry Isolation and One-Month Socialization and Adjustment in Five Residential Settings for the Aged Ranging from High to Low Totality

Setting	N	Correlations			
		Pre-Entry Isol. & Soc.	Pre-Entry Isol. & Integ.	Pre-Entry Isol. & Eval.	Pre-Entry Isol. & Conf.
State hospital (high)	11	.21	.07	.11	.05
Nursing home	20	.15	.57*	-.10	-.15
Home for aged (institution)	100	.27*	.16	.07	.02
Home for aged (apartment)	10	-.01	.21	-.12	-.21
Public housing development (low)	20	.40	.07	-.10	**

*Sig. at .05 level.
**No conformity measure was available for the apartment house.

TABLE 3.13.   Correlations between Socialization and the Integration, Evaluation and Conformity Components of Adjustment after One Month of Residence in Five Residential Settings for the Aged Ranging From High to Low Totality

Setting	N	Correlations		
		Socialization & Integration	Socialization & Evaluation	Socialization & Conformity
State hospital (high)	11	.24	-.37	-.57
Nursing home	20	.32	-.05	.12
Home for aged (institution)	100	.51	.26	.03
Home for aged (apartment)	10	.59	.11	-.09
Public housing development (low)	20	.23	-.16	*

*No data on conformity were obtained in Public Housing Development.

been either isolated or unsocialized usually did not become well integrated into the home's activities. On the other hand, in the mental hospital and the housing development, integration was not as affected by prior isolation or poor socialization.

Table 3.13 shows the correlations between socialization and the three adjustment measures of integration, evaluation and socialization.

There is a marked curvilinear relationship between the correlations and institutional totality. For all of the adjustment indicators, socialization varies positively with adjustment in the middle range of totality, indicating that in such settings lack of knowledge of social norms is a handicap as far as adjustment is concerned.

CURRENT RESEARCH ON THE NEW YORK CITY ELDERLY

The research on social isolation, social adjustment and mental disorders was extended into studying a random sample of the New York City elderly using some of the measures described above, as well as others. (For details see Gurland et al., 1980.)

Although we did not repeat all of the measures used in earlier institution studies in our current studies of the aged in the community, we did include many measures of health, mental health and social problems, as well as the two measures of isolation.

Table 3.14 shows that the AI and PMI yield similar measures of central tendency over time and in a wide variety of settings. This is an indication of the hardiness of these measures. They yield similar correlations with each other in a variety of settings that may attest to their validity. The one exception is their low correlation in a mental hospital, but inconsistency of behavior is thought to be symptomatic of mental disorders.

In the New York City sample, isolation per se is not highly correlated with mental disorders. However, analysis of the New York City data by type of isolate yielded some interesting findings.

Table 3.14 contains measures of central tendency on the Adulthood Isolation Index and the Past Month Isolation Index as well as correlations of the two indexes obtained in 7 samples studied in different New York City settings from 1957 to the present (Bennett, R. 1973a; 1973b). As can be seen, the mean PMI and AI vary across settings, but in a predictable fashion. The most isolated individuals are those who were chosen for this purpose. They were individuals selected for partici-

Table 3.14. Measures of Central Tendency of Adulthood Isolation (AI) Index and Past Month Isolation (PMI) Index and Correlation Coefficients between AI and PMI Indices by Place of Study, Year of Study, and Number of Persons Studied.

Place Of Study	Year	N	Means AI	Means PMI	Correlations AI and PMI
1) Jewish Home and Hospital, NYC New admissions in 1 year	1959	100	16.5*	4.5*	.55**
2) Jewish Home and Hospital, NYC New admissions in 1 month	1965	10	19.0	5.4	.52
3) Towers Home, NYC New admissions in 1 month	1965	20	14.1	2.7	.59
4) Brooklyn State Hospital New admissions in 1 month Geriatric Ward, NYC	1965	11	14.2	3.3	.19
5) Mott Haven Housing Project Tenants in newly opened senior housing	1965	20	14.5	6.3	.66
6) Participants in a Friendly Visiting Program West Side, NYC (selected from low PMI)	1973	11	12.9	1.4	.61
7) NYC (random sample)	1976	AI 395*** PMI 411***	21.7	4.6	.48

*Median scores. All other scores of central tendency are means.
**Rho correlations. All other correlations are Pearson product – moment correlations.
***These numbers are slightly lower than the total NYC sample of 445, due to missing data.

pation in a Friendly Visiting Program precisely because they were isolated (Mulligan, Sr. Mary Anne and Bennett, R., 1978). The least isolated are the community aged, with a variety of institutional groups obtaining scores between the most and least extreme scores.

There is moderate test-retest reliability in AI, which contains background information which should not vary at two points in time. Initially, this was found by retesting 1/2 of the first group of 100 studied at JHHA about two years later and obtaining a correlation coefficient of .62. AI scores from the first five settings are within five points of each other showing a certain consistency over time for admissions to three nursing homes, tenants in senior housing, and admissions to a state mental hospital. PMI scores from these settings are within four points, which is slightly greater fluctuation given the lower range (0–10 versus 0–32) of this measure. The number of recent social contacts would be expected to vary slightly more than the number of lifelong contacts due to short term factors that might level out with time.

There is construct validity to the PMI and AI as indicated by the moderately high correlations in the .5–.6 range between the two over time and in different populations. Only the Brooklyn State Hospital group differed and that makes sense, since these patients were recent admissions and hospitalization and psychiatric disorder would be expected to disrupt their usual patterns of social activity. The correlation obtained in the New York City sample recently is consistent with those obtained in earlier community samples.

We have learned from our research conducted over the past 22 years, as well as the current U.S.-U.K. Study, that isolation is not a unitary concept and perhaps not even an additive one. Measures of isolation are not always highly associated with each other. For instance, AI and PMI are correlated only .19 for a sample of Brooklyn State patients.

Table 3.15 contains the mean scores on 16 "rational" scales of the New York City sample for each category of isolation. (These analyses have been repeated with homogeneous scales and have yielded similar though better results.) In New York City involuntary isolates obtained the worst scores on 12 out of 16 scales. In seven instances isolation pattern differences were highly significant. The recent actives did worst or tied for worst on three scales, all measures of physical disorder. Perhaps this fact reflects increased social contact experienced by physically impaired respondents who move in with relatives. It seems the New York group that is most mentally and physically impaired is the group that early in life showed an inclination to be social but who, for many reasons, became socially deprived late in life. Such persons might be those who are forced to look after an invalided spouse, those who are recently widowed or those whose neighborhood has deteriorated causing them to fear going outdoors. Probably, there are as many reasons for involuntary isolation as there are cases. The involuntary isolates are most socially disadvantaged as well as physically impaired. Both voluntary and involuntary isolates live in crime ridden neighborhoods and suffer environmental deprivation. Coupled with findings on the high rate of institutionalization of voluntary or lifelong isolates, this may mean only those in very good health stay in the community. Early isolates seem to be fairly

Table 3.15. Mean Scores on "Rational" Scales by Isolation Pattern
for New York City

| Rational Scale | Isolation Pattern | | | |
	Lifelong Isolate $N = 126$	Involuntary Isolate $N = 63$	Recent Active $N = 73$	Lifelong Active $N = 127$
Dementia	1.44	1.60	.93	.72*
Depression	3.42	3.52	3.01	2.98
Cancer	.17	.22	.42	.23*
Arthritis	2.24	2.24	2.05	1.97
Heart	.69	.78	.78	.77
Neural Impairment	.07	.10	.10	.03
Total Illness	5.07	6.27	5.89	4.69
Observed Immobility	.99	1.87	.88	.48**
Total Immobility	2.40	4.76	2.30	1.57**
Observed Perceptual Impairment	.24	.25	.14	.19
Total Perceptual Impairment	1.58	2.17	1.18	1.24
Inadequate Activity	4.36	5.17	3.63	2.76**
Finance	.86	.93	.74	.62
Observed Environ. Deprivation	.61	.62	.47	.33*
Crime	.80	.94	.66	.76
Total Environ. Deprivation	3.06	3.19	2.67	2.09*

*F test for one way analysis of variance significant, $p < .05$.
**$p < .01$.

independent, unmarried, poor females who prepare their own meals and are lower in service use than involuntary isolates. Almost a fifth have no confidante, yet most can find some means of summoning help in time of need.

SUMMARY AND CONCLUSIONS

Studying isolation in institutional settings, we found that isolation had a negative impact on the aged. It seemed to lead to desocialization, impaired social adjustment and reduced interaction. Isolation was not synonymous with mental disorder in the aged though it seemed to result in some behavior patterns associated with mental disorder, specifically poor social adjustment and poor cognitive functioning. Those in institutions at the middle range of totality seemed at a greater disadvantage due to isolation than those in the community.

The experience of pre-entry isolation appeared to have a negative effect on socialization in all but one residential setting. The experience of isolation immediately prior to entry was a better predictor of poor socialization than isolation experienced during an individual's entire adulthood. The correlations between pre-entry isolation and integration were generally smaller than those between socialization and integration. The correlations of both isolation and socialization with integration, although positive throughout, were generally higher in the moderately total institutions than in settings at both extremes of totality. Thus, a new admission to a nursing home, home for the aged or apartment resident who had been either isolated or unsocialized usually did not become well integrated into the home's activities. On the other hand, in the mental hospital and housing development, integration was not as affected by prior isolation or poor socialization.

Socialization seemed only slightly related to mental status. Possibly, use of a more comprehensive psychiatric status instrument would have strengthened this finding. (Such a measure is being used in our current studies in New York City and London.) Normative knowledge and, possibly, its internalization did not appear to be a prerequisite for adjustment in residential settings at either extreme of the totality continuum. It was related positively and significantly only in institutions of the middle range of totality. Perhaps only in the middle totality range is how well one does socially a clear reflection of what one knows. It may be that size or degree of cohesion in institutions of the middle range explains why that is where adjustment criteria were found to be explicit and clearly communicated. This finding was thought to reflect the needs of such institutions, which are structured like small communities and serve as permanent homes for their residents. Perhaps such institutions rely most heavily on an individual's learning and, possibly, internalizing norms so that he may be able to regulate his own conduct. Thus, an individual who was not socialized early was seriously disadvantaged in such settings.

At the extreme high and extreme low end of the totality continuum were a state hospital and a public housing development. Neither seemed much of a community, and both were large. Nor is it clear whether those who run them think of themselves as working in institutions serving as permanent communities for residents. In such settings many intervening factors may play a role in the relation between socialization and adjustment. There may be a large difference between a person's knowing what's expected of him and his doing it. The factors of personality and pathology may play a greater role in a large and anonymous setting than in a smaller one. Those who know what to do may feel less inclined to do it in a setting in which they do not feel personally committed to the community norms. Such residential settings may, therefore, rely more heavily on external agents and sanctions to enforce and uphold norms than on individual internalization of norms.

The relationship between isolation and desocialization was thought to be a crucial one for adaptation to institutionalization. However, we were concerned about whether or not our measures of socialization were merely a reflection of intelligence or education level. Thus, we conducted two studies to rule out this possibility. One study was of the relationship between isolation, socialization and cognitive performance in a home for aged; the second study was a one-year follow-up of the same relationships.

We found that socialization is not the same thing as cognitive ability, in that it often improves with time and tenure in an organization, whereas scores on cognitive tests do not. Moreover, age alone does not account for declines in cognitive performance. Nor does education. Those individuals who appeared to be engaged in the socialization process in order to adapt to the role of newcomer showed gains in cognitive performance, despite their age. Former newcomers, who were beginning to settle into and accept oldtimer status, showed some signs of loss in performance on tests of cognitive abilities. Oldtimers showed the greatest percentage of loss in scores of all WAIS subtests of any of the three groups. Furthermore, they seemed most negatively affected by social isolation. Former waiting-list persons, stimulated by new experiences, were socially and cognitively alert.

Institutionalization seemed to affect people differently. After about one year of residence the transition from newcomer to oldtimer status is achieved, and the lack of challenge and new roles and relationships seems to be in evidence. Newcomer status provides residents with daily stimulation and tangible goals, whereas oldtimer status—although not without privileges—provides fewer incentives to learn because the environment and the residents have stabilized to a great extent. Using a longitudinal design, the follow-up study confirmed earlier findings of the first cross-sectional study. The longitudinal design enabled us to determine that the WAIS scores of waiting-list persons improved when they became newcomers, whereas those of the former newcomers and oldtimers did not improve.

Cognitive functioning was affected by patterns of isolation but not in the same manner for all groups. All oldtimers demonstrated a drop in mean total WAIS score, involuntary or old age isolates showing the most precipitous drop. However, in the former waiting-list group, those who had been isolated performed very well on WAIS retesting. All isolates from the former waiting list actually performed better as newcomers on most cognitive measures. This had been true of the newcomer group in the first study. At that time, in newcomers, the involuntary isolates actually performed better on cognitive and socialization measures than did the lifelong nonisolates in the other groups. The implication is that isolates benefitted most from the environmental stimulation encountered on becoming a newcomer in an institution.

Although we did not repeat all of the measures used in earlier institution studies in our current studies of the aged in the community in New York City and London, we did include many measures of health, mental health and social problems, and it was thought appropriate to discuss some of the early findings from these current studies in this chapter.

In the general community the effects of isolation seemed different from those in institutions. Despite the many measures used in this study, it was difficult to determine whether or not there was a relationship between isolation and desocialization. Probably this was because we did not include any direct measures of desocialization in the community. Isolation per se was not related to the various types of mental disorder studied.

However, when we looked at isolation patterns, we found that the results of our earlier studies had some bearing upon the results of the current community studies. For the random sample of the New York City aged studied, patterns of isolation seemed important for health, mental health and social problems. We found that in the New York City elderly, involuntary or recent isolates did more poorly on a number of measures including measures of mobility, mental health and physical impairment. They also used more services than did the others.

This is not inconsistent with the findings of our earlier research, which suggests that involuntary isolates are good targets for social programs because they improve when offered help (e.g., upon institutionalization or when included in therapy groups). Voluntary or lifelong isolates seem to be more socially disadvantaged rather than physically or mentally handicapped. Early isolates, that is, those isolated early in life but not later, seem to be fairly independent, unmarried, poor females, who prepare their own meals and are least likely to use services. Those who are socially integrated throughout life appear to be the best off. Nonetheless, they too might be toppled by a crisis if one is to judge by the fact that they depend on others, usually elderly spouses, to prepare their meals.

REFERENCES

Barrabee, P., Barrabee, E., and Finesinger, J. E. A normative social adjustment scale, *Am. J. Psychiat.*, 1955–56, *112*, 252–259.

Bennett, R. Living conditions and everyday needs of the aged with specific reference to social isolation. *J. Aging Hum. Dev.*, 1973a, *IV*, *3*, 179–198.

Bennett, R. Isolation and isolation-reducing programs. *Bull. N.Y. Acad. Med.*, 2nd Ser., Dec. 1973b, *49*, *12*, 1143–1163.

Bennett, R., and Nahemow, L. Institutional totality and criteria of social adjustment in residential settings for the aged. *J. Soc. Issues*, 1965, *XXI*, 44–78.

Busse, E. W. Psychoneurotic reactions and defense mechanisms in the aged. In P. H. Hoch and J. Zubin (Eds.), *Psychopathology of Aging*. New York: Grune and Stratton, 1961, 274–284.

Gibb, Ceil A. Leadership. In G. Lindzey (Ed.), *Handbook of Social Psychology*, Vol. 2. Cambridge, Mass.: Addison-Wesley, 1954, 891.

Goffman, E. Characteristics of total institutions. In M. R. Stein, A. J. Vidich, and D. M. White (Eds.), *Identify and Anxiety: Survival of the Person in Mass Society*. Glencoe: The Free Press, 1960, 449–479.

Goldfarb, A. I. Summarization of survey findings from the office of the consultant on services for the aged. In New York State Legislature, Joint Committee, Albany, 1961, 37–41.

Gruenberg, E. N., Snow, H. B., and Bennett, C. L. Preventing the social breakdown syndrome. In F. C. Redlich (Ed.), *Social Psychiatry*. Baltimore: Williams & Wilkins Co., 1969.

Gurland, B., Bennett, R., and Wilder, D. Planning for the elderly in New York City: An assessment of depression, dementia and isolation. *Proceedings of Research Utilization Workshop.* Community Council of Greater N. Y. (March, 1980).

Kahn, Robert, Goldfarb, A. I., Pollack, M., and Peck, A. Brief objective measures for the determination of mental status in the aged. *Am. J. Psychiat.*, 1960, *117*, 326–328.

Lieberman, M. A., and Lakin, M. On becoming an institutionalized aged person. In R. H. Williams, C. Tibbitts, and W. Donahue (Eds.), *Processes of Aging*, Vol.*1*. New York: Atherton Press, 1963.

Mulligan, Sister Mary Anne, and Bennett, R. Assessment of mental health and social problems during multiple friendly visits: The development and evaluation of a friendly visiting program for the isolated elderly. *J. Aging Hum. Dev.*, 1978, *8, 1*, 43-65.

Newcomb, Theodore. The study of consensus. In Robert K. Merton et al. (Eds.), *Sociology Today*. New York: Basic Books, 1959, 279-280.

Oberleder, Muriel. Attitudes related to adjustment in a home for aged. Unpublished Ph.D. thesis, Columbia University, 1957.

Parsons, Talcott. *The Social System*. Glencoe, Ill.: Free Press, 1951.

Pollak, Otto. *Social Adjustment in Old Age*. New York: Social Science Research Council, 1948.

Rosen, T. The resident's adjustment to the home. In M. Leeds and E. Shore (Eds.), *Geriatric Institutional Management*. New York: G. P. Putnam's Sons, 1964, 119-130.

Sommer, R., and Osmond, Humphry. Symptoms of institutional care. *Social Problems*, Winter 1961, *3*, 254-263.

Tec, N., and Bennett [Granick], R. Social isolation and difficulties in social interaction of residents of a home for aged. *Social Problems*, 1959-1960, Vol. 7, No. 1, 226-232.

Treanton, Jean-Rene. Some sociological considerations on the problem of adjustment in older people. In C. Tibbetts and W. Donahue (Eds.), *Social and Psychological Aspects of Aging*. New York: Columbia University Press, 1962, 655.

Walton, H. H., Bennett, R., and Nahemow, L. The significance of psychiatric symptomatology for social adaptation. *Br. J. Psychiat.*, 1964a, *110*, 548-554.

Walton, H., Bennett, R., and Nahemow, L. Psychiatric illness and adjustment in a home for the aged. In J. Zubin (Ed.), Can psychopathology be measured? *Ann. N. Y. Acad. Sci.*, 1964b, *105*, 897-918.

Wechsler, D. Intelligence, memory and the aging process. In P. Hoch and J. Zubin (Eds.), *Psychopathology of Aging*. New York: Grune and Stratton, 1961.

Weinstock, C., and Bennett, R. From "waiting on the list" to becoming a "newcomer" and an "oldtimer" in a home for the aged: Two studies of socialization and its impact upon cognitive functioning. *J. Aging Hum. Dev.*, Vol. *2*, 1971, *1*, 46-58.

4
Isolation and Attitudinal Dependency*
Lucille Nahemow, Ph.D.**

At one point in our series of studies, we thought isolation might have some salutary personality effects, possibly resulting in the attitudinal independence of the "old codger," who would do battle against any restraints. This idea was generated from the popular literature of the fifties and early sixties, which contained a typical central character who was a rugged individualist, as in the novel of Ayn Rand or the movies of Humphrey Bogart. This hero was so strong that he did not seem to need other people (or perhaps so weak that he could not bear to test his ego strength in an intimate relationship—but we are getting ahead of our story, drawing upon the insights of the present research and the ideological climate of the seventies). He never discussed his ideas with anyone; his convictions were born full-blown, like Minerva.

The popular stereotype of the aged was similar in some ways. Old people were seen as rigid and stubborn, as folks who were set in their ways and apt to dig in their heels and refuse to listen to reason. A recent Harris poll found that the public view of most people over 65 is that they are *not* "very openminded or adaptable." Unfortunately, it was true that even those who were themselves over 65 "bought the stereotypes of older people as closed-minded" (Harris, 1975, p. 47).

*This research was part of a dissertation presented by the author to Columbia University in candidacy for the degree of doctor of philosophy, where she was advised by Professors R. Christie, J. Zubin and H. Hyman.

The author is grateful for the assistance of Drs. Frederic Zeman, Alvin Goldfarb and other personnel of the Jewish Home and Hospital for the Aged in New York City. She is indebted to Drs. Ruth Bennett, Comilda Weinstock and Henry Walton, who interviewed residents of the home.

This research was supported by XIMH predoctoral fellowship #14, 144 C1, a U. S. Public Health service research fellowship and NIMH grants MH02775 and CD00029.

**Director, Division of Gerontology, Office of Urban Health Affairs, New York University School of Medicine.

We do know that many old people have become socially isolated (Blau, 1957; Clausen and Kohn, 1954; Cumming and Henry, 1961; Drake, 1958; Lundberg and Lawsing, 1949; Parsons, 1942; Tec and Bennett [Granick], 1959; Townsend, 1957). Has social isolation had an impact on attitude maintenance? If so, has it led to rigidly held opinions, or has it led to persuasibility or attitudinal dependency or an acquiescent response set?

Attitudinal Dependency

Hovland et al. (1953) introduced the concept of persuasibility when they noted that two factors simultaneously determine the effectiveness of a persuasive appeal: the reaction to the content of the message, and the individual's susceptibility to persuasion. A factor of general persuasibility appeared to exist independent of subject matter (Janis and Hovland, 1959). Jackson and Messick (1961) defined the "acquiescent response set" as the tendency to agree, or disagree, with items regardless of their content. McGee (1962a) found general agreement in the literature that there was a trait of response acquiescence. Couch and Keniston (1960) considered this tendency to agree a significant and functional part of personality structure.

It has been found that individuals are particularly susceptible to persuasive appeals when they are unfamiliar with the pros and cons of an issue. Hovland et al. (1953) found that people who were uninformed, or perceived themselves as uninformed on a topic, were highly persuasible on items relating to that topic. They also found that when individuals were presented with two-sided appeals and thus became familiar with some of the arguments used by the opposition, they were subsequently better able to resist persuasive appeals presented by the opposition. In a similar vein, Papageorgis and McGuire (1961) found that when subjects were pre-exposed to refutations of some counterarguments, their beliefs were more resistant to change. Manis and Blake (1963) immunized college students by providing them with counterarguments against persuasive messages to which they were later exposed. McGuire (1961) postulated that people tend to defend their beliefs by avoiding exposure to counterarguments rather than by developing positive supports for them. This results in an "ideologically aseptic environment" in which the person tends to remain highly confident about his or her beliefs, but also to be highly vulnerable to strong counterarguments when forced exposure to them occurs.

Individuals who are socially isolated have little opportunity to be exposed to arguments countering their point of view. Thus, it appears that social isolation would lead to attitudinal dependency. If this is true, old people would be expected to show a high level of attitudinal dependency.

Studies of the aged have found them to be an acquiescent group. Kogan (1961a) developed a scale to measure attitudes toward old people. He administered this scale and several others to samples of young and old people (Kogan, 1961b). His data showed that older people were more prone than the younger ones to "set" as opposed to "content" consistency in responding to attitude items. He concluded that the phenomenon of acquiescence could probably be considered an important personality correlate of aging or an aspect of an "old age" syndrome. Gergen and Back (1962) also found aged persons to be less opinionated than younger ones on public opinion polls.

As was seen in the previous chapter, Bennett and Nahemow (1965) found that most of the residents of a home for the aged were extremely isolated in the year preceding their entry. They found that isolated individuals had difficulty in becoming adjusted, and that involuntary isolates had as much difficulty as voluntary isolates. Bennett [Granick] and Nahemow (1961) found that isolates had great difficulty becoming socialized in a home, and that it made little difference if the isolation was recent or lifelong. Walton et al. (1964) found that lifelong isolation was not related to psychiatric diagnosis. A panel study over a two-year period showed that the reports of the residents of a home for the aged concerning the extent of their social isolation prior to entry were reliable over an extended time interval. They also found that individuals who were isolated prior to entry were isolated in the home (Bennett and Nahemow, 1965). Measures of persuasibility were obtained within the home for the aged in order to study the relationship between social isolation and attitudinal dependency.

The research hypothesis was that social isolation of residents in a home for the aged would correspond to heightened persuasibility.

METHOD

Subjects

Ninety-six residents of a home for the aged completed two interviews. The sample included all residents who had been admitted between one and three years prior to the investigation, except those who were unable to speak English, totally deaf or hospitalized. They averaged 82 years of age. Twenty-seven were men, and 69 were women. All were of the Jewish faith. Twenty-five were born in the United States, and the rest came from Europe. The average educational level was grammar school; the range was broad: six residents had no formal education at all, and five had graduated from college. Most had some physical disorder; for 44 these disorders were not greatly incapacitating, whereas the rest required regular nursing care.

Procedure

Every subject was interviewed twice, an average of six months elapsing between the first and the second interviews.* The interviews were conducted by different experimenters who were of the same age and sex. Each experimenter conducted half of the first and half of the second interviews.

Fifty residents were interviewed a third time during this interval by a psychiatrist who measured mental status and feelings of alienation, and made a psychiatric diagnosis.** The psychiatrist was not connected with the Home and did not have access to the data reported here. Details of the clinical assessment are provided in Chapter 3.

All staff members who had contact with residents provided lists of residents they worked with. Those questioned included occupational therapists, physical therapists, nurses, secretaries, volunteer workers, social workers, housekeepers and rabbis. Staff members who directed activities provided names of those who attended. Lists of residents who held office in clubs were obtained, as were lists of those who performed library and telephone duty. Copies of the "Home News" for two and a half years were obtained, and any article written by a resident in the sample was noted.

---

*Seven residents died or were hospitalized during the course of the experiment and were, therefore, dropped from the final analysis. No subjects were lost because of refusal to be interviewed. If a resident could not, or would not, complete an interview, it was completed at a later time. In an extreme case, the aid of the resident physician was enlisted, and ultimately all interviews were successfully completed.
**Scales used were the Mental Status Questionnaire (Kahn, et al., 1961) and Anomia (Srole, 1956).

Description of Indices

Social Isolation   Social isolation was defined as the absence of participation in activities that require interpersonal contact—the opposite of integration. Measures of integration both within and outside the home were obtained. It should be noted that the concept and measures of isolation used in this study refer only to those assessed within the institution.

Because a home for the aged is a self-contained community, social integration in the home could be measured sociometrically, that is, by asking others in the home about their participation with the residents in the sample. Because the sample consisted of all residents who entered the home one to three years prior to the study—a large proportion of the census of the home itself—this procedure could be followed for residents as well as staff without an enormous loss of information.

Sociometric data were obtained from each resident in the sample; everyone named all the people with whom they were friendly. Similarly, each staff member was asked whether the residents in the sample interacted with them in any way, and this information was added to lists obtained of participants in the Home Club, reporters for the Home newspaper, and so on. Every time an individual was mentioned as participating in the Home in any way, he/she received one point, and every time a resident was named as a friend, he/she received one point. A total integration score was obtained by adding together sociometric scores and staff reports of participation. Self reports were also obtained by asking the residents about their own participation.

Integration outside the Home. Most of the residents were permitted to leave the home when they chose, and visiting hours were frequent and flexible. In assessing integration outside the home, the resident's self report of outside contacts was the only measure available.

A point was assigned each time the subject left the home to visit someone, for each outside organization whose meetings the subject attended, for consulting individuals outside of the home or the mass media when faced with the necessity of making a decision and, finally, for maintaining an interest in world events.

Alienation   The five-item Anomia scale of Srole (1956) was administered to obtain a subjective measure of each person's sense of isolation from society.

Persuasibility Persuasibility was defined as a tendency on the part of the residents to agree with contradictory opinions expressed by two interviewers during persuasive appeals. Two measures of persuasibility were used: one dealing with issues of some importance, and another that was relatively topic-free. The first three of 17 pairs of contradictory statements comprising the opinion scale of persuasibility are shown in Figure 1.

Two forms of this scale were administered; in each case the statement was presented as the opinion of the interviewer. The items were balanced for positive and negative wording, conservative and liberal attitudes and oldfashioned and modern ideas. One side of an issue was presented during the first interview; the opposite side was presented during the second. A resident who agreed with both statements was considered persuasible. Theoretically, the scores could range from −17 for complete negativism to +17 for complete persuasibility.

The topic-free measure of persuasibility was administered in a similar manner (see Figure 2). During the first interview the resident was told that the interviewer preferred one pattern, and during the second that the interviewer preferred the other. Again, the persuasible individual would agree with both opposite choices.

Interview 1	Interview 2
I think that special housing should be built for older people so that they can have the companionship of people of their own age. What do you think?	I don't think that special housing should be built for older people because it's more interesting for them to have some young people around. What do you think?
I think that free speech in this country means that even a communist should be allowed to speak to any gathering. What do you think?	I think that free speech is fine but if we know that someone is a communist, he should not be permitted to speak. What do you think?
I don't think that hospital employees should be permitted to join unions because their complete loyalty should be toward the hospital. What do you think?	I think that hospital employees should be permitted to join unions the same way as any other worker in order to maintain their own self-respect. What do you think?

Figure 1. Opinion measure of persuasibility

Figure 2. Sample item from the picture-choice booklet

Results

Social Isolation Within the Home Despite the variety of activities offered in the Home, 65% of the residents did not attend any major activities; that is, they did not regularly attend club meetings, perform any voluntary jobs, hold office in a club or write articles for the Home newspaper. Forty-seven percent were not named as a friend or acquaintance by any of the other residents in our sample. Thirty-six percent of the sample apparently did not participate in any aspect of the social life of the Home. This finding was unrelated to age or sex, but did relate to functional health in that sicker residents tended to be less active. As might be expected, those who attended activities in the Home were likely to have made friends with other residents (see Figure 3).

As though to demonstrate that the Home is indeed a self-contained, total institution, we found that few residents maintained contacts outside the Home. Nearly a third of the sample never went out, and only about half had visited anyone outside the Home during their entire residency. More than half the residents said they would not consult anyone outside of the Home if they had to make an important decision. Only 12 claimed continued interest in world events. Again, it was found that those who were integrated in one sphere were likely

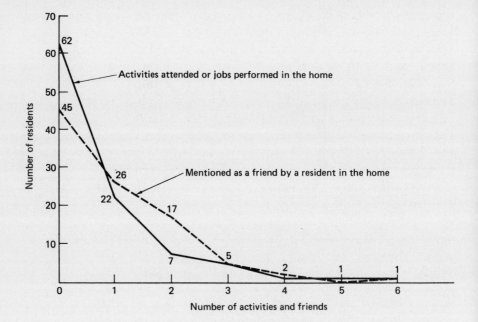

Figure 3.   Relationship between attending activities and being mentioned as a friend. $\chi^2 = 5.41; p < .01$

to be integrated in others. Those residents who were most active in the Home were also the ones who maintained outside contacts ($\chi^2 = 8.70, p < .01$).

Psychiatric Diagnosis and Self-report of Isolation   As would be expected, the self report of friends and activities were significantly related to those obtained from others in the Home ($\chi^2 = 9.43, p < .01$). The socio-metric measures of integration within the Home were considered the better estimate because they seemed less subject to fluctuations in mood than self report measures. This supposition was confirmed by the finding that although *no* relationship was found between integration in the Home, as measured by the reports of others, and psychiatric diagnosis, residents with functional mental disorders *reported* themselves as nonparticipants in the activities of the Home.

Persuasibility The residents were far more likely to agree with both examiners than to disagree with both. For the 17-item pairs comprising the opinion persuasibility scale, 28 to 63% of the residents agreed with both interviewers' contradictory statements. The median double-agreement was 41%. In contrast, only 2 to 10% of the residents disagreed with both statements. The median double-disagreement was 5%. The average subject agreed with both examiners 70% of the time. The distribution on the topic-free picture-choice booklet was similar. The average resident agreed with 62% of the interviewers' statements. The correlation between the meaningful-opinion persuasibility scale and the topic-free picture-choice scale was +.41. (Persuasibility scores are presented in Figure 4 for both types of material.)

Persuasibility was not related to age or to sex (the latter finding is unusual and will be discussed below).

Isolation and Persusibility The hypothesis that social isolates were more persuasible than those who became integrated into the social fabric of the Home was confirmed, as is shown in Table 4.1 and Figure 5. However, the difference was statistically significant only for the meaningful material. Feelings of alienation also correspond to heightened persuasibility to material with meaningful content ($r = .45$). Persuasibility was not related to psychiatric diagnosis.

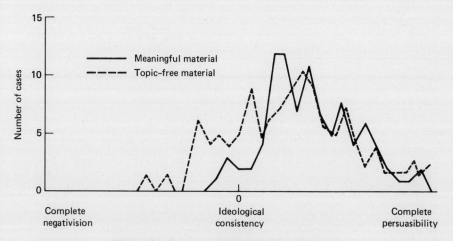

Figure 4. Scores on persuasibility measures

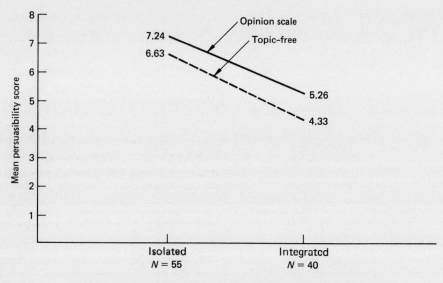

Figure 5. Relationship between isolation and persuasibility

Table 4.1. Mean persuasibility scores of isolated and integrated residents

Persuasability	Isolated[a]			Integrated			Difference	t
	M	N^b	SD	M	N	SD		
Opinion scale	7.24	55	4.03	5.26	39	2.77	.98	2.64**
Picture-choice scale	6.63	51	6.10	4.33	40	5.42	2.33	1.88

[a]Reports of others in the Home were cut at the median. Integrated residents are those with two or more contacts reported.

[b]Two Ss could not take the opinions scale because of language difficulties. Five Ss could not take the picture-choice scale because of blindness or near blindness.

**p $<$ .01 interpolation from E. S. Pearson and H. O. Hartley, *Biometrika Tables for Statisticians VI*, Cambridge University Press, 1956, p. 23. Two-tailed test used.

DISCUSSION

These results demonstrate that those residents of a home for aged who remained isolated from their peers after a year or two in residence were more persuasible than those who became integrated into the social life of the Home. The isolates were not the more obstinate people; far from it, they were vacillating and seemed confused regarding their own beliefs. It would appear that social isolates are deprived of social support for their opinions. They are also deprived of the opportunity to sharpen their opinions by defending them when they conflict with the sentiments of others. Newcomb (1950) first alluded to this mechanism with college students, saying, "One could expect that failure to become affiliated with primary and secondary groups in the community would leave the individual with 'unanchored' attitudes and hence more amenable to change." Abelson and Lesser (1959), who investigated the relationship between social isolation and persuasibility in children, found socially isolated boys more persuasible than sociometric stars in the classroom. Thus the relationship between social isolation and attitudinal dependence has been found at both ends of the life span.

The finding that even within a voluntary home for the aged that took pride in the wide spectrum of social activities provided for residents, people remained quite isolated, can be added to an extensive body of data showing that the aged are a socially isolated group of people and that the institutionalized aged are especially so (Rosow, 1962). In the sample studied, very few people had any interest in or contact with people or groups outside the Home. Within the Home, over one-third of the sample did not appear to have formed any social relationship at all.

Kogan (1961b) attributed the heightened acquiescence of the aged to the energy loss that is characteristic of the aging process. The present study shows that it may be better explained by the social isolation that they experience. In this study, social integration in the Home was not related to the age of the residents or to the length of their institutionalization. Therefore, age per se did not account for the persuasibility found. Neither did it account for the pervasive social isolation experienced. It was found that those residents who were integrated in one sphere of activity were integrated in others as well.

The fact that social isolation resulted in heightened persuasibility in regard to both content-free and meaningful material, almost equally, has profound implications. The bulk of the information regarding this issue shows that people are much more likely to vacillate on topic-free material that does not have great meaning to them (Janis et al., 1953). Perhaps in this case the loss of social support for opinions and sounding boards to test them out has been of such long duration that it has not only produced heightened susceptibility to persuasive communications concerning material with ideological content, but generalized to all areas of cognitive functioning. Thus, aged individuals who have been socially isolated show signs of having a general trait of persuasibility. Another possible explanation for this finding is that the residents were so insulated within the Home that, appearances to the contrary, the opinions items were no more meaningful to them than the picture-choice items. Therefore, they agreed with everything because they really had no point of view.

In the present study it was difficult to determine the extent to which the isolation experienced by a given individual in the sample was voluntary or involuntary. For most isolated residents there was an element of both. For example, some subjects emphasized the voluntary component when they explained that they kept out of trouble by not becoming close to anybody in the Home. Some emphasized the involuntary components when they complained that many of their old associates had died and that they themselves were not in good health. It cannot be said with certainty that because a person was ill, his isolation is of an involuntary nature. Although a statistical relationship was found between physical status and isolation, it was far from perfect.

Women have generally been found to be more persuasible than men. The present study is one of the few that does not report that typical result. We think that this is so probably because the interviewers were women, which was not the usual state of affairs at the time this study was undertaken. Is it that men were more likely to try to please women—or was it that women were more likely to be straight with other women? This issue may not be as trivial as it seems at first. It is possible that there is a tendency to give more socially desirable, less meaningful, responses to a person one perceives as dissimilar from oneself. The acquiescence of the elderly may be affected by the fact that it is always youngsters asking the questions.

Typically, this study raised more questions than it answered:

1. To what extent are the findings reported the result of aging? Would younger people who were equally isolated have been equally persuasible?
2. What role does institutionalization itself play in this syndrome? Would old people residing in the community be less acquiescent?
3. What was the effect of race and ethnicity on the expression of opinion?
4. Would people in different environments respond differently?
5. Did isolation really produce persuasibility, as had been implied throughout, or is it possible that the person who is too eager to please turns people off?

It was concluded that social isolation is related to persuasibility, and that this fact might well account for the findings of others that old people are highly persuasible (or acquiescent). Individuals who are not subjected to the contradictory opinions of others and who, by virtue of their social isolation, are not in a position to argue their opinions for the benefit of others, ultimately become unsure of their own point of view and are, therefore, highly vulnerable to persuasive communications. Thus the aged seem not to know their own minds. Senility? Hardly!—although it often masquerades as such. It can better be seen as the long-term effect of social deprivation.

REFERENCES

Abelson, R. P., and Lesser, G. S. In I. Janis and C. Hovland (Eds.), *Personality and Persuasibility*. New Haven: Yale University Press, 1959, 187-206.

Bennett, Ruth, and Nahemow, Lucille. The relations between social isolation, socialization and adjustment in residents of a home for aged. In M. P. Lawton and F. Lawton (Eds.), *Proceedings of Institute on Mentally Impaired Aged*. Philadelphia: Maurice Jacob Press, 1965, 90-108.

Bennett [Granick], R., and Nahemow, L. Preadmission isolation as a factor in adjustment to an old age home, in P. Hoch and J. Zubin (Eds.), *Psychopathology of Aging.*, New York: Grune & Stratton, 1961, 285-302.

Blau, Zena. Old age: A study of change in status. Unpublished doctoral dissertation, Columbia University, 1957.

Clausen, J., and Kohn, M. The ecological approach in social psychiatry. *Am. J. Sociol.*, 1954, *30*, 140-151.

Couch, A., and Keniston, K. Yeasayers and naysayers: Agreeing response set as a personality variable. *J. Abnorm. Soc. Psychol.*, 1960, *60*, 151-174.

Cumming, Elaine C. and Henry, William, *Growing Old*, New York: Basic Books, 1961.

Drake, J. T. *The Aged in American Society*. New York: Ronald Press, 1958.

Gergen, K. J., and Back, K. W. Communication in the interview and the disengaged respondent. Tech. Rep. 4. Paper read at American Psychol. Association, St. Louis, Sept. 1962.

Harris, L. *The Myth and Reality of Aging in America*. National Council on Aging, Washington, D. C., 1975.

Hovland, C., Janis, I., and Kelley, H. H. *Communication and Persuasion*. New Haven: Yale University Press, 1953.

Jackson, D. N., and Messick, S. Acquiescence and desirability as response determinants on the MMPI. *Educ. Psychol. Meas.*, 1961, *21*, 771-790.

Janis, I. L., and Hovland, C. *Personality and Persuasibility*. New Haven: Yale University Press, 1959.

Kahn, R. L., Goldfarb, A. I., Pollack, M., and Peck, A. Factors in selection of psychiatric treatment for institutionalized aged persons. *Am. J. Psychiat.*, 1961, *118*, 241.

Kogan, N. Attitudes toward old people: The development of a scale and an examination of correlates. *J. Abnorm. Soc. Psychol.*, 1961a, *62*, 44-54.

Kogan, N. Attitudes toward old people in an older sample. *J. Abnorm. Soc. Psychol.*, 1961b, *62*, 616-622.

Lundberg, G. A., and Lawsing, Margaret. The sociography of some community relations. In L. Wilson and W. Kolb (Eds.), *Sociological Analysis*. New York: Harcourt Brace, 1949, 271-286.

Manis, M., and Blake, J. B. Interpretation of persuasive messages as a function of prior immunization. *J. Abnorm. Soc. Psychol.*, 1963, *66*, 225-230.

McGee, R. K. The relationship between response style and personality variables: I The measurement of response acquiescence. *J. Abnorm. Soc. Psychol.*, 1962a, *64*, 229-233.

McGuire, W. J. The effectiveness of supportive and refutational defenses in immunizing and restoring beliefs against persuasion. *Sociometry*, 1961, *24*, 184-197.

Newcomb, T. M. *Social Psychology*. New York: Drysden Press, 1950.

Parsons, T. Age and Sex in the social structure of the United States. *Amer. Soc. Rev.*, 1942, *7*, 604-616.

Papageorgis, D., and McGuire, W. J. The generality of immunity to persuasion produced by pre-exposure to weakened counter-arguments. *J. Abnorm. Soc. Psychol.*, 1961, *62*, 475-481.

Rosow, I. Retirement housing and social integration. In C. Tibbits and W. Donahue (Eds.), *Social and Psychological Aspects of Aging*. New York: Columbia University Press, 1962, 329-339.

Srole, L. Social integration and certain correlaries: An exploratory study. *Am. Sociol. Rev.*, 1956, *21*, 709-716.

Tec, N., and Bennett (Granick), R. Social isolation and difficulties in social interaction of residents of a home for aged. *Social Problems*, 1959, *7*, 226-232.

Townsend, P. *The Family Life of Old People*. London: Routledge and Kegan, Paul, 1957.

Walton, H. J., Bennett, Ruth, and Nahemow, Lucille. Psychiatric illness and adjustment in a home for aged. *Ann. N. Y. Acad. Sci.*, 1964, *105*, 897–918.

PART II
REDUCING ISOLATION
IN THE COMMUNITY AGED

5

Reduction and Prevention of Isolation in the Community Aged: Friendly Visiting*

Sr. Mary Anne Mulligan, Ed.D.**

By the time the study of the effects of friendly visiting was begun, we were fully convinced that isolation had no salutary effects. We were also convinced that its prevention made more sense than trying to undo the effects of much exposure to isolation. The friendly visitor program discussed in this chapter was designed as an isolation-reduction program based on the social-gerontological theory that reduction or prevention of social isolation of the aged results in improved mental state, cognitive functioning and social adjustment. This chapter will discuss to what extent the program had an impact on social adjustment as seen in a change in grooming and apartment upkeep of the elderly people visited. The discussion will also include evidence of an improvement in cognitive awareness and mental health of the visitees. Finally, some recommendations will be made as to the place a friendly visitor program should have in a multi-service delivery system to help prevent and/or delay institutionalization of older people.

Friendly visitor programs are not new to our society; they existed as organized services as far back as 1869 in London (Maurice, 1913), 1885 in Boston (Richmond, 1907) and 1946 in Chicago (AOA Publication 129, 1971). The American Society of Directors of Volunteer

*Parts of this chapter were referred to in (1) Ruth Bennett, Social isolation and isolation-reducing programs, *Bulletin of the N. Y. Academy of Medicine*, second series, Dec. 1973, *49, 12,* 1143–1163; (2) Sr. Mary Anne Mulligan and Ruth Bennett, Development and evaluation of a friendly visitor program for the community aged, *Int'l. Journal of Aging and Human Development*, 1977–1978, *8,1,* 43–66; and (3) Sr. Mary Anne Mulligan, Friendly visitor program: Its impact on the social and mental functioning of the elderly, *Issues in Mental Health Nursing*, Spring 1978, *1,* 1–11. Data in this chapter were presented in Sr. Mary Anne Mulligan, Development of a friendly visitor program and evaluation of its impact on community-based elderly, unpublished Ed. D. thesis, Teachers College, Columbia University, 1973. The early stages of this research were supported by small grants from the N. Y. City Chapter of Red Cross and the N. Y. State Department of Mental Hygiene. Partial support was provided by an AOA traineeship.
**Sr. Mary Anne Mulligan, Ed. D., Director, Gerontology Program, Ohio Dominican College, Columbus, Ohio.

Services in its 1970 annual report listed friendly visiting as part of the service programs of 740 member institutions of the American Hospital Association.

Over the past 15 years in response to the needs of community-based aged, friendly visiting programs became an integral part of project programs organized under civic, industrial and private auspices; to name but a few, Project FIND, Project PATH, Project PILOT and the famous ILGWU (International Ladies Garment Workers Union) Friendly Visiting Program.   Their target population was primarily the aged population who were most likely to become socially isolated and possible victims of the deleterious effects of the isolation phenomenon.

In spite of the magnitude of the problem of social isolation, and especially of its attendant negative consequences as seen among the isolated aged population residing in urban settings, no major programmatic effort to combat it has been evidenced even up to now. This may be so because the problem of social isolation of the aged seems insurmountable, or, perhaps, because some of the solutions seem so simple, though expensive, that they have no news value.   It is possible that because these community programs that have aimed specifically at the aged have not been evaluated systematically, it is assumed that they have not reduced social isolation or improved the social or emotional functioning of the people visited.

PROBLEM OF SOCIAL ISOLATION

American cities today more than ever before are housing greater numbers of aged people, particularly the aged poor. This phenomenon may be attributed to the inability of the aged to join the younger and more affluent families who move to the suburbs to avoid the "noise, smog, dirt, social stress, and poor housing of the central city" (Birren, 1970).

It is likely that many of the aged population, whether in urban or rural areas, and regardless of their socioeconomic levels, become victims of factors beyond their control that probably contribute to their becoming social isolates. These factors may be due to one or more of the following circumstances: loss of spouse, family and friends; reduced mobility; retirement; fixed income; social and geographic mobility of offspring; and many others.

But the problem of social isolation of the aged is not a new one. Bennett, a sociologist (1968)*, claims that because isolation and segregation of the aged seem normative and acceptable to both young and old in our society, little has been done to alter the situation.

Yet the phenomenon of social isolation as it affects the aged has been the subject of investigation in the works of Bennett (1968; 1971a, b; 1972), Tec and Bennett (Granick) (1959), Bennett [Granick] and Nahemow, (1961), Rosow (1973), Tunstall (1966), Weiner (1972) and Weinstock (1968). It has been suggested that the isolated person becomes insensitive to the behavioral standards of the community because he is cut off from the pressures by which standards become operative on the individual (Weinstock and Weiner, 1970; Tec and Bennett [Granick], 1959). Moreover, because he is virtually living in an obsolete world, he is not only deprived of the opportunity for ordinary conversations but has no opportunity to learn new experiences (Weinstock, 1968). Worse still, isolation subjects him to loneliness and depression, both of which have been found related to psychiatric impairment (Lowenthal, 1968).

Effect on Social Adjustment

There is a common assumption that deterioration of social skills in the aged is a consequence of the biological and psychological aging processes. Weinstock and Weiner (1970), however, attribute this loss of social skills to a disuse of them as seen in the isolated aging person who finds he has little or no opportunity to practice them. Moreover, isolation removes the opportunities to obtain the feedback that is necessary for controlling or mediating social behavior. Thus, behaviors characterized as rude, withdrawn or inappropriate are adopted by the isolated person, leading to further isolation (Weiner, 1972). Bennett asserts that, given the assumption that frequency of contact, interpersonal significance and reward can influence behavior, then if old people are offered such opportunities, they should be able to relearn what has been lost through disuse and even to add new learning for appropriate social roles (Bennett, 1971b).

---

*Many of the studies cited here are reviewed in Chapters 1–4 of this book.

Effect on Cognitive Awareness

In a series of studies, Weinstock and Bennett (1971) found that social contacts are necessary as stimulating learning experiences for maintaining a high level of cognitive performance. Moreover, Weiner (1972)* investigated the effects of a resocialization program on the cognitive functioning of isolated, community-based geriatric clinic patients and found that an increase in intellectual performance was related to a decrease in recent isolation. This research would seem to indicate that if the lack of social interaction accounts for lack of knowledge of appropriate behavior, then it may be possible to intervene at critical times in the life of the aged person and prevent further desocialization.

Effect on Mental State

That such conditions as isolation, loneliness and poor social adjustment are related to psychiatric impairment in the aging has been substantiated by Lowenthal et al. (1967), Weiss (1967) and Roth and Kay (1962). It was found that in relation to morale among the healthy aged, the crucial role of intimacy appreciably influences a sense of well-being more than either an increase or a decrease in other social relationships. With the loss of such relationships, the individual seems to be subject even more to isolation's damaging effects.

The above studies have also confirmed that social interaction and mental stimuli are of great importance in maintaining the mental health of older people. Few personal contacts, no memberships in organizational groups and feelings of loneliness have been found to be associated with psychiatric impairment.

THE FRIENDLY VISITOR PROGRAM

It was thought that a program that reconnected the elderly to others, gave some indication of an awareness of their presence in the community and showed concern for their well-being would bring about some improvement in the social and mental behavior of those receiving this service. Such a program was the friendly visitor program (Mulligan, 1973) discussed in this chapter. As mentioned previously, it was

---

*This study is summarized in Chapter 6 of this book.

designed as a resocialization program with a built-in evaluative study to determine its impact on the behavior patterns of community-based, isolated elderly people.

Sample

The major portion of this study was conducted over a six-month period in the fall of 1971 on a small nonrandom sample of isolated, aged people living in the upper West Side of New York City, a catchment area known as the "Crime Hub." A follow-up study was conducted six months after the major portion of the study to investigate the possibility of some evidences of delayed deterioration in those receiving regular visiting as compared to those who were not visited regularly.

The sample consisted of 24 persons, aged 65 years and over, who were divided into an experimental and a control group. The median age was 77.5. Individuals with gross impairments, such as total deafness, senility syndrome and a language disability, were excluded from the study. Moreover, the group was limited in number to make possible the continuance of the program using community volunteers as back-up visitors upon completion of the study.

Visiting Procedure

The major procedure was hour-long structured visits made to each visitee in the experimental group every two weeks for six months by one of five pairs of trained volunteer visitors. The control group was visited by the same pair of visitors once in the beginning and once at the end of the study.

The visitors traveled in pairs to ensure their safety. A pair of visitors, moreover, helped to ensure continuity in the friendly relationship in case one member of the pair dropped out of the program. Two visitors would also be a help to keep the conversation going, especially in the initial visits.

An interview schedule, designed to assess the greeting behavior, grooming, apartment upkeep, cognitive awareness and mental state of the visitee, was part of each visit. Because a too rigidly structured interview would tend to inhibit rather than aid the visitor to be a friend to the visitee, the interview schedule was set up in such a way that it could be part of the conversation of the friendly visit.

After each of the 12 visits to the experimental group and two to the control group, the visitors, on the basis of what they observed during the visits, gathered data on the appropriateness of the behavior of the visitees. Only on the first and last visits, when a pre- and a post-test were administered, was any writing done in the presence of the visitees.

Two other evaluative procedures were: the follow-up study and a questionnaire evaluating the impact of the program on the visitee, e.g., timing and length of the visits, training of the volunteers, visiting in pairs and evaluating the effects of the program on the visitors themselves. The questionnaire was answered by the friendly visitors at the end of the study.

Impact of the Friendly Visitor Program

One of the strongest findings for judging the effectiveness of the friendly visitor program was the number of subjects who participated in the follow-up study. The experimental group outnumbered the control group two to one. Three visitees in the control group were found in nursing homes, and another was deceased. None of the experimental group was reported to have been institutionalized since the program ended. Because this finding is not subject to investigator's bias, nor does it depend on data analysis to confirm its validity, it was seen to be a major criterion for evaluating the effectiveness of the program.

Social Isolation

The *hypothesis* that social isolation would be reduced with friendly visiting was not supported by the findings in the major portion of the study. The follow-up visit, however, found a significant improvement. As seen in Table 5.1, the mean of 3.6 for the experimental group on the follow-up visit is double that of the mean on the last visit made in the major part of the study. The control group, however, were found to be as isolated on the follow-up visit as they were when the program ended six months before this visit.

The increase in social contacts for the survivors of the experimental group after the program terminated may have been due to the "sleeper effect," that is, the visitees, aware that their friendly visitors

Table 5.1. Distribution Scores of Past Month Isolation Index for Survivors in Experimental and Control Groups on First (T_1), Last (T_2) and Follow-up (T_3) Visits

| Past Month Isolation Scores | Frequency | | | | | |
| | Experimental | | | Control | | |
	T_1	T_2	T_3	T_1	T_2	T_3
10						
9						
8						
7			1			
6					1	
5			1			
4		1	3	1		1
3	1	1	1			1
2	2	2	1	2	1	2
1	3	3	1	1	2	1
0	1	1	1	1	1	
	$N = 7^a$	$N = 8$	$N = 8$	$N = 5$	$N = 5$	$N = 5$
Mean	1.4	1.8^b	3.6^b	1.8	2.0	2.4
SD	1.0	1.2	1.7	3.1	2.1	1.0

[a]One subject showed indifference and was not asked to respond to the interview schedule.
[b]t between $\bar{x}$ for T_2 and T_3 was 3.3; $p < .05$ for the survivors of the experimental group.

would no longer be coming to visit, were prompted to make social contacts on their own. Moreover, this resocialization of the visitees, who had been receiving regular visits, may be due, in part, to the opportunities afforded by the back-up community visitors in the way of escort services and invitations to social gatherings.

Social Adjustment

Greeting behavior, grooming and apartment upkeep were the indices used to measure social adjustment. There was no significant change over time in the manner in which the visitors were greeted by the visitees in either group. There was a steady improvement in personal appearance and the condition of the home during the major portion of the study for the experimental group.

As can be seen in Table 5.2, there was an improvement in grooming for those receiving regular visits. An improvement in appearance may best be understood from the notes of one of the visitors:

Mrs. K. was clothed in a soiled, woolen, tattered dress. Her hair was unkempt and she looked depressed. (Visit II)
On different occasions Mrs. K. wore a special dress and had her hair cut and set because, as she said, "I knew you were coming." (Visit VII)

Moreover, the improvement in personal grooming was only exceeded by the improvement in apartment upkeep for the experimental group. As can be seen from Table 5.3, the final visits showed significant improvement since the first visits. Some visitors even noted that the apartment upkeep showed improvement before personal grooming. One report read: "Mrs. G. had cleaned her room but she herself was still in the dirty housecoat she had on at the last visit." Another read: "Mrs. K. had groomed herself for the visit but made a special effort to improve the appearance of the room. She added a floral piece on the table, hung curtains and a couple of inexpensive paintings on the wall." It would seem that the visitees did not see how they themselves looked but were aware that their apartment was not ready for visitors. As can be seen from Table 5.3 there was little change in the appearance of the living quarters of those in the control group.

Some indication of the dynamics of change that were observed in the social adjustment over the 12 visits was seen in the visitors' reports as cited below:

Initially Mrs. K. was met on the street. When she learned of the Friendly Visitor Program she was eager to participate because she claimed to be "lonely and with no friends." Mrs. K. is a widow with no children. She lives alone in a single room occupancy hotel. She has no phone, television, or radio. She gets the daily paper and reads the current magazines at the library. When the visitors paid the first visit to Mrs. K. she was found lying on her bed, covered with a single blanket perforated with cigarette burns. She was reading *True Confessions* under a 40-watt bulb. The room was cold, cluttered, and dirty. The window looked as if it had not been washed for years. The floor and walls were in need of repair. Both Mrs K.'s room and the communal kitchen (with its padlocked refrigerator and one-burner stove) were infested with roaches. Mice were evident in the hallway. (Visit I)

Table 5.2. Distribution of Scores of Grooming Index for Experimental Group on Visit I (T_1) and Visit XII (T_2) and Control Group on Visit I (T_1) and Visit II (T_2)

		Frequency			
		Experimental		Control	
Grooming Index Scores		T_1	T_2	T_1	T_2
4		5	8	3	3
3		3	1	4	4
2		2	2		3
1		1		5	2
	Total	11	11	12	12
	Mean	3.1[a]	3.5[a,b]	2.4	2.7[b]
	SD	1.0[a]	0.8[a,b]	1.3	1.2[b]

[a] t between $\bar{x}$ for T_1 and T_2 in experimental group was 1.8; $p < .05$.

[b] t between $\bar{x}$ for T^2 in experimental group and control group was 2.0; $p < .05$.

Table 5.3. Distribution of Scores of Apartment Upkeep Index for Experimental Group on Visit I (T_1) and Visit XII (T_2) and Control Group on Visit I (T_1) and Visit II (T_2)

		Frequency			
		Experimental		Control	
Apartment Upkeep Scores		T_1	T_2	T_1	T_2
4			9	1	3
3		7		5	5
2		1	2	3	
1		3		3	3
	Total	11	11	12	11
	Mean	2.4[a]	3.6[a,b]	2.3	2.7[b]
	SD	0.9[a]	0.8[a,b]	1.0	1.2[b]

[a] t between $\bar{x}$ for T_1 and T_2 in the experimental group was 2.78; $p < .05$.

[b] t between $\bar{x}$ for T_2 in experimental and control groups was 2.10; $p < .05$.

Mrs. K. was most happy to see visitors; immediately she invited us to come in and sit down. She apologized for the appearance of her room explaining that "all the places in this neighborhood are the same." Mrs. K. at this time was clothed in a soiled, woolen, tattered dress. Her hair was unkempt and she looked depressed. She told of her hard life with her alcoholic husband whom she "supported with my hard earned money." She was a graduate of a business college and had held several positions such as stenographer, secretary, receptionist, and housekeeper. (Visit II)

In the course of the visits, Mrs. K. not only made an effort to improve the appearance of her room by scrubbing the floor and having the walls painted, but her personal appearance also improved. On different occasions she wore a special dress and had her hair cut and set just because "I knew you were coming." (Visits III-XI)

Mrs. K. has changed her pattern of living. She has become more outgoing to the manager and clerk in the hotel whom, on the first visit, she had called "scum." Even they commented on Mrs. K.'s change and their attitude toward her has changed accordingly. She has begun to attend meetings at a neighborhood center. (Visit XII)

In this next case, the visitors reported that there were no marked improvements observed over time. However, they did report that, as far as they could judge, there was no regression over the six-month period but rather a stabilized condition.

Mrs. G., age 72 lives in one of the crime-ridden single-room occupancy hotels on the upper West Side. She is obviously malnourished and though only mildly arthritic, she is too weak to ever leave her room. The room where she spends her life is tiny, shabby, filthy, and smelly. She has resigned herself to living in a building inhabited by drug addicts and pushers and where robbery and forcible entry are the rule rather than the exception. She is in remarkably good spirits—her brother lives two doors down the hall and they are both grateful that they have each other. The hotel owner "manages" her welfare check and buys her food and cigarettes. (Visit I)

Although Mrs. G. expressed pleasure at seeing us, it became immediately obvious that she much preferred watching her routine afternoon soap operas. She participated practically not at all in the conversation, except when we very pointedly asked her a question. Her response was adequate but never lengthy. At one time in the visit she unabashedly spit into a can she had on the windowsill. (Visit III)

Mrs G. had cleaned her room. I think she and her brother, who visits with us, really made some effort for us. But Mrs. G. was still fairly lethargic. However, she "looks forward to our next visit." (Visit IV)

This visit was spent listening to Mrs. G. as she related the story of the latest intruder. At 2 P.M. Mrs. G. and her brother, while watching TV heard a noise outside her door. As he opened the door to investigate, a hand was clapped over his mouth, knocking his glasses off, and the owner of the hand entered the room, locking the door behind him. He searched the brother and then turned to Mrs. G. She explained that all her money was downstairs with the owner. He then went to Mrs. G.'s "kitchen" (such as it is), heated himself a can of soup, drank it, and asked the brother to open the door. The intruder then departed with a reminder to re-lock the door. At this visit both Mrs. G. and her brother were quite shaken up and seemed to be grateful to have someone with whom they could share their fears and anxieties. (Visit VI)

Mrs. G. was so much more alive today. (Visitor's note: The vitamins I brought two visits ago may have had some ameliorating effect on her.) She talked more, seemed much happier, even a trifle euphoric. Mrs. G. was having her lunch—a piece of toast. She even mentioned going downstairs herself to the lobby to get her daily ration of cigarettes from the owner. (Visit VII)

Today the TV was blasting as usual, yet Mrs. G. ignored it for long intervals to speak with us. (Visit VIII)

Mrs. G. was in much better humor this week and even seemed glad to see us. We chatted a bit, mostly about inconsequential things sandwiched in during commercial breaks. Even so, today's visit was much more satisfactory than most (even all) of our previous visits. (Visit XI)

As it became clearer during the visit that this was our last visit, Mrs. G. became a little distant and somewhat irritable. She answered the questionnaire fairly well. (She had refused to do so on the first visit.) At one point she inquired just what good this visiting did her. (Visitor's note: Probably this is one reason for her consistent TV viewing during visits. She would always have her TV with her.) (Visit XII)

On the follow-up visit there was a decided drop in the mean scores of both groups, indicating a deterioration in both grooming and apartment upkeep as can be seen in Table 5.4. It would seem that the termination of the visits in the major part of the program deprived the visitees of a motivating factor for caring about their appearance and living quarters. Moreover, the control group showed little change in apartment upkeep over the entire period and a marked negative change in grooming on the follow-up visit.

Mental State

It is not known how many former mental patients were numbered among the isolated elderly found in this study. The following results

Table 5.4.   Mean Scores and Standard Deviations for the Greeting, Grooming and Apartment Upkeep Indices for the Survivors in the Experimental and Control Groups for the First (T_1), Last (T_2) and Follow-Up (T_3) Visits

Index	Statistic	Experimental			Control		
		T_1	T_2	T_3	T_1	T_2	T_3
Greeting	Mean	0.9	0.8	0.8	0.8	1.0	1.0
	SD	0.2	0.3	0.3	0.2	0.0	0.0
Grooming	Mean	3.1	3.5	2.6	2.4	2.8	1.8
	SD	0.8	0.9	1.3	1.2	0.8	1.0
Apartment upkeep	Mean	2.4	3.6	2.9	2.3	2.7	2.6
	SD	1.3	0.5	1.5	1.3	0.5	1.4
		$N = 8^a$	$N= 8$	$N = 8$	$N = 5$	$N=5$	$N=5$

[a]One subject showed indifference and was not asked to respond to the interview schedule.

might have multiplied if the program had continued longer than six months.

As visits continued, Mrs. M.'s trust in her visitors was revealed when she shared her secret with us. She blamed her brother and sister for placement in a mental institution at the age of 29 where she remained until she was discharged at 72 years of age. In speaking of her experiences at the mental institution, she seemed to have a clear and precise knowledgeable recall.

Another visitee took 14 weeks before she could feel free to share her "secret" with the visitors, as evidenced by this report:

It was the seventh visit before Mrs. K. felt comfortable enough to tell us that she had been in a mental hospital. She was 49 years old when she was committed by her husband. She blames her commitment to the mental hospital on the suffering she endured because of her husband and her family. The latter rejected her when she married Mr. K. Mrs. K. was very dramatic while relating her experience.

Mental functioning was measured by the change in the number of symptoms of inappropriate behavior observed by the visitors during the course of the visits. Since the visitees were a community-based group capable of independent living, it was not expected that serious

Table 5.5. Distribution of Observation Items, Means and Standard Deviations of Scores of Mental Status Schedule and Mental Status–Geriatric Supplement that Indicated Change or No Change in Mental State in Experimental Group and Control Group on First Visit (T_1) and Last Visit (T_2)

Symptoms	Frequency			
	Experimental		Control	
	T_1	T_2	T_1	T_2
Decreased or remained the same:				
constantly gay	5	2	6	2
keeps same posture	6	2	1	1
sad expression	2	1	2	2
cries	1	0	4	1
talks on and on	2	1		
frightened expression	1	0		
speaks, no hand or body gestures	2	0		
impassive face	1	0		
expresses hatred	1	0		
exalted, serene expression	1	0		
appears preoccupied	2	1		
appears indifferent	1	1		
circumstantial	2	1		
keeps smiling	2	0		
cuts visit short			1	1
long pauses in speech			1	1
voice faint			1	1
speaks slowly			1	0
keeps asking advice			1	1
Increased:				
harps on physical ills	1	2	2	4
cuts visit short	0	1		
occasionally incoherent	0	1		
frequently incoherent	0	1		
speech often halting	0	1		
ignores visitor	0	1		
irrelevant	1	2		
refuses details	0	1		
talks on and on			0	1
frightened expression			0	2
has panic attack			0	1
reintroduces hallucinations			0	1
distractible			0	1
emotionless on problems			0	1
speaks, no hand or body gestures			0	1
impassive face			0	1
	$N = 11$		$N = 12$	
Total	31	19	20	23
Mean	2.8[a]	1.7[a]	1.7	1.9
SD	2.4	2.2	1.4	2.8

[a] t between $\bar{x}$ for T_1 and T_2 in the experimental group was 2.3; $p < .05$.

disorders would be found. It was thought, however, that the presence of the visitors would have some effect on the visitees' talking on and on, or harping on some physical illness, or crying throughout visits—all signs of inappropriate behavior usually found in an isolated elderly population.

Table 5.5 shows the data resulting from Spitzer's Mental Status Schedule and MSS—Geriatric Supplement (Spitzer et al., 1967), which assessed the mental state of both the experimental and the control groups.

As can be seen in Table 5.5, there was a significant drop in the number of symptoms in the experimental group, from 31 to 19, whereas there was no improvement in the mental state of the control group. The significant improvement in the mental state of those receiving visits may be due to the presence of the visitors, who gave evidence that they had not abandoned them.

Some of the observed symptoms of disorder, such as "keeps same posture," "talks on and on," "muttering to oneself," could be considered more as oddities than as symptoms of disorder. It is possible that circumstances, such as long periods of loneliness, can foster these "oddities." The report on this lonely woman is a case in point:

Invariably as we get ready to go, Mrs. M. becomes more talkative and stands against the door in order to prolong the visit. She begs us to stay longer than we plan. She never fails to beg us to return and always asks when our next visit will be.

Another report of one of the visitors gave instances to support the positive finding in the mental state of the experimental group.

Mrs. K. showed definite improvement in her mental state and sociability over time. During the first few visits she used vulgar language and was derisive and suspicious of people and us. In her opinion everyone is mean and no good. She seemed depressed and gave the impression there was no reason to live. As visits increased, she became more outgoing and seemed to look forward to seeing us.

Cognitive Awareness

On each visit to the experimental group the visitors planned to introduce items on a Social Issues Index* as a topic of conversation.

---

*This index was designed for this study with the assistance of Elizabeth Sanchez.

Issues such as food stamps, social security and crime were thought to be relevant to the older person. This index was specially designed to measure the cognitive awareness of the visitees receiving regular visits.

When the issues were brought up again at a later visit, there was no significant change in cognitive awareness as evidenced by the visitees' inability to carry on a conversation about the particular issue. It is possible that the issues thought to be relevant to an older population did not hold the interest that "soap operas" might have had for them.

The following report of one of the visitors gives evidence of an exception to this finding.

Mr. C. was extremely glad to see us. In fact he brought up the matter of busing: asked our opinions as educators. We talked that over for several minutes—he's against busing on two counts: (1) parents should have the right to decide where their children will attend school; and (2) schools in economically and/or socially deprived areas should be brought up to the standards of schools in more well-to-do neighborhoods, thus eliminating the need for busing.

CONCLUSION: FRIENDLY VISITING AS AN ALTERNATIVE TO INSTITUTIONALIZATION

In summary, the influence of the friendly visitors apparently was evidenced more quickly and more clearly in the improvement shown by visitees in social functioning than in any other measure in the study. It is possible that over a longer period than six months a greater change would have been noticed in mental as well as social functioning owing to continued stimulation through conversation with the visitors.

It seems that it is only over time that the impact of a friendly visitor program or any other similar program can be evaluated positively (i.e., as bringing about changes that have some degree of stability to them).

A friendly visitor program is a social service program that provides the support to promote independent living for aged persons as well as mentally disturbed and physically incapacitated people remaining in the community. It is a program that tries to locate and assess those at risk in the community by providing routine, regular and frequent home visits. Moreover, it is a service that educates the friendly visitor to know the person in his natural surroundings, rather than as an institutionalized person conditioned by norms and forms.

The friendly visitor program, however, cannot function independently of auxiliary services. Hence, it is imperative that it be organized as an outreach program in a multi-service delivery system. In this way problems of the visitees that would present themselves to the visitors could be referred to a professional staff in the sponsoring agency. The friendly visitor program, whether based in a community hospital, medically related facility (e.g., nursing home) or private organization with multiple back-up services such as homemaker, home health care and the like, has as its goal to preserve health and promote the overall adjustment of aged and other persons incapacitated in the community.

In conclusion, friendly visitor programs can be vital links between the isolated aged, particularly the poor, isolated aged, and community services available for their physical, mental and social welfare. Moreover, if visitors are trained to recognize signs of crisis in aged persons in their own homes, the program becomes a crisis-prevention measure. This is a major goal of a friendly visitor program because preventing a crisis may prevent relocation of the aged, a stress that is fatal to many elderly persons. Finally, the friendly visitor program can be an alternative to institutionalization, and as such, promote continued viable, independent community living for aged persons in society.

REFERENCES

Administration on Aging. *Let's End Isolation.* Publication No. 129. Washington, D.C.: U.S. Department of Health, Education, and Welfare, Social and Rehabilitation Services, June 1971.

Bennett, Ruth. Distinguishing characteristics of the aging from a sociological viewpoint. *J. Am. Geriatr. Soc.*, 1968, *16, 2*, 127–135.

Bennett, Ruth. Community mental health programs with specific reference to those aimed at the aged. Paper read at Institute of Gerontological Society, Ashville, N. C., August 1971.

Bennett, Ruth. Program of gerontological research for fiscal year 1972–73. Submitted to Department of Mental Hygiene, New York, 1971b. (Mimeo.)

Bennett, Ruth. Living conditions and everyday needs of the elderly with particular reference to social isolation. Invited address read at 9th International Congress of Gerontology, Kiev, U.S.S.R., July 2–7, 1972.

Bennett (Granick) R., and Nahemow, L. Preadmission isolation as a factor in adjustment to an old age home. In Paul Hoch and Joseph Zubin (Eds.), *Psychopathology of Aging.* New York: Grune and Stratton, 1961, 292–293.

Birren, James E. The abuse of the urban aged. *Psychol. Today*, March 1970, *3, 10*, 37–38.

Lowenthal, Marjorie F. Social isolation and mental illness in old age. In Bernice L. Neugarten (Ed.), *Middle Age and Aging: A Reader in Social Psychology.* Chicago: University of Chicago Press, 1968.

Lowenthal, Marjorie F., Berkman, Paul E., Bressette, Gerard G., Buehler, John A., Pierce, Robert C., Robinson, Betsy C., and Trier, Melba L. *Aging and Mental Disorder in San Francisco.* San Francisco: Jossey-Bass Inc., 1967.

Maurice, C. Edmund (Ed.). *Life of Octavia Hill as Told in Her Letters.* London: Macmillan & Co., 1913.

Mulligan, Sister Mary A. The development of a friendly visitor program and the evaluation of its impact on the community-based elderly. Unpublished Ed. D. thesis, Teachers College, Columbia University, 1973.

Richmond, Mary E. *Friendly Visiting Among the Poor.* London: Macmillan & Co., 1907.

Rosow, Irving. The social context of the aging self. *Gerontologist*, Spring 1973, *13, 1,* 82–87.

Roth, Martin, and Kay, D. W. K. Social, medical and personality factors associated with vulnerability to psychiatric breakdown in old age. *Gerontol. Clin.*, 1962, *4,* 147–160.

Sanchez, Elizabeth. Social Issues Index. For a description and scoring of this index, see Mulligan, Sister Mary Anne. The development of a friendly visitor program and the evaluation of its impact on the community-based elderly. Unpublished Ed. D. thesis, Teachers College, Columbia University, 1973.

Spitzer, R. L., Fleiss, J. L., Endicott, J., and Cohen, J. Mental Status Schedule. For a full description of the construction and scoring of this index, see Spitzer, R., et al. in *Arch. Psychiat.*, April 1967, *16,* 479–493.

Tec, Nechama, and Bennett (Granick), Ruth. Social isolation and difficulties in social interaction in residents of a home for aged. *Social Problems*, 1959, *7,* 226–232.

Tunstall, Jeremy. *Old and Alone.* London: Routledge and Kegan, Paul, Ltd., 1966.

Weiner, Marcella Bakur. The effects of a resocialization program on the functioning of isolated, community-based geriatric clinic patients. Unpublished Ed. D. thesis, Teachers College, Columbia University, 1972.

Weinstock, Comilda Sundeen. The relations between social isolation, social cognition and related cognitive skills in the aged. Unpublished Ed. D. thesis, Teachers College, Columbia University, 1968.

Weinstock, Comilda S., and Bennett, Ruth. From "waiting on the list" to becoming a "newcomer" and an "oldtimer" in a home for the aged: Two studies of socialization and its impact upon cognitive functioning. *Aging Hum. Dev.*, Feb. 1971, *2,* 46–58.

Weinstock, Comilda S., and Weiner, Marcella. Development of a socialization program for geriatric outpatients. Paper presented at Annual Meeting of Gerontological Society, Toronto, Canada, Oct. 22, 1970.

Weiss, Robert S. Social relationships and the aged individual. Boston, 1967. (Mimeo.)

6
The Short-Term Effects of A Resocialization Program on the Functioning of Isolated, Community-Based Geriatric Clinic Patients*

Marcella Bakur Weiner, Ed.D.**

Not all isolated elderly can be reached in the community. Many congregate in bus stations, parks and clinics simply to be in contact with others. However, often no communication occurs among them. An investigation was carried out to bring together a group of those who "hang around" a hospital clinic. This study was concerned with the effects of a resocialization program on a sample of isolated, community-based geriatric outpatients attending a neighborhood medical clinic.

BACKGROUND

Psychotherapy has never been easily available to the aging. Because therapy, in general, demands so much time and effort, it is considered better to expend them on those who have a long life ahead. In particular, insufficient attention has been paid to group therapy involving aging persons (Lowy, 1967) in which the older person may exercise the wish to change identity and preserve a sense of possibility and future growth. There is, therefore, sparse material relating to group formations for the older person—the use of interpersonal relationships to attain specific goals and the changing of the group's emotional components to match the expressed needs of the older adult (Feil, 1967).

Few studies have been conducted on the impact of a group approach as an intervention method in relationship to the cognitive, social and physical functioning of the aged. Usually poor cognitive functioning,

*Part of unpublished Ed.D. thesis, Teachers College, Columbia University, 1972. This study was accomplished through the aid of an Administration on Aging (AOA) grant to the investigator while a doctoral candidate at Teachers College, Columbia University for a three-year period.
**Adjunct Professor, Brooklyn College, City University of New York and Executive Director, Geriatric Problem-Solving, Inc., New York City.

decreased social awareness and increased physical ailments are attributed to organic deterioration considered as natural to the aging process.

In order to study the effects of a resocialization program on the functioning of aging persons, test scores of a population of aging persons were compared before and after exposure to the resocialization process. The tests, in particular, were intended to measure cognitive, physical and social functioning before and after participation in the groups. The population was divided into groups designated "experimental," "talk" and "controls" for purposes of the research.

SAMPLE

Samples were selected from a normal, aged, relatively well-functioning, lower middle class, urban population. These samples were similar with respect to most personal and demographic characteristics including age and living conditions. The entire population may best be characterized as living in an environment greatly devoid of stimulation. This environment contained little opportunity for receiving varied input, in that it offered few possibilities for interaction with other persons. In general, it constituted a state best defined as isolation. It was thought that experiences in a resocialization group might counteract some of the damaging effects of such a deprived environment.

The study took place within the confines of Coney Island Hospital, after a pilot study at another Brooklyn general hospital, Maimonides Hospital. Coney Island Hospital serves a total of 638,636 persons, of whom 223,523 or approximately 35% are over the age of 65. Basically, the area is predominantly white, low to high middle class, but with substantial concentrations of working class populations. It has been estimated that of the total population, 81.5% are Jewish, and more than a third of the total are foreign-born. As of 1970, 11.3% of the total population were receiving public welfare assistance. Coney Island Hospital is thus one of four municipal hospitals which provides general hospital care and treatment for those of the 2,627,319 Brooklyn residents who are unable to pay for their own medical care. In the hospital, there are 43 different clinics, such as the cardiac clinic, the hematology clinic, the X-ray clinic, and so on. Elderly persons and others located in that catchment area may walk into the hospital, and are then directed to the screening clinic and undergo a battery of medical tests; most aging persons utilize the clinics on an average of every four to six weeks. When there are no acute, but only chronic ailments, the usual spacing of clinic visits is one every three months.

In order to help carry out the resocialization study, eight nurses were selected for participation by their supervisory personnel. The study was conducted as part of an in-service training program in which nurses were trained in interviewing, data collection and observational techniques. This training program was established by the hospital as part of its effort to train staff in methods of research involving aging persons, and the training included trial interviewing and role-playing in which alternate roles of both patient and nurse were assumed by the nurses. Use of this technique furthered an understanding of the theoretical aspects of aging, considered most relevant to staff working with this age group.

METHOD

Before initiation of the group program itself, community-based aging subjects attending the medical clinic at Coney Island Hospital were selected for participation in this study. Subjects were then given a battery of tests to assess cognitive, social and medical functioning. Tests included:

1. *Cornell Medical Index*, (modified for this study) referring to hypochondriacal and psychosomatic symptoms.
2. *Social Isolation Scale* consisting of: (a) *Adulthood Isolation Index*, measuring the extent of lifetime social contacts with family, friends, work and organizations; and (b) *Past Month Isolation Index*, measuring the number of social contacts in the month prior to the interview.
3. *Socialization Index*, measuring information learned by the subjects about the hospital setting.
4. *Group Evaluation Form* (post-test only), measuring types of experiences members had in the group itself.
5. *Wechsler Adult Intelligence Scale* (WAIS), consisting of three subtests: Information (measuring basic knowledge); Comprehension (measuring the ability to combine information into new forms); and Similarities (intended to measure conceptualizations). These three subtests were selected because, with older adults, they correlate highly with total WAIS scores.

Tapes recorded at the beginning (session 2), middle (session 6) and end (session 11) of group sessions were collected. These sessions were selected because session 1 was, as is typical of first meetings primarily an orientation session, concerned with establishing identities and the "rules of the game"; session 6 is representative of the middle of group progress because by then four sessions had taken place, and group progress could be charted; session 11 rather than 12 was chosen to represent the end phase because the last, or end, session usually manifested signs of depression/loss at the group's termination and would thus not be as representative of the later stages of the group in progress as would the preceding session.

The sample was divided as follows: 27 in the experimental or resocialization condition, 20 in the intermediate or talk condition and 20 in the zero-control (no group) condition. The mean age of the entire sample was 73.8 years; the majority or three-fifths of the total sample were in the 65–74 age range. Within that age range, slightly more than one-third were in the 70–74 age group.

In the total sample there were 58 women and 9 men, or 86% females and 14% males. This makeup is representative of sex ratios in the later years. Because there were fewer males, the males were distributed equally into groups such that each of the groups contained equal numbers of men with only one group containing fewer. The majority of the sample had had some elementary schooling; most were skilled workers, having come to this country in the early part of the century. Most were also of Eastern European descent. Everyone in the sample had been living alone, a criterion established for selection purposes. The average number of years of living alone was five, the time ranging from several months (recent) to ten years. Individuals with gross physical impairments such as total blindness or deafness were excluded from the study.

All of the subjects were pre-tested on the instruments indicated and then randomly assigned to one of the three group conditions. Groups were to be conducted for a period of 12 weeks, once a week.

As defined for this study, the experimental group was that manipulated by the leader; the talk group established the leader as "just another person"; and the control group did not meet at all. The experimental group was conceptualized as moving through phases and stages (Rosenbaum and Berger, 1963), with the typical phase movements throughout each session taking the form of moving qualitatively from a relative emphasis on attempts to solve problems of orientation (what is it) to attempts to solve problems of evaluation (how do we feel about it) to, last, attempts to solve problems of control (what shall we do about it). Reflective of group therapy literature (Rosenbaum and Berger, 1963), this emphasis allowed orientation to reach its peak in the first phase of the group experience, evaluation in the second and control in the third. This group condition created a situation wherein there existed an active, trained leader, familiar with group techniques, who, as such, used her knowledge of group principles and, in particular, verbal reinforcement as a means of manipulating the group within a problem-solving orientation.

It has been observed that widespread and consistent changes in behavior may be influenced by no more than a nodding of the head and repeating of the words "uh-huh" or "hmmmm-mmm" on the part of a group leader (Wolberg, 1967). Verbal reinforcement has thus been considered a most effective technique. Both in psychotherapy and in daily life, selected reinforcement of special aspects of behavior takes place (Wolberg, 1967). Accepting and approving responses from the group leader thus act as reinforcing stimuli in learning (Verplanck, 1955; Yates, 1970).

The experimental group's stages may be traced as follows: Early sessions or weeks 1 through 3 (Stage I) devoted some time to listening to members' complaints about their health; however, because one of the major goals of the group resocialization experience was to redirect the existing focus on medical symptoms, within a few sessions members, encouraged by the leader and their peers, would be suggesting possible ways of coping with health problems. Nonreinforcement, according to the model, would lead to sessions soon turning to the expression of consistent fears and experiences deemed common to aging persons (Stage II). It could be projected that one common theme that would emerge would be that of isolation (Bennett, 1968). This stage would lead naturally to Stage III (final stage), in which group members would possibly both organize a "buddy system," each lending support to the other, and utilize themselves in ways indicative of attempts at mastery, competence and belongingness.

To accomplish these goals, traditional group principles were utilized with the resocialization group only. These principles were: (a) interrogation—used by the leader to help her document points that promised to be clinically decisive; (b) clarification—used by the leader to elucidate some point that had not been adequately dealt with; (c) illustration—the use of an anecdote, simile or comparison following a successful confrontation for the purpose of reinforcing the confrontation; (d) confrontation—the use of information to disconcert the patient by pointing out an inconsistency; and (e) explanation—an attempt on the leader's part to strengthen the patient (Slavson, 1964).

The process of group intervention itself may be further clarified by the following steps taken during the group meetings:

Step 1. Formulating the Core Problem: This step consisted of the formulation, in the therapist-leader's thinking, of the current core problem as expressed by the group members. This was essentially a process based on unifying the major threads of the group members' discussion and pinpointing the critical, core issue as presented by them.

Step 2. Expressing the Core Problem: This step was the expression, by the therapist-leader, of the group's thinking in terms of clarification and summation of the core problem as offered by the group. This step permitted members' participation and helped stimulate group cohesion.

Step 3. Extending the Core Problem: This step was based upon the therapist-leader's skills of extending the presented core problem to all group members so as to involve the group in its core-thinking process. This was accomplished by calling on silent, more passive members, as well as by consistently reinforcing verbal communications of group members showing group participation.

Step 4. Directing the Core Problem: This step was based upon the therapist-leader's directing the core problem toward a realistic goal. It allowed the leader to offer the group a possible goal whereby the core problem, as expressed, might be resolved through members' manipulation of themselves and their environment.

Step 5. Resolving the Core Problem: This final step allowed the resolution of the current core problem, suggesting to the group alternate means of pursuing the goal as well as outlining appropriate strategies for its achievement. This was accomplished by calling on various group members and enlisting the aid of members who were socially active ("models") and experienced in the process.

The technique of verbally reinforcing appropriate behaviors such as social involvement in the group, expression of problem-solving strategies and the offering of novel means to attain group goals was utilized through the means of simple positive reinforcing statements such as "good," or "that is very helpful," and "the group can certainly benefit from that."

The leader's role during each group session thus consisted of five generic functions: formulating, expressing, extending, directing and resolving current core problems as presented by the group members. The leader herself may be conceived of as being an instigator or catalyst with her role defined as one who stimulates the group toward significant verbal productions, interactions and resolving of problems within a here-and-now focus. The general group goal, as specified above, was always the reinforcment of problem-solving strategies.

The talk (intermediate) group met with the leader also. However, in this condition, the leader defined her role as that of "just another group member"; no attempts at reinforcement or manipulation of any form was attempted. She was, in effect, a passive member of the group, never assuming an active leadership role, or using any problem-solving approaches.

The zero-control group was pre- and post-tested, as were the other groups, both experimental (resocialization) and intermediate (talk), but controls never attended any group sessions. This was consistent with the experimental design.

RESULTS

One way in which results may be viewed is to examine progress-over-time. Thus, the actual recorded, edited tapes of the two groups may be examined for changes-over-time. These tapes are offered in the following pages for such examination.

The Progress of the Experimental Group Over Time

As stated in detail elsewhere, the resocialization process, using problem-solving techniques with a here-and-now focus, was offered only to the experimental group, congruent with the aims of the study. Thus, it was only during these group sessions that the leader took an active role and used simple reinforcement techniques previously referred to. Because a major aim of the study was to help the group acquire alternate ways of functioning in response to the expressed needs of the group members, the leader consciously manipulated the group, indicating that the aging group members themselves were capable of utilizing both their own internal resources and the external resources available to them in the environment. In addition, "solution" models would be used, that is, members considered by the group leader to have some of the strengths and resources lacking in less adequately functioning members. It was understood that these models could then be imitated by the other members to heighten the latter individuals' own sense of mastery and competence.

The Experimental Group—The Beginning (Session 2) (Introductions had been made, all group members greeted and the purpose of the meeting explained; the group was now in progress. The tape recorder had been placed in a convenient location, and it had been explained that it was part of the study.)

Mrs. R.: I didn't do much this weekend. My son was supposed to come and visit me but he called at the last minute to say he couldn't make it.

Mrs. T.: My children want to come, but I tell them to stay home. They have places to go to besides seeing me. After all, they are young people and have their own lives to live. What can they do for me? They will ask, "Ma, what are you doing?" They can ask that over the phone. What they can do is come and spend a lot of time with me, not just a quick visit.

Leader.: Then what you are saying, Mrs. T., is that you resent their not coming to spend time with you. How about the rest of the group members—do you feel the same way?

Mrs. F.: I don't. I see my daughter even though she has four children. But they come, even though I'd like them to come more. And besides, there is a difference between a daughter and a daughter-in-law.

Mrs. M.: I wouldn't want anyone if only I could go someplace, but my legs won't carry me. Years ago it was different. You stayed with your parents. You showed them respect. Now it's different. Even when I had boyfriends, in the old days, they had to ask my father. Not now.

Mrs. T.: Now what I do is stay home and watch television. I'm not so crazy about the T.V., but what else is there to do? I don't even need the drama on television. I've had enough drama in my own life.

Mrs. S.C.: You said it.

Leader.: What I hear you saying is that you're lonely and would want to either be able to get out more by yourselves or have people come to visit you. What can we do about that? Do some of you belong to community centers in this neighborhood, or how do you solve this kind of problem?

Mrs. S.C.: There are plenty of places to go around here, but you can't stay out too late. But places to go, yes, there are many. There are a lot of old people living around here.

Mrs. M.: That's right. Even I know that.

Leader: Then there are places around. Can you tell me what they are and what they offer?

Mrs. T.: There's the Brighton Y, there's Haber Houses' Community Center . . . [she elaborated and listed several community and senior citizen centers] .

The leader, in this group, used such group techniques as interrogation, clarification and confrontation. Thus, because loneliness was the theme for this session, the leader established the fact that this was the central idea being expressed by reflecting back the group's thoughts, but then she moved the group into a problem-solving direction.

Alternate ways of responding were suggested by using Mrs. S.C., for example, as a solution model. The fear of staying out too late was thus not responded to, for the time being, but the content relating to the fact that community centers did exist was attended to through the leader's response of asking for clarification and extension on that point. At that point the group moved, through Mrs. T., to furnish the elaboration asked for by the leader, responding to the reinforcement and problem-solving techniques offered. The reinforcement, in terms of verbally agreeing with what a member said, or making positive comments in response to a member's statements, was used as a means of adding credence to that member's judgment; it offered acceptance and approval.

Consistent with the literature on group process, ignoring the theme of loneliness as a critical phenomenon will lead to that theme being extinguished, so that the group content can then be moved into a problem-solving direction.

The Experimental Group—The Middle (Session 6) (Preliminaries such as greetings, and so on, had been attended to.)

Mrs. S.C.: My grandson bought me a tape recorder, very much like yours. [Reference is to tape recorder placed in the room by the leader.]

Mrs. K.: That's nice. Maybe I can hear myself on tape. I never did [laughs] .

Mrs. R.: That's why I like to come here. There is so much to see and do.

Leader: Can you explain that?

Mrs. B.: Well, what I think Mrs. R. means is we are all here to help each other. And that is very nice. Otherwise, what can you do alone in the house all day?

Mrs. K.: That's right. For example, Mr. B. has not been here lately. I called his house many times to see what was wrong but I can't seem to reach him.

Leader: That was very kind of you, Mrs. K. I think one of the good things about meeting like we do is that perhaps we can call one another if someone does not show up for a meeting. What do you all think?

Mrs. M.C.: That is very nice. I think I would like that too. Maybe I'll call Mr. B.

Leader: I'm sure he would be pleased.

Mrs. K.: That's right. It makes you feel good if someone calls. I know because it happened to me.

Mrs. S.C.: I have also called other people to come to the group.

Leader: Good.

Mrs. M.C.: We went to a community meeting last night. The only thing wrong was that there was not enough food.

Mrs. K.: So next time we'll cook more.

Mr. S.: What we need besides more food, is more men in this group [laughs].

Mrs. K.: So go out and bring them in. We also want men in this group, no? [Group laughs.]

Mrs. B.: Men are not so much around. Husbands die too soon.

Mrs. K.: I too have been alone for a long time.

Leader: But some people marry again after their husband or wife dies.

Mrs. S.C.: I think that second marriages are no good.

Mrs. B.: I don't agree. Some people are happy and some are not, in a first or a second marriage.

Mr. S.: I think that all second marriages stink.

Mrs. M.C.: Some second marriages are better than the first. What you say is not so.

Leader: How do the rest of you feel about this?

Mr. S.: I have a widow I have been seeing but she has a grown son. So now if I want to get married, do I have to take both her and her son?

Mrs. R.: Why not? If you love her, you can take her son too because she is the mother.

Mrs. K.: You can't just take one.

Mr. S.: Why not? He's had her for 28 years. Now it's my turn.

Mrs. S.C.: You want her to yourself.

Leader: What do you think, the rest of you, about later marriages and the fact that both sides may have grown children?

Mrs. K.: If I found someone good, I wouldn't mind.

Leader: Have you had opportunities? What has happened?

Mrs. K.: Yes. Years ago, but I was foolish. Only I didn't know it then.

Mr. S.: What I don't like about being alone is I don't like shopping.

Mrs. S.C.: So find a woman and get married and she will help you shop.

Mr. S.: I told you I have someone.

Mrs. K.: So if you love her, marry her.

Mr. S.: I don't believe in love. It's just physical attraction.

Mrs. K.: I believe in love. Why not? You're never too old for that.

Leader: Is that how the rest of you feel, like Mrs. K.?

Mrs. M.C.: Why not? You marry a second time not just for what Mr. S. said [group laughs] but also for companionship. For instance, why do people come to this group [laughs]?

Leader: Why?

Mrs. M.C.: Well, for companionship and maybe, I don't want to say too much, but maybe to also meet someone.

Leader: You're not saying too much. What you're saying sounds fine. How does it sound to the rest of you?

Mr. S.: O.K. She sounds fine, but bring more men in the group, and then everyone can have a chance. [Group laughs.]

The above demonstrates the basic resocialization orientation using reinforcement and accepted group process approaches. Thus, members were asked to clarify a point (leader, to Mrs. R.'s comment of why she, Mrs. R., likes to come to the group: "Can you explain that?") through the technique of "interrogation" as a means of helping the leader document points that promised to be clinically decisive. In this case, the leader has attempted to extend Mrs. R.'s expression of her positive reactions to the group by a form of positive reinforcement, verbal praise and encouragement. Later on, positive reinforcement was again used in responding to Mrs. K.'s remarks about her attempts to seek out another group member. This was done to encourage members to interact with one another outside of the group limits as well as within the group. Reinforcement was also used as a means of encouraging appropriate behavior for the group. Mrs. M.C. was thus set up as a solution model. Her response, about coming to the group possibly to meet a man, was responded to by the leader as being perfectly acceptable. Reinforcing statements such as "good," or "that's very kind of you," were used consistently during the session.

Because this type of group was not psychoanalytic in nature, intrapsychic interpretations were avoided. For example, the leader used techniques of circumvention and intervention when Mrs. S.C. confronted Mr. S. At this point, the leader intervened and involved the entire group in an open-ended question ("How do the rest of you feel about this?"), which deflected the confrontation. Techniques of positive reinforcement, clarification and extension were thus used as tools by the leader in order to strengthen group members' available behaviors for a problem-solving group approach.

The Experimental Group—Approaching the End (Session 11) (Preliminaries such as greetings had been taken care of.)

Mrs. R.: It's good to be here for all reasons.

Leader: What reasons?

Mrs. R.: Well, because otherwise you stay home alone for so long. It's a pleasure to come to talk to other people and to you, darling.

Mrs. M.C.: That's it. When I stay home alone, sometimes I talk to myself [laughs]. I talk to the walls too. Then I find something to do, like cleaning the house, watching T.V.

Leader: How about the others?

Mrs. B,: We come here to be with everyone and with you and the nurses.

Mrs. K.: How was Washington? Did you tell the President about us? [Everyone laughs. Reference is to conference the leader had attended.]

Leader: [Spent some time telling relevant details of conference.]

Mrs. M.C.: We have to make things better for older people.

Mrs. K.: But 30 or 40 years ago we didn't even have this much. We just have to fight for things; then, maybe you get some.

Leader: Right. What kinds of things in particular were you thinking of?

Mrs. M.C.: Well, poor people have to be helped.

Leader: Could you spell that out—in what way?

Mrs. M.C.: Well, the poor are poor, and the rich are rich. It could be better. But not only with money. Some people don't care for the poor people or the old people. It would take three hours to tell you [sighs].

Leader: We don't have three hours, but we have some time and I think maybe we can all discuss this. What do the rest of you think?

Mrs. M.C.: Mrs. R. can tell you.

Mrs. R.: I can tell you that now it's better. We never had social security. Now we have that and they even send somebody to clean your house if you need it. From this hospital, they sent a girl three times a week to the man next door whose wife died. They never used to do this.

Mrs. K.: If everybody pushes and fights, we'll get what we need.

Leader: Good point.

Mrs. S.C.: Believe me, we all worked all our lives and we should get things from this country.

Leader: Absolutely.

Mrs. K.: Will we be meeting some more?

Leader: Next week is our last time.

Mrs. K.: This helps. Coming to the group is good.

Leader: How?

Mrs. K.: Well, in the group we talk to each other, see each other. Only in the evening, we can't go out.

Leader: You belong to community centers, don't you Mrs. K.?

Mrs. K.: Yes. But we have to have more groups for all older people, not just the one hour. That flies. The one hour is good but what is one hour? Last week Mrs. R. [from group] came to visit me and it was a pleasure.

Mrs. R.: Then I invited her back. I wanted to give her tea or something, but she said she just wanted my company.

Leader: I can understand that.

Mrs. R.: That's right. But we have to get company for ourselves. We have to keep ourselves busy, right, doctor?

Leader: What do the rest of you think?

Mrs. S.C.: Right. We all have to help each other.

Mrs. K.: I belong to clubs. That's the only thing that helps me. We pass the time. We have a community center in the building, and two evenings a week we go down and sing and tell stories. All the elderly people go. It's very nice.

Mrs. R.: We need more community centers.

Leader: That's a good idea. Maybe we can pick up on that next time. [Session ends.]

As in previous sessions, the leader here used a problem-solving orientation with a focus on the here-and-now. When a member (e.g., Mrs. M.C.) expressed a theme such as loneliness, it was picked up but thrown to the group so that her peers could contribute their problem-solving approach, which, by then, had become one of the ways in which the group examined problems. Thus, for example, when Mrs. M.C. expressed feelings of isolation, Mrs. B. commented that one way to deal with this was to come to the group. Mrs. K. then appeared to reflect the problem-solving approach when she followed Mrs. B.'s comments with statements referring to a recent conference concerned with political and social action for older persons. This theme was then explored with the group, the leader using resocialization techniques previously referred to (e.g., reinforcement of appropriate behaviors, the sanctioning of realistic problem-solving approaches and the use of peers as solution models).

The theme with which the session ended was the need for a social restructuring of our society ("more groups for older people") and an assertion of the aging person's rights to the fruits of his many years of labor. Expressed, too, were views, encouraged by the leader, of the need for the individual to use problem-solving for himself (in members' comments such as "but we have to get company for ourselves") rather than rely on an authority-leader figure to solve problems for the members.

The emphasis was thus always on the present; the techniques used were those of resocialization (i.e., finding alternate ways of responding to one's environment, making use of one's own adaptive resources rather than relying on authority figures and modeling after peers who cope and function very adequately). Based upon accepted knowledge in the field of human behavior, this approach would lead to the reactivation, possibly lost through disuse, of the feelings of competence, mastery and the aging member's ability to manipulate and order his environment in order to make it more fitting to his own needs.

The group's progress, over time, moved from an expression of themes common to aging (e.g., isolation and loneliness) to the ways with which to deal with them. The group also learned to use each other as possible resources.

In addition, subjects generally considered "out of bounds" for aging persons (dating, remarriage, sex, etc.) were encouraged and allowed free ventilation. Once encouraged, the members did express these themes freely. Similarly, themes of a social action nature were encouraged and group members stimulated to become active participants in political struggles.

The basic group goal was thus expressed in stages, geared first to the expression of problems and finally to effective ways of dealing with them. This development was consistent with the major purpose of the study.

The Progress of the Talk Group Over Time

This group met with the leader for the same time period as the experimental group. Preliminary matters were also attended to in a similar way; for example, greetings were extended, and the tape recorder was identified, when in use. However, consistent with the design of the study, no attempts at group manipulation were made; the leader did not use her group training and knowledge of technique. Reinforcement was not attempted, and the leader's role was that of "another group member" who listened passively, accepting what group members said but exercizing no leadership. Her presence was explained as being due to the hospital system of encouraging patients to get together for some discussion on particular days.

The Talk Group-The Beginning (Session 2) (Introductions had been made and all preliminaries attended to.)

Mrs. Z.: How was your week, Mrs. S?

Mrs. S.: How could it be—I have nobody [cries].

Mrs. Z.: I don't want to make Mrs. S. feel bad but she has to take herself in hand. You're always crying. Last time you cried too [referring to opening session]. I see her upstairs in the clinic, and she's always crying.

Mr. B.: I'm having trouble managing the house. I clean a little, but then I get short of breath. I don't know what to do.

Mrs. S.: What can you do? Everyone has problems. I too am alone and in an apartment. You have to try to manage as best you can. I even have a sick daughter in the hospital, and I don't know what to do either.

Mrs. G.: I have a little grandson. He is brain-damaged and my daughter twice had a nervous breakdown. What can you do? You have to take it.

Mrs. K.: My feet bother me and even if I shop for a couple of blocks, I have to take the bus back. What can you do, doctor?

Leader: I can understand your problem.

Mrs. S.: I wish I could get a job. The doctor told me to do that but I can't get out of the house, so how can I get a job?

Mrs. Z.: Everyone has problems. I lost a sister and a brother and they were both in their early fifties. It's just no good to think too much. When I start to think, I want to run out altogether.

Mrs. K.: When I start to think, I take a pill. You have to take a little dope to forget. What can you do? If I don't sleep, I also have to take a pill. You want to forget but especially at night, you think.

Mr. B.: Everyone has something.

Mrs. G.: That's right. Everyone has problems. I have a refrigerator. It makes such noise at night I can't sleep.

Mrs. K.: You have to make the best out of it. Is that right, doctor?

Leader: It would seem so. [Session ends.]

Since resocialization was not a goal with this group, established principles of group resocialization process were not used. Thus, the group was not interrupted in its theme of isolation ("I too am alone"), helplessness ("I don't know what to do either") and medical ailments ("My feet bother me"). When the group turned to the leader for solutions, her comment of "I can understand your problems" was a passive acceptance of the fact that problems do exist. No attempt at intervention was made; problem-solving approaches were not offered to the group as coping devices. Thus, when Mrs. K. suggested to the group that all one can do is accept the existing problems, the leader's comment of "It would seem so" indicated an acceptance of the group's approach without attempts to move it into any specific direction, unlike the approaches used with the experimental group. As anticipated, lack of intervention approaches made for an increase of expressed medical symptoms and an extension of the theme of overwhelming problems.

The Talk Group—The Middle (Session 6) (Preliminaries, as usual, had been attended to.)

Mrs. Z.: How are you Mrs. K.? I didn't see you last week.

Mrs. K.: Not so well. I passed out twice. I went to see Dr. H. here at the clinic, and he told me to come back tomorrow.

Mrs. S.: My pressure is up. I feel very weak [begins to cry]. My son is coming, the one who lives far away. He lives in Baltimore. He can't stay. He has a wife.

Mrs. K.: I was at my son's house last week because I didn't feel well. I blacked out, and so I came home. I had fallen and was all bruised. I fell in the street, and people picked me up. And my stomach—I don't know if it's my nerves or what. I never used to have this trouble. My sugar also was high, and my pressure was 240. I asked the nurse for a cardiogram, and she wouldn't give it to me. I asked for a tranquilizer, and they wouldn't give it, just vitamins. Who needs vitamins? They also tell me to relax. How can I?

Mrs. S.: [Cries] I also feel so weak. I asked the druggist for a new medicine but I couldn't get it. He told me to ask the doctor, but she doesn't do anything for me.

Mrs. K.: The doctors here don't help me at all. I don't know why. Maybe I could change doctors. The one I have I don't like from the day I got her. A lady sitting next to me, her husband had a stroke, and she also didn't like her doctor. The doctor told the lady, "Your husband is an old man—what do you expect."

Mrs. S.: If this hospital threw out all the old people, they would have nothing to do. I fell this winter. I was coming out of my son's car and he drove away and didn't know that. So people came over and said, "Don't do this, or don't do that." But I told them to go get my son. I told them please stop the green car. Maybe they didn't believe me. There are so many liars, you don't know when someone is telling the truth [laughs]. But anyway, I told them it was my son and to please get him at the red light because I could see he stopped his car for the light. So he came back and took me to the hospital. I had stitches. Then I came to this hospital. But I wanted to go stay with my son because I was scared. So I went to him and saw doctors there. We paid $7.00. We told him we belonged.

Mrs. K.: You mean to Blue Cross and Blue Shield?

Mrs. S.: That's right. But it didn't help. We had to pay. Why should that be? Tell me, why should that be?

Mrs. K.: I don't know. I really don't know. Maybe you should ask somebody.

Mrs. S.: Who is there to ask?

Mrs. K.: Ask the doctor here.

Leader: Ask outside, at the screening desk. They should have that information. [Session ends.]

The theme of this session appeared to be that of medical complaints ("My pressure is up," "I blacked out"), unmet needs ("I asked for a tranquilizer, and they wouldn't give it"), anger at society's attitudes toward the aging ("Your husband is an old man—what do you expect") and inability to master the environment ("but it didn't help. We had to pay"). When the members, as in the previous recorded session, turned to the leader for solutions, she suggested they take their complaints to official hospital personnel. Specific directions, problem-solving approaches and extensions or explorations of statements by the group members were not offered, unlike the case of the experimental group. Thus, medical complaints, as in previous sessions, were elaborated upon, as was the theme of isolation. Neither appropriate nor inappropriate ways of responding were reinforced, and thus the session, unlike the parallel session of the group in the experimental condition, showed no movement or change in the direction of accepting and implementing a problem-solving orientation.

The Talk Group—Approaching the End (Session 11) (At this session, only one subject appeared, Mrs. S. It was learned, through the "grapevine," that other members had stated that the group was depressing because Mrs. S. cried a lot, and that they "didn't seem to be getting anywhere.")

Mrs. S. was greeted, as always.

Mrs. S.: I don't blame the others for not coming because when they come to the hospital, they sometimes don't treat you so good. I also don't feel so good [cries] and so I came here, to the clinic, and saw the colored doctor [cries] . The nurse told me that if I bother her, she will give me the card back [reference to clinic card] . So I didn't bother her. But I told her I feel very bad. Then the doctor looked at me [cries]. Why shouldn't the hospital have only good doctors and not the other ones? It's the doctor who takes $500.00 a day. So why shouldn't he take care of me? Why?

Leader: I don't know why. Doctors should give good medical care.

Mrs. S.: But they don't. This doctor gave me pills and I don't know what to do. I don't want to bother him. You should see how red it was. I mean my leg. See. Look at it.

Leader: Yes. I see. It does look red.

Mrs. S.: Why doesn't the doctor take the part of women? When the old lady last week said she fainted, why didn't they believe her? I blacked out last week three times [cries] . The last time I blacked out I had three stitches. Remember. I told you. When the others were here, and when my son was with me. Remember?

Leader: I remember.

Mrs. S.: I think that is a terrible thing. I would like you to take more interest, I told the doctor. The nurses take an interest. This nurse is wonderful. You know, the redhead, don't you?

Leader: Yes. I do.

Mrs. S.: If I come here, I want them to make my life a little easier, not harder, right [cries]?

Leader: Yes. I can understand that.

Mrs. S.: I once went to the doctor in screening when I had a stroke years ago. I had a very high pressure. I felt very bad, and the machine to take the high pressure takes a second, and so I asked him to take it. He said that I don't have to take it, that every six months is enough. What kind of doctor is that? I could do a better job myself. The doctors come here to rest up. A nice patient respects doctors, and a nice doctor respects patients. They think if you are older, you are crazy. They sent me to a psychiatrist, but I didn't want to go. I told Dr. H. the whole story, and that I didn't want to go. They sent me because I don't know my telephone number. They think I'm crazy because I cry since my daughter died last year [cries]. Dr. H. said I didn't have to go; so I didn't. He said if I didn't want to go, I didn't have to. I came home and figured if I wouldn't go, they will hold it against me. So I saw Dr. H., and he said that I don't have to come back again. He said that I was old and had had a very hard life and that that was all that was wrong [cries]. [Session ends.]

The theme at this session was one of depressed affect (much crying), helplessness ("So why shouldn't he take care of me?"), dependency ("I want them to make my life a little easier") and self-pity ("He said that I was old and had had a very hard life and that that was all that was wrong").

As in previous recorded sessions of the talk group, the leader, consistent with the role assumed for this group, responded to the subject's comments with sympathy and some support ("I don't know why. Doctors should give good medical care"), but did not offer a directed, problem-solving approach or use techniques consistent with that orientation. The mood of the session was thus depressed, and because no attempts at manipulation were introduced as a means of stimulating change, the mood and content remained fairly constant. Thus, whereas in the resocialization condition group members appeared to have moved from an identification of problems to a problem-solving direction, over time, the talk group moved from an emphasis on medical symptoms and an elaboration of isolated living, to an intensification of focus on these elements. Because, as stated, no attempts were made to reinforce appropriate behaviors and extinguish inappropriate ones, the latter type of behavior (e.g., crying) persisted. In fact, crying increased in terms of number of times this behavior was engaged in, over time. In addition, in contrast to the final recorded session with the group members in the experimental condition, society was not seen by the talk group as a possible ally for social change, but was, rather, blamed for not caring for its aging members, without the aging individual attempting to use himself as a resource for social and political change. Though the past was reflected upon, in a way similar to the behavior indulged in by the experimental group, unlike them members of the talk group did not view it within the framework of a perspective-in-time, with a visible future, but only within the context of what had occurred in one's life, which was then seen as a finality.

In summary, the results of the edited tape recordings indicate that there were major differences in group functioning, over time, between the experimental and talk groups. Whereas the leader in the experimental group used resocialization, problem-solving techniques and orientations, this was not done with the talk group. Thus, only with the resocialization group did the leader move the group from a statement of the problem to seeking its solution. Focusing on the here-and-now, members were encouraged to reactivate feelings of mastery, competence and control over both self and the environment. The content of the group's edited speech recordings appears to reflect this as they move from the stage of "what is it" to that of "how do we feel about it" to the final "what can we do about it," typical of group process.

In contrast, the talk group, never manipulated by the leader, remained fixed in either Stage I or Stage II and never reached Stage III or felt competent enough to use a problem-solving direction to meet the needs and stresses of the aging individual. Medical complaints were thus enumerated, and sessions remained at this point for their entire time span. In addition, whereas the experimental group appeared to seek out members of the group for companionship outside the group's limits, such behavior was nowhere evident in the talk group. It would thus appear that the results confirm the hypothesis stating that there would be differences in social functioning favoring the experimental group.

Also confirmed was the hypothesis that the experimental group would show less medical symptomatology (see Tables 6.1 and 6.2). Clinical impressions attested to this; nurses and doctors in the hospital stated that this group became less anxious about seeing "the specialist" (physician) and more excited about participating in the group. Of interest is the fact that the talk group, meeting with the "passive" leader also showed some decrease of medical symptoms, whereas the control group, never involved in group activity at all, showed an increase of medical complaints, as recorded by hospital charts.

A striking finding, too, was the tempo of the sessions in each of the two group conditions. The experimental group had many more active sessions as recorded by the nurse-observers. Thus, in this group, persons addressed other persons (there was much cross-conversation); questions and answers were parried back and forth, and dialogue was vibrant and "alive." This was in direct contrast to the situation of the talk group, where, with few members present, persons often carried on a monologue, and the tempo was a depressed, slow one. Consistent with these findings was the fact that group attendance remained high for the resocialization or experimental group, whereas attendance consistently dwindled in the talk group to the point where, as noted previously, only one member attended the last session! Consistent with the high attendance and vibrant tempo of the experimental group was the fact that those members sought out other group members; the talk group members did not do so, claiming that the others in the group "depressed them."

It was also hypothesized that the experimental group would show positive changes in intellectual functioning. This was found, with the WAIS "Total" scores yielding an F value of 4.310 ($p < .05$)(see Table 6.3). The experimental group showed the greatest overall increase of intellectual skills, the talk group a small amount and the control group none at all. The last group, conversely, showed a decrease in that their scores, in pre- and post-test analysis, dropped. A simple but possibly valid explanation for this finding is that the experimental group was in the most stimulating environment. This type of environment seems to be related to an increase in overall cognitive or intellectual functioning; an environment devoid of such stimulation seems to depress intellectual acuity.

Of the isolation scales used, although all groups were equal on the Adulthood Isolation Index, the experimental group showed significant differences on the Past Month Isolation Index; that is, they sought out other persons (other than their group members) with whom to interact, after exposure to the experimental condition.

The Socialization Index yielded no differences between the groups. Perhaps it is not sufficiently sensitive for an intact (i.e., nonhospitalized) population.

Table 6.1. A One-Way Analysis of Variance for Change Scores on
the Cornell Medical Index "Yes" for the Experimental, Talk and
Control Groups

SOURCE	SUM OF SQUARES	DF	MEAN SQUARE	F	P
Between	178.33	2	89.16	5.553	$<.01$
Within	786.51	49	16.05		

Table 6.2. A One-Way Analysis of Variance for Change Scores on
the Cornell Medical Index "No" for the Experimental, Talk and
Control Groups

SOURCE	SUM OF SQUARES	DF	MEAN SQUARE	F	P
Between	654.88	2	327.44	4.625	$<.05$
Within	3468.65	49	70.79		

Table 6.3. A One-Way Analysis of Variance for Change Scores of the WAIS
"Total" Scores for Experimental, Talk and Control Groups

SOURCE	SUM OF SQUARES	DF	MEAN SQUARE	F	D
Between	345.04	2	172.52	4.310	$<.05$
Within	1962.94	49	40.06		

The Group Evaluation Form yielded significant differences favoring
the experimental group in that, whereas both the talk and the experimental group stated that feelings were openly expressed in the
group, only the experimental group wanted to join a group similar to
this. The talk group did not wish a repeat of the experience.

SUMMARY AND IMPLICATIONS

In summary, an intervention approach, in the form of a resocialization group process, applied to community-based aging using a

medical center's clinic setting, may be responsible for the significant results noted. Apparently the intervention approach, which allowed for the creation of both a stimulating environment and the use of accepted reinforcement techniques by a trained group leader, best explains the significant differences between the groups. Noting the lack of significant results in the talk group, it may also be posited that stimulation per se (without a trained leader) may be inadequate for changing behaviors.

Regarding future research and implementation, perhaps groups of this nature should be incorporated into settings such as offices of medical doctors, community clinics and senior citizen centers where aging persons assemble, as a means of formalizing preventive approaches. Future research and social action might thus include early-intervention techniques in the lives of the aging as a means of reversing the "aging means illness with concomitant decreases in cognitive functioning and socially inappropriate behaviors" model projected upon the aging, and, indeed all, members of this society.

REFERENCES

Bennett, R. G. Distinguishing characteristics of the aging from a sociological viewpoint. *J. Am. Geriatr. Soc.*, 1968, *16*, 127-134.

Feil, N. W. Group therapy in a home for the aged. *Gerontologist*, 1967, *7*, 192-195.

Lowy, L. Roadblocks in group work practice with older people: A framework for analysis. *Gerontologist*, 1967, 190-113.

Rosenbaum, M., and Berger, M. A review of some recent group psychotherapy methods for elderly psychiatric patients. In *Group Psychotherapy and Group Function*. New York: Basic Books, Inc., 1963, 445-495.

Slavson, S. R. *A Textbook in Analytic Group Psychotherapy*. New York: International Universities Press, 1964.

Verplanck, W. S. The control of the content of conversation: Reinforcement of statement of opinion. *J. Abnorm. Soc. Psychol.*, 1955, 668-676.

Wolberg, L. W. *The Technique of Psychotherapy*. New York: Grune and Stratton, 1967.

Yates, A. J. *Behavior Therapy*. New York: John Wiley and Sons, Inc., 1970.

PART III
TREATING THE CONSEQUENCES OF ISOLATION: EXPERIMENTS IN RESOCIALIZATION OF THE INSTITUTIONALIZED AGED

7
Project SHARE:
The Therapeutic Use of
"Social Hours for
Adult Recognition Exchange"*

Frances B. Arje, Ed.D., R.N.**

In the ongoing search for therapeutic social contexts, program gimmicks that are simple and inexpensive to use are very attractive to personnel in facilities for care of the aged. Once established, these gimmicks tend to be perpetuated—usually because they serve the interests of personnel and rarely because their effect on residents has been systematically studied and evaluated.

The above statement just paraphrased one of CORAD's (1969) statements of priority needs for research in social gerontology. The original statement was a dignified—and printable—reflection of some thoughts and feelings when it was evident that a "new" group discussion technique being used in some homes for the aged, was, in fact, a technique specifically designed by Robinson (1967) for use by psychiatric aides to "remotivate" mentally ill patients in state hospitals.

REMOTIVATION TECHNIQUE: A BRIEF HISTORY OF ITS DEVELOPMENT

The technique was devised in 1949 by Dorothy Hoskins Smith, a teacher of English literature who also worked as a volunteer in a state hospital in California. Ms. Smith used the technique with a small group of regressed male patients in what was then referred to as a "back ward." The results were astonishing—men who hadn't uttered a sensible word in years began conversing with Ms. Smith and with each other. Word of this phenomenon reached the East Coast, where the Southeast Chapter of the Pennsylvania Mental Health Association persuaded

*Part of an unpublished doctoral dissertation, Teachers College, Columbia University, 1973. Partial support was provided by an AOA traineeship.
**Assistant Director of Education and Training, South Beach Psychiatric Center, Staten Island, New York. Adjunct Associate Professor, Department of Leisure Studies, SEHNAP, New York University.

Smith, Kline and French to provide funds so that Ms. Smith could be brought to the Philadelphia State Hospital to demonstrate her technique. She showed how it could be mastered by personnel with a high school education or less. After Ms. Smith's sudden death in 1957, some of her former trainees, led by an aide named Walter Pullinger, Jr., taught the Smith technique to other personnel in 40 state hospitals. Somewhere along the way, someone dubbed it "remotivation" technique.

By 1970, there were 14 Regional Remotivation Training Centers in the United States, and remotivation programs were being conducted in 248 institutional settings. An unspecified number of these programs were in nursing homes and homes for the aged (APA, 1970).

The Smith remotivation technique has been defined by Pullinger and Sholly (n.d.) as "very simple group therapy, of an objective nature, used by an attendant with his own patients on his own ward, in an effort to reach the 'unwounded' areas of the patients' personality and get them moving again in the direction of reality." Robinson (1967) defined it as "a technique of simple group interaction which can be used by the psychiatric aide with his own patients," and as "a structured activity which enables her (the nurse or the aide) to reach patients in a meaningful and constructive way, over and above daily custodial care."

A remotivation program usually consists of a series of 12 sessions held once or twice a week with groups of 10 to 15 patients. Each session may require from 30 minutes to one hour of time, depending on the topic and the patients' responses. Patients are encouraged, but not required, to attend.

The discussion leader is referred to as a "remotivation technician." The remotivation technician is one who has attended a 30-hour course in remotivation technique at a regional training center or a nearby hospital.*

The remotivation technician selects topics—and develops written plans for presentation of topics—in accord with recommendations made in manuals published under the auspices of the American

---

*In Project SHARE, the remotivation technician was Deolinda Clark, L.P.N., of the staff of the Society of St. Johnland, Kings Park, N. Y. Ms. Clark was trained in the technique by Ms. J. Houpt, Remotivation Coordinator and Director of Inservice Education, Northeast Nassau Psychiatric Hospital, Kings Park, N. Y.

Psychiatric Association/Smith, Kline and French Remotivation Project. For example, Robinson (1967) recommended that topics be selected that:

have to do with everyday, ordinary things which many of us take for granted—the way a tree grows, the history of our native state, what wares one might find in a department store, what smoke means in our daily lives, what makes weather, and all the multitude of things with which we live and the people with whom we must interact . . . . Some of the more obvious limitations on the selection of subject matter would preclude such topics as religion, sex, prejudice, marital problems, family relationships, and similar "touchy" areas.

Pullinger and Sholly (n. d.) wrote that "Almost anything may be used as topic material," and suggested that subject matter could be chosen from geography, history, hobbies, literature, nature, science, sports and industry.

A sample meeting plan presented by Robinson illustrates the method recommended to remotivation technicians for using a written plan as a guide to discussion of a preselected topic:

Step 1. The Climate of Acceptance.

Step 2. "What kinds of animals are found in Africa?" (Several answers until someone says, "Lion.") "What does a lion look like?" (Allow for some descriptions, then show pictures of lions.) Poem: "Lion" (Mary Britton Mille).

Step 3. "Why are men afraid of lions?" "What other wild animals are fearful?" "What else is Africa famous for?" (List several other related questions.)

Step 4. "What products come from Africa?" (There will be a number of answers which can lead to a discussion of work and jobs in Africa. Show pictures from *National Geographic* of African diamond mines, Egyptian cotton and oil, etc.)

Step 5. Thank patients for coming and express pleasure at meeting. Plan for next meeting.

As indicated in the sample plan, a remotivation technician takes five basic steps in leading a discussion of a preselected topic. The five steps taken during each session in a series of remotivation sessions are:

1. *The Climate of Acceptance:* greeting each person by name, telling the group that it is good to be with them, establishing a warm, friendly ambience. (Suggested time span: 5 minutes)

2. *A Bridge to Reality:* introducing a topic of general, everyday interest using poetry, props, displays and other visual aids to attract attention and stimulate discussion. (Suggested time span: 15 minutes)

3. *Sharing the World We Live In:* developing the topic by asking planned, objective questions; encouraging participants to speak to the remotivation technician and to each other. (Suggested time span: 15 minutes)

4. *An Appreciation of the Work of the World:* with mental patients, the aim of this step is to stimulate thinking about work in relation to themselves; with nursing home patients, the aim of this step is to stimulate reminiscence and sharing of experience, ideas and opinions regarding activities that have past, present and possibly future interest for participants. (Suggested time span: 15 minutes)

5. *The Climate of Appreciation:* expressing enjoyment of being together; showing pleasure that each person attended the session; inviting participants to bring poems, songs, props, artifacts, newspaper clippings and other items relevant to the topic planned for the next session. (Suggested time span: 5 minutes)

It is evident that the foregoing five steps *are* simple for most people who are interested in working with small groups—and the costs, in terms of manpower hours and equipment, *are* low. As CORAD suggested, such gimmicks are attractive to personnel working with residents of facilities for care of the aged. However, consultants in the Divison on Aging, Federation of Protestant Welfare Agencies were concerned and wanted some answers to the question, "How will the residents—in the voluntary homes for the aged served by this Division—react to this particular group discussion technique?"

A search of the literature on remotivation technique showed that at that time only three systematic studies of the Smith technique had been done; none of these three studies dealt with a population that could be considered comparable to the residents of the homes served by the Federation's Division on Aging (Long, 1962, 1965; Wolfe, 1965).

The consultants of the Division could not generalize the findings of these studies of the effect of the Smith technique upon samples of mental hospital patients to the needs and interests of residents of the Federation's homes for the aged. So, we decided to try the technique in a representative home, the Society of St. Johnland in Kings Park, N. Y.

DESCRIPTION OF THE STUDY

The study, which was referred to as Project SHARE (Social Hours for Adult Recognition Exchange), combined an experimental design with an action research approach.* Reactions of residents of a home for the aged who attended a series of remotivation sessions were compared with reactions of residents of the same home who did not attend the sessions. The sessions were planned and conducted in accord with the specific methods of the Smith five-step remotivation technique.

The purpose of Project SHARE was to obtain information that would be useful to consultants and other concerned personnel in making decisions as to suitability of the technique for use with the heterogeneous populations served in homes for the aged.

The Project SHARE sample of 72 residents was considered representative of populations served by member homes of the Federation of Protestant Welfare Agencies, Inc., New York, N. Y., in relation to the following key characteristics: number of residents served; age range of residents; ratio of men to women residents; religion; education; occupational background; need for levels of care (independent living, intermediate care and long-term care).

The Attender group of 36 residents was subdivided into four subgroups of about 10 persons because the Smith five-step remotivation technique was designed for use with small groups. The procedure for forming and scheduling the four subgroups consisted of staff examining each Attender's usual pattern of participation in recreational and restorative services, schedule of nursing care and treatments, rest periods, visits by physicians, hairdressing appointments, entertaining visitors, going out to visit with family and friends, shopping trips and other activities of daily living.

The instruments used to measure reactions of the SHARE sample to the Smith five-step remotivation technique were selected for relevance to hypotheses, reliability and ease of administration by persons

---

*The experimental design consisted of administering a "post-test only" interview schedule to an experimental group of 36 residents who had attended a series of 12 remotivation sessions for a period of seven weeks and to a control group of 36 residents of the same home who had not attended the sessions. The action research approach involved the home's administrative and direct service staff in planning, obtaining special training and using selected unobtrusive measures to record observations of resident behaviors for a 21-week interval, which began seven weeks prior to and ended seven weeks after the series of remotivation sessions.

with minimal experience in use of forms for recording observations. Four questions that served as research questions of the study were:

1. Do residents who have been exposed to the selected remotivation technique have measurably higher levels of socialization, mental status and morale than residents of the same home for the aged who have not been exposed to the technique?
2. Do residents who participate in a series of remotivation sessions show measurable changes in behavior during the series of sessions?
3. Do residents who have been exposed to the selected remotivation technique engage in measurably higher levels of participation in regular recreation program activities than residents of the same home who have not been exposed to the technique?
4. Are residents who have been exposed to the selected remotivation technique measurably more independent in activities of daily living than residents of the same home who have not been exposed to the technique?

Statistics used to determine significance of findings were unsophisticated, and included small-sample statistics to examine similarities and differences in experimental and control groups prior to and following exposure of the Attender group to the Smith five-step remotivation technique.

MAJOR FINDINGS

The Attender group obtained significantly better scores on three post-test interview indices used to find answers to the hypothetical question, "Do residents who have been exposed to the selected remotivtion technique have measurably higher levels of socialization, mental status and morale than residents of the same home who have not been exposed to the technique?" The answers to this question appeared to be "yes," as may be seen in Table 7.1.

Socialization

Attender group mean scores on this index were significantly better than Nonattender group scores. The Socialization Index (SI) (Bennett and Nahemow, 1965) was a measure of information known by

Table 7.1. Means, Standard Deviations and Z-Values for Total Scores
on Socialization Index, Mental Status Schedule and Geriatric Supplement,
and Morale Scale, by Attender and Nonattender Groups, Project SHARE,
Society of St. Johnland, Kings Park, N. Y., January 1971

INDEX	ATTENDING (N=36)		NONATTENDING (N=36)		Z-VALUE
	MEAN	SD	MEAN	SD	
SI: Socialization Index	29.88	3.57	13.44	5.67	+14.235[a]
MSS-GS: Mental Status and Geriatric Supplement	16.13	10.42	45.63[c]	24.20	+ 6.715[a,b]
PGS: Philadelphia Geriatric Center Morale Scale	15.77	3.82	10.11	4.11	+ 6.047[a]

[a] Significantly different at the .01 level (for a one-tailed test).
[b] The Z-value was computed from the F-ratio of 45.11 (D.F. = 1.70) given for total MSS-GS scores on the computer analysis print-out.
[c] Higher scores for MSS-GS indicated greater degrees of emotional disturbance.

residents about social norms at St. Johnland. The SI used in Project SHARE was adapted from one that had previously been used (described by Bennett in earlier chapters above).

Mental Status

Attender group mean scores on this index were significantly better than Nonattender group scores. The Mental Status Schedule and Geriatric Supplement (MSS-GS) was designed to offer clinical judgments of current pathology based on data collected during an interview; however, it also offers indicators of relative degrees of mental health/ illness in groups of nonpsychiatrically diagnosed aged persons (Spitzer et al., 1964, 1966).

Morale

Attender group mean scores on this index and its principal components were significantly better than Nonattender group scores. The Philadelphia Geriatric Center Morale Scale (PGS) contains 22 items related to six components that indicate the multidimensional nature of the concept generally referred to as "morale" (Lawton, 1972).

Table 7.2. Means, Standard Deviation and Z-Value for Time I and Time II Total APA/SKF Group Interaction Scores, Attender Group Project SHARE, Society of St. Johnland, Kings Park, N.Y., October/December 1970

Time of observation	Total APA/SKF Group Interaction Score		
	Mean	SD	Z-Value
Time I	24.771	9.248	+15.337
Time II	42.222	5.356	

An unobtrusive measure was used to find answers to the hypothetical question, "Do residents who participate in a series of remotivation sessions show measurable changes in behavior during the series of sessions?" The answers to this question appeared to be "Yes," according to observations by teams of participant observers (assigned to each of the four Attender subgroups). Observations were recorded on a form adapted from two instruments developed by the American Psychiatric Association/Smith, Kline and French Remotivation Project (APA/SKF). Use of this form yielded Time I and Time II total interaction scores as well as scores for 16 discrete items listed on the form.

Attenders showed impressive improvement over time in their interactions with the SHARE leader (remotivation technician) and with other members of the SHARE subgroups, as is seen in Table 7.2.

Individual Attender Reactions

The most impressive changes in behavior among Attenders during the series of SHARE sessions were in the areas of interest and appreciation, improved relations with other members of the group, enjoyment of sessions, improved behavior during sessions *and* on the ward, reduction of tendencies to be restless or withdrawn and increased interest in group activities.

One member of the Attender group, who had accepted during the first round of randomly extended invitations to attend SHARE sessions, evidently had some second thoughts about the matter. Miss "S" did not attend the first two sessions, saying she did not feel up to going over to the Lawrence House Solarium "today." She then attended ten consecutive sessions when Miss "C," another resident of the Inn, persuaded her to join the Delta subgroup. They explained to the SHARE leader that Miss "S" had been reluctant to attend because of a hearing impairment, but that she was happy to be with the Delta group because Miss "C" sat next to her and kept her informed of what was being said.

During administration of the post-test interview, Miss "S" was one of a total of 33 respondents who expressed appreciation of the value of SHARE sessions for those who are lonely, for newcomers and for those with ambulatory, visual and manual impairments. Miss "S," who was 95 years of age, prefaced her remarks with the statement, "It was wonderful to see what happened to those *old* people in the wheelchairs!"

In Time II ratings, a total of 26 persons, or 72.22% of the Attender group, were judged to have improved greatly in participation in intergroup comments and to have established very good relationships with others. They became more attentive to each other, assisted those who needed help in seeing, hearing or ambulation—either directly or by asking a participant observer to do so—or tried to assist the leader in various ways, such as helping to clean up after a session or speaking up when there was a lull in the conversation during a session.

With respect to being attentive to one another, by the end of the fifth session the majority of Attender group members had begun to take an active part in the greeting and farewell behaviors referred to in the remotivation literature as Step I, "The Climate of Acceptance," and Step V, "The Climate of Appreciation." This was quite a contrast to earlier observations, in which it had been noted that Attenders tended to cling together.

Also, in early sessions, some overt evidence of rejection of residents with visible disabilities was observed. For example, Mrs. "H," a legally blind but partially sighted resident of the Inn, might nudge her neighbor, another resident of the Inn, point across the room to Mrs. "K" (a wheelchair-bound resident of Lawrence House, with severe parkinsonism) and say in a loud stage whisper, "What's she doing here? She doesn't belong with this group!"

Attender group members who exhibited reactions similar to those of Mrs. "H" during early sessions were not spoken to directly about their behavior.

The changes in attentiveness to each other and acceptance of others among members of SHARE subgroups apparently evolved spontaneously. These changes appeared to be emulations of behaviors of the SHARE leader and participant observers. These behaviors were based on recognition of three responsibilities of group observers, which had been described in the literature on group development: (1) considering oneself a member of the group rather than an outside person; (2) making contributions that can be constructive for the stage of growth a group is in at a particular time; and (3) passing on to the group itself observer functions or roles.

In regard to an APA/SKF item listed under "Group Relations" as "does not resent being interrupted," the two persons who had shown this behavior during early sessions changed in this respect: They were eventually able to say something like, "Please let me finish what I was saying." This was thought to be a possible indicator of improved self-image and ego function.

Observations of enjoyment of early sessions were based primarily on whether or not a person continued to attend. The Time II observations, however, were based on apparent comfort in speaking up, interest in listening to others, smiling, nodding, laughing appropriately, joining in spontaneous singing or play-acting, shaking hands or patting or stroking others and similar evidences of pleasure and satisfaction. In this respect, the change from Time I to Time II was remarkable. The behaviors described in the foregoing passage were evidenced by 33 persons, or 91.65% of the Attender group; whereas in early sessions, only five persons, or 13.88% of the group, had exhibited any of the "enjoyment" behaviors.

Of the 24 persons, or 66.66% of the Attender group, who in early sessions had seemed to enjoy the sessions "sometimes," only two, or 2.77% of the Attender group, were observed to continue to show signs of not enjoying themselves from time to time. One of these two persons was Dr. "M" of Lawrence House, who attended all 12 sessions with his subgroup.

Dr. "M" had a tendency to dominate conversations during early sessions, became visibly angry (red in the face) when interrupted and would retire behind his newspaper when other members of the group "talked too much." Toward the end of the sessions, however, Dr. "M" seemed more interested in and more attentive to others. During the post-test interview, he remarked: "Some of these old fools around here seemed to get a lot out of SHARE. Why, for the first time in five years, I've been able to have sensible conversations with [mentioned names of other Lawrence House residents]. I had given them up as hopeless cases."

The other person who seemed to enjoy sessions "sometimes," according to the Time II rating, was Mrs. "F," whom Dr. "M" had considered a "hopeless case."

Three incessant "chatterers," who had originally been rated by participant observers as talking too much, modified their behavior to the point where they listened attentively to others and made appropriate responses to what was being said.

One extremely shy resident became a "star" in her subgroup during the third session, in which the topic was flowers. She astonished everyone by reciting, in full, every stanza of Wordsworth's "I Wandered Lonely as a Cloud." In a gentle, low-pitched but perfectly clear voice, Miss "C" of the Inn managed to fill the Lawrence House Solarium with a "host of golden daffodils." Word of this achievement spread, and Miss "C" was invited by another SHARE subgroup to repeat her performance. She accepted.

Mrs. "N" was a SHARE enthusiast. Her responses were very positive. She emphasized its value for "lonely persons" who needed something to "take their minds off their troubles" and needed help in "making friends."

Mrs. "O" was an outgoing, active, friendly and cheerful person, well liked by everyone. She, too, was a SHARE enthusiast. One of her ways of helping the SHARE leader was to say, "Oh, that reminds me of a song." She would then sing a few bars, stop and ask other members of her subgroup to join in, asking them to help her "remember" the words. Evidently she mentioned this ploy to other subgroup members who were residents of the Inn, because they began to do this with their subgroups, all of which expressed particular enjoyment of this aspect of the group interactions and activities that characterized the second half of the series of SHARE sessions.

Creative Activities

It was found that almost half of the SHARE sample of residents exposed to the Smith five-step remotivation technique appeared to have potential for assisting a remotivation technician. Although participant observers considered only 27.77% of the Attender group able to do so, self reports of Attender group members indicated that 44.44% felt willing and able to assist the SHARE leader.

Table 7.3. Means, Standard Deviations and Z-Values for Time II Highest Levels of Participation in Creative and Competitive Activities by Attender and Non-attender Groups, Project SHARE, Society of St. Johnland, Kings Park, New York, December 11, 1970–January 22, 1971

Type of activity	Attender Group (N=36)		Nonattender Group (N=36)		Z-Value
	Mean	SD	Mean	SD	
Creative	5.444	2.117	4.250	2.285	+2.301[a]
Competitive	5.944	2.203	3.000	2.842	+5.493[b]

[a]Significantly different at the .05 level (for a one-tailed test).

[b]Significantly different at the .01 level (for a one-tailed test).

Another unobtrusive measure was used to find answers to the hypothetical question, "Do residents exposed to the selected remotivation technique engage in measureably higher levels of participation in regular recreation program activities than residents of the same home who have not been exposed to the technique?" Again, the answer appeared to be "Yes," according to observations recorded by recreation staff members on Individual Progress Records (IPR) (Margulies, 1968), which were recorded for the total population of 89 residents over a period of 21 weeks. The IPR is a graphic form for recording the highest levels of an individual's participation in activities classified as creative or competitive during each week over a period of months. In Project SHARE, the highest level of activity recorded for the sample of 72 residents during the first and the twenty-first week provided a basis for Time I and Time II comparisons, as may be seen in Table 7.3.

Over a period of 21 weeks, Time II observations showed that the Attender group had moved up to significantly higher levels of creative activity. On the other hand, the Nonattender group showed an insignificant reduction of engagement in creative activities.

Competitive Activities

Over a period of 21 weeks, Time II observations showed that the Attender group had moved up to even higher levels of competitive activity. The Nonattender group showed no improvement at all in terms of engaging in competitive activities.

A third unobtrusive measure was used to find answers to the hypothetical question, "Are residents who have been exposed to the select-

Table 7.4. Means and t-Values of Time I and Time II Summary ADL Scores of Nonattender Group, by House, Project SHARE, Society of St. Johnland, Kings Park, New York, October 9-16, 1970/December 11-18, 1970

House	Nonattender Group (N=36)		t-Value
	Time I Mean	Time II Mean	
The Inn	1.083	1.083	(D.F.=11)
Thomson House	1.667	1.888	1.005 (D.F.=17)
Lawrence House	4.167	4.000	0.543 (D.F.=5)

ed remotivation technique measurably more independent in activities of daily living than residents of the same home who have not been exposed to the technique?" Again, the answers to the hypothetical question appeared to be "Yes," according to around-the-clock observations recorded by nursing personnel for each of the 89 residents of the home two weeks before and two weeks after the series of remotivation sessions. The Index of Activities of Daily Living (ADL) was used to obtain scores on Time I and Time II performance of the SHARE sample of 72 residents, as is shown in Tables 7.4–7.6. The ADL form is a checklist of levels of independence in performance of six functions: bathing, dressing, toileting, transfer, continence, and feeding (Katz et al., 1963).

Time II observations indicated that Attender group members who required long-term care improved significantly in independence for dressing, going to the toilet, transfer from bed to chair and from wheelchair to regular chair, and in ability to feed themselves. Attender group members who required intermediate care improved significantly in independence in bathing themselves.

In contrast to the significant improvement in activities of daily living in the Attender group, Time II observations of the Nonattender group yielded summary ADL scores that indicated a significant increase of dependence in residents who required intermediate care.

Further scrutiny of ADL data on the total Nonattender group, however, indicated no significant differences for each of the six functions of activities of daily living for Time I and Time II observations.

Table 7.5. Mean Scores and *t*-Values of Time I and Time II Ratings of Levels of Independence in Six Activities of Daily Living for Attender Group, by House, Project SHARE, Society of St. Johnland, Kings Park, New York, October 6–16, 1970/ December 11–18, 1970

House, Time and *t*-Value of Rating	Activity of Daily Living					
	Bathing Mean	Dressing Mean	Toileting Mean	Transfer Mean	Continence Mean	Feeding Mean
The Inn (*N*=11)						
Time I	1.273	2.000	2.000	2.000	2.000	2.000
Time II	1.273	1.818	1.909	1.909	2.000	2.000
t-Value (D.F.=10)		–1.000	–1.000	–1.000		
Thomson House (*N*=6)						
Time I	0.833	1.833	2.000	2.000	2.000	2.000
Time II	1.167	2.000	2.000	2.000	2.000	2.000
t-Value (D.F.=5)	+1.587	+1.000				
Lawrence House (*N*=18)						
Time I	0.316	0.526	1.316	1.211	1.368	1.474
Time II	0.526	0.789	1.474	1.478	1.421	1.684
t-Value	+1.455	+2.041[a]	+1.845[a]	+2.538[a]	+0.326	+2.186[a]

[a]Significantly different at the .05 level (for a one-tailed *t*-test).

Table 7.6. Mean Scores and *t*-Values of Time II Ratings of Levels of Independence in Six Activities of Daily Living for Attender and Nonattender Groups, by House, Project SHARE, Society of St. Johnland, Kings Park, New York, December 6–12, 1970

House, Group and *t*-Value of Rating	Activity of Daily Living					
	Bathing Mean	Dressing Mean	Toileting Mean	Transfer Mean	Continence Mean	Feeding Mean
The Inn						
Attenders (*N*=11)	1.273	1.818	1.909	1.909	2.000	2.000
Nonattenders (*N*=12)	1.250	2.000	2.000	2.000	2.000	2.000
t-Value (D.F.=21)	+0.078	–1.047	–1.047	–1.047		
Thomson House						
Attenders (*N*=6)	1.167	2.000	2.000	2.000	2.000	2.000
Nonattenders (*N*=18)	0.444	1.444	1.944	1.944	1.944	2.000
t-Value (D.F.=22)	+3.426[a]	+1.712	+0.575	+0.575	+0.575	
Lawrence House						
Attenders (*N*=19)	0.526	0.789	1.474	1.478	1.421	1.684
Nonattenders (*N*=6)	0.333	0.667	1.333	1.500	1.167	1.333
t-Value (D.F.=23)	+0.803	+0.302	+0.508	–0.090	+0.622	+1.063

[a]Significantly different at the .01 level (for a one-tailed *t*-test).

IMPLICATIONS OF MAJOR FINDINGS

Because of the problem of resistance to random selection, bias of experimental and control groups was not overcome in Project SHARE. A systematic sampling method was used as a compromise. Thus, there must remain some doubt as to the validity of any probability statements that might be made as generalizations from the SHARE sample to other hetrogeneous populations served in homes for the aged. The quest for scientific precision—as exemplified in the use of a multiple comparison method to find out if refusers retained in the Nonattender group because of the small size of the sample had inflated the Project SHARE findings—helped to diminish some of these doubts. However, as Lind and O'Brien (1971) pointed out, researchers must never lose sight of the reality that human reactions are "difficult to anticipate, control or even measure."

Socialization

It may be inferred from Project SHARE findings that, when used with small groups of residents, the Smith five-step remotivation technique promotes socialization by increasing the number of social contacts among residents, and that those exposed to the technique do become better integrated into the social system of a home for the aged.

An implication for action, therefore, is that the technique be tried on a one-to-one basis with residents who are social isolates and those who refuse to attend group sessions. This one-to-one approach might be initiated by a resident who has been exposed to the technique and who is acceptable to the isolated individual resident.

Selection of resident remotivators to work with social isolates and others who refuse invitations to attend group remotivation sessions might be based on observations of leadership qualities demonstrated by individuals who have participated in a series of remotivation sessions. These leadership qualities, as described by Ross and Hendry (1964), are referred to as empathy, consideration and surgency. These authors define empathy as ability to "identify with, and respond to, the emotional needs of members of the group and/or to be the object of identification for group members"; consideration is defined as ability to "give help in very practical ways, to be ready to explain actions, to

give detailed instruction, to improve the welfare of his followers relative to their work or activity in the group"; and surgency is defined
as "talkativeness, cheerfulness, geniality, enthusiasm, expressiveness,
altertness and originality."

A resident serving as a remotivator would undoubtedly need supportive supervision from a staff member. The supervising staff member might help the resident remotivator plan a gradual increase in complexity of demands upon the social isolate, with the goal of persuading
the isolated resident to engage in socializing interactions with a gradual-
ly increasing number of other selected residents of the home.

In the early spring of 1975, the recreation consultant who had
served on the SHARE action team reported that two surviving members of the original Attender group were still informally engaged in
serving as one-to-one remotivators of social isolates and newcomers,
with informal supportive supervision of recreation and nursing personnel at the Society of St. Johnland.

In 1975, it was also reported that one surviving member of the
original Nonattender group had mastered and was still using the technique during the social hour preceding meals, when residents get together for a light repast of juice, sherry or port, and cookies. This
was all done on a spontaneous, unplanned basis. However, it appears
evident that such use of "graduates" of a series of remotivation sessions might very well be attempted in a systematic manner, in planned
experiments in other homes for the aged.

Mental Status

Project SHARE findings suggested that the Smith five-step remotivation technique may well be a simple, inexpensive and effective intervention method for improving mental status of residents of homes
for the aged. The need for such intervention has been suggested by
the findings of a survey that indicated that institutionalized aged persons with physical illnesses also have severe emotional problems. The
SHARE sample did indeed have multiple physical disorders and impairments, which could be expected to have an adverse effect upon their
feelings about themselves and others, and upon their reactions to
environmental as well as internal stresses or frustrations.

In this respect, it seems reasonable to assume that the relationship
of physical deficits to mental status is probably a universal problem

among older people—in or out of institutional settings. Because significantly better mental status scores were obtained by SHARE sample Attenders of remotivation sessions as compared to mental status scores of Nonattenders, it seems likely that adapted use of the technique with older persons—in or outside of institutional settings—should be encouraged.

For example, workers in a community mental health center might want to consider teaching the technique to families of older persons who have been or are about to be discharged from general hospitals, or from psychiatric units of general hospitals, or from state mental hospitals. For those who do not have families to return to, and who must be transferred from hospitals to nursing homes, halfway houses, foster homes or single-room occupancy in hotels (or other living arrangements), the technique might be readily taught to paraprofessional personnel who provide follow-up services. Expanded use of the technique might be a step toward enabling older persons to maintain gains in mental status and to prevent or minimize the need for readmission to hospital settings.

Morale

Again, Project SHARE findings seem to support the notion that this simple, inexpensive method of intervention has a beneficial effect on the general morale of the older person who lives in a home for the aged. Because morale seems to be influenced by—and also seems to influence—a person's ability to accept social norms, take part in the activities available in the "community" in which he lives and adjust to the limitations imposed by physical aspects of aging, the SHARE findings may have implications for action to maintain or restore maximal levels of functioning in relation to the older person's socialization, mental status and morale.

Use of the Smith five-step remotivation technique may be a basic approach to enabling older persons, wherever they may be living, to overcome feelings of uselessness imposed by attitudes toward "old codgers," which have detrimental effects on the morale of older people in our society. An older person who could be enabled to serve as a "remotivator" for other older people would probably score highest on a morale scale, and older people who have had the attention of a selected elderly remotivator would probably obtain higher morale-scale scores than those who have not had this type of helpful intervention. The possibilities of extending this morale-building service to older persons seem endless.

What would be needed is probably some type of adult education and practicum program for older persons who have the leadership qualities described in this chapter. Such a program could conceivably be offered through the education and training department of a community mental health center. Graduates of the program could be assigned to the health center's aging client population, to work with supportive supervision of staff members who are conversant with the case histories of individual aged clients. The elderly remotivators might work as volunteers, or perhaps arrangements could be made to pay for their services.

Group Interaction and Leadership

The findings of Project SHARE suggested that almost half of the older persons who have been exposed to the Smith five-step remotivation technique may have potential for becoming resident remotivators and could, with adequate supervision, work effectively with aged social isolates and others who are reluctant to join group activities. An education program offered by a community mental health center could probably provide the skill training and supervision elderly remotivators would need to function comfortably and effectively with other older individuals and small groups.

Creative and Competitive Activities

Among the activities referred to as competitive on the IPR form, serving on resident councils or planning committees occupied the highest level. Surviving Attenders who had been judged to have potential for assisting a SHARE leader have tended to engage in this highest level of activity, according to reports of the recreation consultant who was a member of the SHARE action research team.

It may be inferred from this finding that residents of a home for the aged who have observable leadership qualities should be encouraged to help plan remotivation sessions, select topics and conduct sessions with isolated individuals or small groups.

An implication for action is that recreation personnel can make good use of the time, experience and talent of older people to plan programs that are meaningful, interesting and stimulating to themselves and to their aged cohorts. It is likely that, when a series of remotivation sessions has been planned with or by a group of older persons, the topics for discussion might be less bland and more controversial than those selected by the SHARE remotivation technician. Such sessions might lead to action supporting legislation beneficial to themselves and other old people, writing letters to government officials, getting out their votes and other behavior that might help to effect needed change in existing social systems.

Activities of Daily Living

Project SHARE findings suggested that the Smith five-step remotivation technique is useful in encouraging older people with chronic physical disabilities to try to engage in more independent levels of self-care. An implication of this finding is that the technique be used as part of a rehabilitation program for older people with visual, manual and ambulatory deficits, such as those recovering from a stroke. Another implication for action is that use of the technique may help prevent increased dependency among residents who are currently capable of independent living or who require intermediate care.*

For residents whose poor physical disability adjustment seems to preclude initial interest in attending group activities, the adapted use of the Smith five-step remotivation technique on a one-to-one basis might be helpful in improving morale. In working with this type of resident, all personnel, including recreation workers and nursing assistants, might profitably be taught Smith's five-step remotivation technique and how to use these steps while giving physical care aimed at maintenance or restoration of physical functioning.

In general, SHARE findings seemed to indicate that the Smith five-step remotivation technique is most effective in improving socialization, mental status, morale, group interaction and general interest in group activities, and in stimulating active participation in regular

---

*This implication for action stems from the observation that 14 out of 15 residents who refused an initial systematically extended invitation to attend SHARE sessions obtained significantly lower MSS–GS scores for adjustment to physical disability than did other members of the Nonattender group. These refusers, who had said they did not feel well enough to attend, also did not do as well on two of 22 items in the PGC morale scale as other Nonattenders. The two morale-scale items that received significantly more incorrect responses from refusers were related to *feelings* about physical disabilities.

recreation-program activities of a competitive nature. The technique seemed to be somewhat less effective in promoting independence in activities of daily living.

It may be inferred from these findings that improvements in social and psychological functioning of aged residents of homes for the aged do not necessarily have dramatic effects on their levels of independence in activities of daily living. However, the SHARE findings did indicate that some improvement in self-care can be expected among residents of homes for the aged who are exposed to the Smith five-step remotivation technique. An implication for action, therefore, is that personnel who are responsible for physical care of aged residents of homes for the aged should be exposed to in-service education programs that emphasize the need for actively involving the patient in the physical as well as the emotional and social aspects of the rehabilitation process. That is, the Smith five-step remotivation technique can probably be adapted and used to enable chronically ill older persons to function as co-managers of their total treatment regimes.

THE HUMAN IMPACT OF SHARE

Statistically significant findings of Project SHARE suggested that the selected remotivation technique is (1) suitable for use by paraprofessional personnel in homes for the aged and (2) useful in overcoming deficiencies in human contact, social stimulation, morale and social adjustment of residents of homes for the aged.*

However, without being informed of the statistical findings, administrative, nursing and recreation personnel who served as members of the SHARE action research team seemed to consider the technique useful in relation to economic, technical and social values, for they continued to utilize and adapt the five-step technique in their interactions

---

*For information concerning social isolation versus socialization as factors affecting social adjustment of aged institutionalized persons, see R. Bennett (Granick) and L. Nahemow, Preadmission isolation; Ruth Bennett, The meaning of institutional life, *The Gerontologist,* Fall, 1963 *III,* 117-125; Bennett and Nahemow, Institutional totality; Bennett and Nahemow, A two-year follow-up study of the progress of social adjustment in residents of a home for the aged, paper presented at Gerontological Society meeting in Los Angeles, Nov. 12, 1965 (typewritten); Bennett and Nahemow, Socialization and social adjustment in five residences for the aged, *International Association of Gerontology,* July 1966; Bennett, Distinguishing characteristics of the aging from a sociological viewpoint, *Journal of the American Geriatric Society,* 1968, *XVI,* 127-34; and Nahemow and Bennett, Attitude change. All of these papers are summarized in Chapters 1, 2 and 3 above.

with residents on a one-to-one as well as a small-group basis. This also suggested that the problem of the Hawthorne effect was a minimal one in the present study. The purpose of the study appeared to have been achieved. Consultants of the Division on Aging, Federation of Protestant Agencies, began to encourage training of nursing home personnel as remotivation technicians and advocated use of the technique in homes for the aged, in view of the results of Project SHARE.

SUGGESTIONS FOR FURTHER RESEARCH

Project SHARE was a first attempt systematically to study the impact of the Smith five-step remotivation technique on a heterogeneous sample of residents of a home for the aged. The limitations of the study (i.e., the small sample size, the sampling method, uncontrolled variables and lack of evaluation of long-term effects of the selected remotivation technique) indicated the need for caution in attributing importance to findings simply because they were statistically significant.

A major suggestion for improving research on use of this technique would be for researchers to obtain large, randomly selected samples of heterogeneous populations served in homes for the aged.

It would probably improve the research if more unobtrusive measures were utilized with larger samples of older persons, to minimize the reactive measurement effect of error from respondents.

A study of the impact of the Smith five-step remotivation technique in homes for the aged that do not provide the excellent living conditions of the SHARE sample at the Society of St. Johnland might show very different results from those obtained in the present study.

Comparative studies of economic, technical and social impact of (1) use of the Smith five-step remotivation technique by paraprofessional personnel and (2) use of other resocialization techniques by professional personnel should be done to determine total human impact of these types of intervention with residents of homes for the aged.

The person who served as the SHARE action research team leader is currently interested in initiating a new project, in which reality-orientation, followed by exposure to remotivation technique (using pertinent selected topics), would be examined as a method of preparing psychogeriatric patients in a mental hospital for transfer to resident status in a home for the aged.

Another possibility for research would be to videotape a series of remotivation sessions, then use the tapes to help train older persons to become one-to-one remotivators with elderly social isolates and others who are unable to accept invitations to attend group activities.

Action research with residents and other groups of aged persons to obtain data for differential topic analysis and to explore use of the Smith five-step remotivation technique to raise social and political consciousness of older persons could be conducted in homes for the aged, multi-service geriatric centers, day care centers, senior citizen centers and other community-based service settings.

Studies of adapted use of the technique with aged members of minority groups to compare effects of use of cohort remotivators, paraprofessional personnel trained as remotivation technicians and clinical specialists who use more sophisticated group intervention techniques would probably also be useful.

SUMMARY: SHARE FINDINGS AND CONCLUSIONS

A systematic study referred to as Project SHARE was conducted on a sample representative of populations served by member homes of the Federation of Protestant Welfare Agencies, Inc. Project SHARE utilized a five-index post-test interview schedule and three unobtrusive measures to find some answers to four hypothetical questions concerning the impact of the Smith five-step remotivation technique on socialization, mental status, morale, group interaction, participation in regular recreation-program activities and independence in activities of daily living among residents of a home for the aged.

Statistically significant findings suggested that the selected remotivation technique is suitable for use by paraprofessional personnel and beneficial to residents of homes for the aged. However, these findings must be considered tentative. Further research is considered necessary to substantiate the findings of Project SHARE.

REFERENCES

APA Roster of Active Remotivation Programs. Washington, D. C.: American Psychiatric Association Hospital Service, July 1970.

Bennett, Ruth G., and Nahemow, Lucille. The relations between social isolation, socialization, and adjustment in residents of a home for the aged. In M. P. Lawton and F. Lawton (Eds.), *Mental Impairment in the Aged*. Philadelphia: Maurice Jacob Press, 1965.

Committee on Research and Development (CORAD). Proposed priority investigations and experiments. In Robert J. Havighurst (Ed.), The status of research in applied social gerontology: Status report. *Gerontologist*, Winter 1969, *9*, 86.

Katz, Sidney, Ford, A. B., and Moskowitz, R. W. Studies of illness in the aged: The index of ADL: A standardized measure of biological and psychosocial function. *J. A. M. A.*, 1963, *185*, 914–919.

Lawton, M. Powell. The dimensions of morale. In D. P. Kent, R. Kastenbaum, and S. Sherwood (Eds.), *Research, Planning and Action for the Elderly*. New York: Behavioral Publications, 1972.

Lind, S. Donna, and O'Brien, John E. The general problem of program evaluation: The researchers perspective. *Gerontologist*, Winter 1971, *11*, 43–50.

Long, Ralph S. *Remotivation—Fact or Artifact*. Washington, D. C.: American Psychiatric Association, 1962.

Long, Ralph S. A study of staff–patient changes in expectancy, attitude and behavior following the introduction of a remotivation technique into the ward routine of a mental hospital. Unpublished Ph.D. dissertation, Washington University, 1965.

Margulies, Martin S. Motivating institutionalized aged through a system of graduated activity levels. Paper presented at the 21st meeting of the Gerontological Society, Denver, Colo., Nov. 1, 1968.

Pullinger, Walter F., Jr., and Sholly, Esther, M. *Outline for a Remotivation Training Course*. Philadelphia: Philadelphia State Hospital, n. d.

Robinson, Alice M. *Remotivation Technique*, rev. ed. Washington, D. C.: American Psychiatric Association, 1967; and *Remotivation Technique: A Manual for Use in Nursing Homes*. Washington, D. C.: American Psychiatric Association/Smith, Kline and French Remotivation Project, n. d.

Ross, Murray, and Hendry, Charles E. Qualities of the leader. In C. Gratton Kemp (Ed.), *Perspectives on the Group Process*. Boston: Houghton Mifflin Co., 1964.

Spitzer, Robert L., Burdock, Eugene I., and Hardesty, Anne S. *Mental Status Schedule*. New York: New York State Department of Mental Hygiene, 1964.

Spitzer, Robert L., Endicott, Jean, Cohen, George M., Bennett, Ruth, and Weinstock, Comilda S. *Mental Status Schedule: Geriatric Supplement*. New York: New York State Department of Mental Hygiene, 1966.

Wolfe, Richard Russell. Remotivation of the chronically ill and aged patient. Unpublished Ph.D. dissertation, University of Pittsburgh, 1965.

8

Initial Reactions of Newcomers of A Residential Setting for the Aged to A Resocialization Program: an Exploratory Study*

Eugene Barron, Ed.D., M.S.W.**

This research focused on the development and evaluation of a group resocialization program for new residents of two proprietary facilities in order to facilitate the adjustment process. It was an attempt to test the notion of using residents as resocializers. Few studies have focused on the implications of a group approach geared to the resocialization needs of residents in a proprietary setting. Usually studies of programs concerning the elderly have occurred in and have been geared to the voluntary, nonprofit sector. The reality is that many of the institutionalized aged population reside in profit-making proprietary facilities. It is, therefore, relevant that research be conducted on programs that not only assist in the adjustment of residents but would be economically and realistically suitable to the proprietary sector.

Although it is rather uncommon for a program in therapeutic intervention to be based on a theoretical sociological model, some of the principles of socialization developed by Parsons (1951) and elaborated most explicitly by Zelditch (1955) seemed useful for formulating the resocialization program. We wished to put into operation, in a resocialization program, their concepts of socialization as it applies to leadership. Four groups were established, divided on the basis of different styles of leadership. The effects of the groups on the adjustment of the aged participants were ascertained by comparing test scores before and after participation in the resocialization process.

Because the sample population consisted of residents of two Domiciliary Institutional Proprietary Homes for Adults (DIPHA) homes

*Part of an unpublished Ed.D. thesis, Teachers College, Columbia University, 1976. Partial support was provided by an AOA traineeship.
**Director of Social Service, Metropolitan Hospital, New York, N. Y., Clinical Assistant Professor, New York Medical College, New York, N. Y.

which are privately owned senior citizen hotels, a secondary but important goal of the study was to gain an understanding of the Dipha home system and how it related to the aged residents. The two homes selected were located in one geographic area and provided similar living conditions. Both were old, dilapidated-looking facilities, providing the basic necessities of food and lodging, and offering meager recreation programs. Their populations were similar in respect to most personal and demographic characteristics: mostly poor elderly individuals, discharged from a general or psychiatric hospital, or dislocated* from the community.

The official establishment of Dipha homes in about 1967, under the authority of the New York City and New York State Departments of Social Services, represented an effort to control a growing unregulated system in which elderly welfare recipients were residing in privately owned senior citizen hotels that had no responsibilities in terms of defined services or regulations. The importance of these homes rests in the fact that they serve as an alternative living arrangement for a growing number of dislocated elderly persons and discharged elderly hospital patients who are still ambulatory but for various reasons are unable to manage in the community. For these elderly individuals, although it does not represent as drastic a change as admission to the closed system of a nursing home, entrance to the Dipha setting can pose many problems. An elderly person must not only face the implications of relocation but the demands of making his way alone in the Dipha home. Considering the fact that he is possibly made more vulnerable by an illness, entry into a new setting requires an adaptation process that may prove difficult.

Upon transfer into the Dipha home, it is more likely than not that the new resident enters the facility unaccompanied. Arriving, he is given a cursory orientation to the home; and, thereafter, unless he creates a disturbance or has a medical problem, he is generally ignored. Although this will be his permanent residence, he is likely to be escorted to his room without an introduction to the other residents. Henceforth, he must make his own way, indirectly learning the rules

---

*Dislocation, which is a form of displacement for one's home and community, occurred for many reasons. An extended illness and consequent loss of funds forced some elderly persons to abandon their apartments. Others abandoned their homes because of criminal dangers. Urban renewal projects often caused the destruction of their homes, and forced them to relocate. Once they relocated, many lost contacts with friends and relatives who in the past had given them the support needed to maintain themselves.

and regulations and remaining for a long period ignorant of his rights. Exacerbating the problem of adjustment for the newly arrived resident is the effect of relocation (Brand and Smith, 1974). Relocation can be destructive to his capacity to function in that it often involves separation from friends, possessions, home and familiar surroundings. As a new resident he is faced with a loss of continuity with his former life patterns. Excluded in part from the community, economically dependent and no longer productive, he is confronted with being transformed into a societal reject. His major interests are to unlearn much of his former life style, to tolerate congregate living and to cope with a loss of privacy and individuality. Having to learn new patterns of behavior, he is also affected by a normative system new to him and must face the possibility that "adjustment" in the Dipha setting might actually mean becoming disengaged, emotionally flat, without motivation and mentally withdrawn.

SYSTEM CHARACTERISTICS

In order to realize the importance of developing resocialization programs and the tremendous barriers to succeeding with this population, one needs to gain a sense of the impoverishment of their lives, which is further reinforced by the structure of the setting and the system.

Passivity

Passivity was one of the major hallmarks of many of the residents. When one inquired about why they did not speak to management about their complaints, the inevitable reaction was, "It will pass in one ear and out the other." An excellent example of this was a description given during one of the meetings of a theft that occurred during the early morning hours.

R.: I heard some sounds, and looking up I noticed this guy walking out with my pants. I ran after him and finally caught him outside, but he beat me. Look at my legs. [They were deeply cut and bruised.]

Q.: Did you call the night watchman, or wake up your roommate, who was also being robbed?

R.: No, I didn't say anything, and the night watchman was sleeping, and I didn't want to bother him.

Q: Does administration know about what happened?

R.: No, it wouldn't do any good.

Q.: How about you, Stanley, you also lost everything?

R.: [Stanley shrugs, as if to say, "What is the use?"]

Mutuality

In contrast to the above incident, there was a sense of mutuality among some of the residents. The pattern seemed to be one in which a healthier resident assumed the protective role for a more helpless resident, particularly if there was a physical handicap involved such as blindness. It was observed in the homes visited that there were a few blind residents, and in every case another resident assumed the responsibility of ensuring that the blind resident was properly fed and directed. An example of this protective pattern was an incident concerning a blind, non-English-speaking, Chinese resident seated in the lobby, who was in physical distress. The staff ignored him, but the other residents spoke up and requested that arrangements be made to bring him to his room. Inquiring about this resident, it was learned that he had been cared for by another Chinese resident, who had recently died. Now he was almost totally isolated, although one of the residents did assume responsibility for much of his care. Later, in a confidential conversation with a member, it was learned that his companion had committed suicide in his room. There was a general silence about the incident, which reflected the tendency to suppress all negative information.

Isolation and Loneliness

Another feature of the life of many of the residents was their apparent isolation and loneliness. Some waited by the phone for several hours in anticipation of an expected phone call. Several days before they had an appointment, they made preparations and continually reminded the switchboard operator, as if this were to be a major event. They also gathered around any receptive person and "latched on" in an attempt to make contact. Fortunately for the residents in H. home, the switchboard operator was receptive to their gestures and responded warmly.

Community Rejection

Although there were some recreational and shopping facilities located near the homes, it was rare to find a resident leaving the premises. Some were unaware of the existing community facilities, and others were fearful of a new environment. Several residents had never ventured across the street to view the boardwalk and ocean, though they had lived in this seaside home for several months. When a resident did venture forth, he usually did so in an isolated manner. For example, one resident who participated in the meetings spent her entire day seated alone on a box in front of the local supermarket. On the other hand, it was difficult for residents to make contact in the community, as evidenced by the abortive attempt of two participating members to join a local senior center. After they returned to the group meeting and discussed their failure, this researcher contacted the center. The director of the center claimed that they were rejected because she feared allowing state hospital residents into the center (only one applicant was from a state hospital). Because of subsequent intervention after the program's completion, they were eventually allowed to join. However, this situation was indicative of how the community reinforced their isolation pattern.

Poverty

Another factor reinforcing patients' isolation was their meager grant. As a result of small allowances, their clothes were shabby, and they couldn't afford the amenities of the outside world. Consequently, their self-image was negatively affected, as clearly articulated by a resident: "There is a degradation of not having money, especially after having worked one's entire life and then to be made to look like a beggar."

Demoralization

Considering this situation, it was no wonder that bickering and cursing were commonplace. Tragically, each complainer blamed the other for his condition. Further signs of demoralization, particularly in the S. home, were complaints about thievery and the excessive use of liquor.

Staff Pressure and Tipping

The residents also resented the tipping system but felt entrapped by it with the reflection that it was the only way to receive services. It was not uncommon for residents to be pressed indirectly to tip by staff who coaxed them to receive a service that was not then needed. The residents felt obliged to offer a gratuity, and, as one participant said, "I feel bad if I don't tip because then they will be cold to me."

FRAMEWORK FOR RESOCIALIZATION

Among the theoretical guidelines that seem particularly helpful in formulating a conceptual basis for a resocialization approach is that suggested by Parsons and elaborated by Zelditch. Parsons wrote that socialization is an ongoing process that occurs whenever newcomers enter a social system, for they learn a new pattern of life by interacting with others. They acquire a self-image, normative values, beliefs and sentiments of the social group into which they are socialized. Within the social system, for order to be established so that successful socialization occurs, there must exist a "differentiation of the context of instrumental and expressive activities" (Parsons, 1951). It is this differentiation that serves as one of the keys to the stability of the system. On the primary level socialization begins with the nuclear family, and this process is central to the stabilization of the adult personality. In the family system, the differentiation occurs between the parental models along expressive and instrumental lines. A similar process occurs in secondary social systems where activities are directed and encouraged by expressive and instrumental leaders. It is the differentiation of these roles that maintains the "integrity of a normative system," for it fosters the development of collective goals or interests and promotes the authority to "bind and to coerce members of the collective" (Parsons, 1951).

Zelditch (1955), in his research on the family, formulated the concepts of instrumental leader and expressive leader. The instrumental leader is considered to be the one involved with task patterns such as setting rules and giving orders, directions and suggestions. On the other hand, the expressive leader, sometimes described as the "sociometric star," shows a pattern of behavior and attitudes reflecting emotion and supportive relationships with others. According to Zelditch

(1955), in the family, for socialization to be successful, the socializing agent must remain constant, serving as a focal point of identification for the changing socializee. In order to prevent the expressive socializing agent, the mother, from losing a sense of distance and being manipulated to comply with all the socializee's demands, another leader is necessary. The father, as the instrumental leader, is in less intimate contact with the child, and thus not only gives the mother the support to set down limits but can more easily discipline the child when necessary.

Socialization is not only important for the young but has relevance throughout adulthood whenever an individual must enter a new social system. All social systems use socializers to teach the socializee what is expected of him and also to press for conformity to a well-defined hierarchy of statuses.

It is the function of the expressive-instrumental leaders, as socializers, not only to be sources of information but to serve as the role models. The absence for children of such role models or specific identification figures with its consequent deprivation was documented as far back as the forties and early fifties by Linder (1944) and Redl and Wineman (1951). They found that, where there was an absence of a significant person to emulate, the development of personality, feelings and behavior was retarded and thwarted. At the other end of the age continuum, Bennett and Nahemow (1965) reported that the more social contacts an individual had prior to entry in a home for the aged, the more successful he later was at learning the norms of the institution. They also found that pre-entry isolation affected a resident's initial as well as long-term adjustment, and that those newcomers into a home for the aged who were quickly socialized reflected better adjustment on both a short-term and a long-term basis. Conversely, those who were not socialized at the beginning phase of their stay continued their isolation, thus perpetuating the desocialization process (Bennett and Nahemow, 1972). The findings seem to indicate that early socialization is crucial to bringing about subsequent adjustment, and that it is a most persistent predictor of long-term integration into activities by residents of a home for the aged (Bennett and Nahemow, 1972).

Whether or not isolation patterns once established in an aged person can be fully remedied by therapeutic interventions is a question that has not been completely answered. It has been noted that isolation in the aged does not seem to be correlated with age, sex, mental status or education. Although it may result in some behavior patterns symptomatic of mental disorder, specifically poor social adjustment and cognitive function, it is not synonymous with mental disorder. The risk of isolation, if it is not reduced in time, is that it may result in serious cognitive and other impairments. However, unlike some senile mental disorders, the effects of isolation may be reversible (Bennett, 1973).

Findings of Weinstock and Bennett (1971) indicate that newcomers to a home for the aged are faced with the challenge of adapting to a new situation and that the ensuing stimulation has a positive impact on general intellectual functioning. These researchers showed that newcomers performed better than waiting-list persons or oldtimers on cognitive tests. Scores on tests of cognitive performance related to socialization socres only for the newcomers, thus implying that they benefited from their entrance into the home. On becoming oldtimers and facing an absence of new learning demands, they made lower test scores. One of the implications of this study is that the effects of social isolation experienced by a resident of an institution in the pre-entry phase can be counteracted by his being resocialized on becoming a newcomer.

Given the capacity for resocialization of individuals in the later years, it seems reasonable to develop a program to facilitate the process. Because in the Dipha settings there are no formal mechanisms for the integration of newcomers, it seemed important to intervene at an early stage. The intervention focused on a type of program that would permit evaluation of a concept that socialization is contingent upon differential leadership modeled along expressive and instrumental functions. Thus, the purpose of this research was to determine whether the establishment of a resocialization program in a Dipha home, involving the mediating function of significant others in the form of expressive and instrumental leaders, could assist in the social adjustment of newcomers.

PURPOSE OF THE STUDY

This study had several purposes:

1. To design, implement and evaluate a resocialization program for elderly newcomers in a proprietary residential facility (the major purpose).

2. To determine the program's impact on initial social adjustment, socialization and morale of residents.
3. To ascertain which combination of socializers (expressive-instrumental; expressive alone; instrumental alone) is most conducive to facilitating the resocialization process.
4. To learn about the feasibility of instituting resocialization programs led by elderly individuals in proprietary settings for old people because we were not only trying to develop a model for resocialization but also to create a program that could be adopted by paraprofessionals. .
5. To explore the conditions in Dipha homes.

HYPOTHESES

General

Residents subjected to a resocialization program will reflect higher initial social adjustment, socialization and morale, as compared with the residents who have not participated.

Specific

A. Residents subjected to a resocialization program with combined expressive and instrumental leadership models will reflect higher initial social adjustment, socialization and morale than those involved in resocialization programs with other types of models (only expressive or only instrumental).

B. Socialization that is reflected in instrumental behavior and attitudes occurs most commonly with instrumental leadership.

C. Socialization that is reflected in expressive attitudes and feelings occurs most commonly with expressive leadership.

DESIGN

The total sample numbered 71 and included all newcomers (six months or less) in two Dipha homes. Randomly divided, they were placed in four separate groups in each home. For both homes, the four groups were directed along specific lines: expressive ($N=17$), instrumental ($N=18$) and control ($N=19$).

Initially, only senior citizen leaders were to be used; however, because of complications of illness of one of the elderly leaders, professional leaders (social workers) were utilized in the second home. The leaders were expected to conform to their respective, assigned roles: expressive and instrumental. The expressive role focused on feeling factors, as emotional and supportive relations. The instrumental role focused on task patterns such as sharing rules, regulations and information about the home. The leaders were guided by a manual, programmed with resocialization topics.

The group sessions were held for about one hour with a total of seven sessions. Prior to the onset of the program, the leaders were trained in a pilot program that duplicated the planned group sessions. Thereupon, the leaders assumed their respective differential roles in their assigned groups. Table 8.1 reflects the experimental and control conditions. Control groups discussed current events only.

The expressive and instrumental functions were assumed by the trained socializers and generally included the following:

Table 8.1. Delineation of the Groups into Four Programs

Program I Control groups	Program II Expressive- instrumental group	Program III Expressive group	Program IV Instrumental group
Home H. (nonprofessionally led):			
11 participants	10 participants	10 participants	10 participants
No program of re-socialization; current events only were discussed.	Leaders were responsible for conveying information related to expressive-instrumental functions.	The leader related to expressive functions.	The leader related to instrumental functions.
Home S. (professionally led):			
8 participants	8 participants	7 participants	7 participants

Expressive Functions

1. Mediator and conciliator: trouble with roommate or staff, etc.; how to interact so that one will be accepted.
2. Support: helping residents to express feelings and giving reassurance.
3. Interaction: how to go about making contact with other residents; "If you gossip or curse, they will not like you."
4. Newcomer status: "You are expected to make mistakes while finding your way, but as you remain here and become more familiar with the home you will feel more comfortable."
5. Importance of moving outward: "Many residents seem bored, and, therefore, it is important that you maintain interest and participate in activities."

Instrumental Functions

1. Location of things: orientation of residents both to the home and to how to travel within the community.
2. Key people: whom to contact when in difficulty and how to complain effectively.
3. Sanctions, rules and regulations: tipping, smoking in bed, cleanliness, bathing, table manners, leaving the home without notifying staff.
4. Sources of assistance: services available in the home or community.
5. Financial status: how much is received in allotments, and how funds can be managed.

ANALYSIS OF LEADERSHIP ROLE AND CONTENT

To ensure that the leaders conformed to their respective roles, an examination was made of their tape-recorded statements by codifying them into expressive and instrumental categories. The analysis of the findings seemed to show that not only the professionals but also the nonprofessionals were capable of assuming their assigned leadership roles. A significant correlation was noted between the expressive leadership role and expressive statements. There was, however, evidence of differences in style between the professional and nonprofessional leaders in terms of how they responded to the group. The difference probably reflected the greater group-work skill and experience of the professionals. The professionals as compared to the nonprofessional leaders shifted less in their discussions and tended to be more group-oriented. They also seemed to be more directive and interpretive in their statements to the group members.

This seemingly greater flexibility on the part of the professional leaders might have had an effect on the attendance rate. The rate of attendance in their groups was generally consistently higher than for the nonprofessional group. However, the control group in both homes showed a lower attendance rate as compared to the other groups. A possible explanation could be that, regardless of leadership skill, membership attendance will diminish when there is an absence of meaningful material in the meeting.

GENERAL OBSERVATIONS

The development of a sense of trust was initially a major factor in enlisting the participation of residents. The residents were anxious and suspicious of the questionnaire and the reason for the group program.

In H. home, which was led by the nonprofessionals, discussion in the group seemed to focus on gossip and the day's events. The experimental groups in S. home tended to concentrate on problems common to the group members: poverty, loneliness and lack of services. The direction of themes seemed to reflect the areas in which the leaders felt comfortable.

On an individual level, a resident mentioned that, "It was good to talk with each other." Two participants who had previously never spoken to each other visited together and eventually joined a local senior citizens' center. A romance even blossomed between two participants in one of the groups. Fanny and Joe, like many of the residents, lived in their own noncommunicative world. At the end of a session, Fanny remarked to Joe, "Why don't you get some money together and treat me to coffee?" She then remarked to the group that, "He is a handsome man since he got his haircut." The worker centered on Joe, declaring, "It must be a good feeling to get compliments." Joe, who had been extremely reticent, responded that all his life people had said he was ugly, "and this is the first time someone said something nice." By the next session they were holding hands. The impact of the meetings was evident not only in the improved grooming of Joe; other participating residents also reflected greater sensitivity to their attire when attending the group.

Another example of making contact with the withdrawn resident occurred with Mr. L. He claimed to be hard of hearing and rarely participated in the early sessions. However, by the final session he was quoting Latin to the group and proudly admitted that he was a retired Latin professor.

In the professionally led groups, discussion occasionally touched on the death fantasies of some of the participants. A few admitted to past attempts at suicide, and others responded that their main vision of the future was death. However, because the program was not established as group therapy, the leaders tended to avoid developing discussions in this direction.

TRENDS IN THE RELATIONSHIP BETWEEN EXPRESSIVE AND INSTRUMENTAL LEADERSHIP AND TREATMENT GROUPS

Central to the study was an attempt to evaluate whether a trend could be found establishing a relationship between types of leadership and the effects on participants in a resocialization group. It was of interest to ascertain whether certain types of leadership emphasis would produce corresponding changes; that is, whether an expressive emphasis in leadership would result in greater changes in the expressive feelings of those affected, and whether instrumental leadership would produce greater changes in instrumental functions. It was also important to evaluate whether combined leadership would have a more marked effect on participants than individual forms of instrumental or expressive leadership.

For operational purposes the six instruments that were utilized to evaluate the possibility of change were divided into two categories: instrumental and expressive. The instruments used to evaluate social knowledge, conformity and integration were classified in the former category, and the evaluation, anomia and morale instruments in the latter category.

Data were collected for groups in H. and S. homes, as depicted in Table 8.2.

Table 8.2. Summary of Individual Groups Evaluated for Internal Before and After Change Using a t Test for Paired Samples and Reflecting Significant Change

Groups	Home	t scores[a]	Measures[b]
Instrumental	S.	4.4783	Socialization
	H.	3.9427	Socialization
	S.	4.5961	Integration
	S.	5.2842	Morale
Expressive	S.	2.2478	Morale
Expressive-instrumental	S.	3.6602	Socialization
	S.	2.2237	Anomia
	H.	2.0895	Conformity
Control[c]			

[a] $p < .05$.

[b] No significance was noted for some measures tested for their respective groups, and thus they were not listed.

[c] No significance was noted for any measures tested for the control group.

In Table 8.2 it is noted that significant change occurred for individual groups on eight measures. Considering the possibility for change on all the variables, this accounts for 16.7%.* If the control group is excluded and only the experimental groups are included, significant change is found in 22.2% of the measures.** Given these findings, it would seem there was evidence to support the general hypothesis that the resocialization program had an effect on the participants.

If we view the results noted in Table 8.2 in regard to the issue of differential leadership, significant change occurred for the group participants with the instrumental leader in four instances, with the expressive-instrumental in three instances and in one instance with the expressive leader. No change was found for the control group on any measure. These findings therefore do not substantiate a hypothesis concerning the greater effectiveness of dual leadership as compared to individual forms of leadership.

The instrumental leadership groups showed significant change on two (socialization and integration) of the three measures that were classified under the instrumental category. The expressive-instrumental groups also showed greater change on the instrumental measures (socialization and conformity), reflecting two instrumental

*4 groups $\times$ 2 homes $\times$ 6 instruments = 48 possibilities.

**3 experimental groups $\times$ 2 homes $\times$ 6 instruments = 36 possibilities.

measures compared to one expressive measure (anomia). The expressive groups reflected significant change on only the morale measure, which was categorized as an expressive instrument. The findings tend to give support to the hypothesis that socialization, reflected in instrumental behavior and attitudes, occurs most significantly with instrumental leadership. In contrast, there was a lack of evidence to support the hypothesis that socialization that is reflected in expressive attitudes and feelings occurs most significantly with expressive leadership.

It would seem that it was easier to meet the instrumental needs of subjects as compared to the expressive needs. The participants could more easily respond to learning new norms and developing knowledge of the home, than be influenced in terms of mood and problems of alienation. In light of the depressing conditions found in the Dipha setting, this was understandable.

Of the several variables, the social knowledge or socialization measure was most responsive to the impact of the resocialization program, since the experimental group showed significant improvement on this instrument. This might be understood in terms of the fact that social knowledge is easiest to transmit because it focuses on concrete, tangible dimensions of institutional living. From the residents' vantage point, it might be considered a crucial variable because it is necessary for successful functioning in the Dipha system. Given the strong response to this measure, which covers basic information such as dinner hours and financial rights, social learning could be considered an important element in developing a resocialization program.

IMPLICATIONS FOR A RESOCIALIZATION PROGRAM

It has been recognized that socialization is contingent upon role models. It has been suggested that the basis for successful socialization rests in models who assume expressive and instrumental leadership roles. This research has been unable fully to support the idea of the usefulness of combining both expressive and instrumental leadership for bringing about socialization. It seems that an important factor influencing socialization is the environment of the socializee. A poor environment may hinder the socialization process, particularly as it pertains to expressive behaviors.

It was found that when change occurred, the direction was generally toward the area of leadership emphasis. Instrumental leadership seemed to be more conducive to change in instrumental functions such as learning rules, regulations and information about the home. To a lesser extent, expressive leadership appeared to be conducive to change in expressive functions relating to emotional and supportive relationships and the improvement of morale. It would seem that a major implication of this study is that one can gear the direction of resocialization, and the corresponding change in subjects, through the type of leadership emphasis. For example, if it were felt that it would be most helpful for newcomers first to gain a great deal of information about their new environment, leaders could emphasize instrumental factors. Conversely, if it were thought to be of greater importance for newcomers to receive emotional support, then the leader could emphasize expressive factors. Both elements (expressive and instrumental) would be involved in the socialization program, the difference mainly being one of emphasis.* In either case, whether there is a greater emphasis on expressive or instrumental functions, the resocialization program not only has value in supporting the resident on an affective level, but helps the newcomer to find roots in the setting and to envision other alternatives to the observed living patterns in the home.

IMPLICATIONS FOR SENIOR CITIZEN LEADERSHIP

On the basis of experience gained from this research, it is believed that elderly community members can be utilized as group leaders as long as the program is developed in a concrete and comprehensible fashion. In utilizing senior citizens, a twofold benefit accrues: Residents receive a necessary service, and a new type of meaningful role is provided for retired individuals willing to serve as leaders.

RECOMMENDATIONS FOR PRACTICE

The potential for paraprofessional elderly leaders of peer groups has been noted in this research. It would seem highly feasible to encourage the establishment of resocialization programs utilizing senior

---

*Therefore, in a home with extremely poor living conditions, as was found in this study, the major emphasis would be on the expressive needs of residents. A greater number of sessions in terms of time or frequency could thus be conducted under expressive leadership.

citizens because of the nominal cost involved. Using a simplified but well-structured format, a good manual and supportive supervision, senior citizens could be prepared to conduct resocialization programs. This would both enhance their role in society and offer a needed service.

A striking element of the findings is that poor living conditions limit the effectiveness of a resocialization program, particularly as related to the expressive component. Therefore, it should be recognized that there is a need to go beyond individual programs and focus on the restructuring of the particular social system (e.g., Dipha home) in question.

SUMMARY

Given the conditions of the establishment of a short-term, four-week program in a natural setting, having a limited sample and being confronted with many confounding variables such as difficult living conditions, it is remarkable that any useful results were obtained. It was found that a resocialization program does have an impact, particularly on the instrumental learning of the elderly participants.

REFERENCES

Bennett, R. Living conditions and everyday needs of the elderly, with particular reference to social isolation. *Int. J. Aging Hum. Dev.*, April 1973, *4*, 179–198.

Bennett, R., and Nahemow, L. The relations between social isolation and adjustment in residents of a home for the aged. In M. P. Lawton (Ed.), *Proceedings of the Insititute of Mentally Impaired Aged*. Philadelphia: Maurice Jacob Press, 1965, 90–108.

Bennett, R., and Nahemow, L. Socialization and social adjustment in five residential settings for the aging. In D. Kent, R. Kastenbaum, and S. Sherwood (Eds.), *Planning and Action for the Elderly*. New York, Behavioral Publications, Inc., 1972, 501–513.

Brand, F. D., and Smith, R. T. Life adjustment and relocation of the elderly. *J. Gerontol.*, April 1974, *29*, 336–340.

Linder, R. *Rebel Without a Cause*. New York: Granite & Stranton, 1944.

Parsons, T. *The Social System*. Glencoe, Ill.: Free Press, 1951.

Redl, F., and Wineman, D. *Children Who Hate*. Glencoe, Ill.: Free Press, 1951.

Weinstock, C., and Bennett, R. From "waiting on the list" to becoming a "newcomer" and an "oldtimer" in a home for the aged: Two studies of socialization and its impact upon cognitive functioning. *J. Aging Hum. Dev.*, 1971, *23, 1*, 46–58.

Zelditch, M. Role differentiation in the nuclear family: A comparative study. In Talcott Parsons (Ed.), *Family, Socialization and the Interaction Process*. Glencoe, Ill.: Free Press, 1955, 300–345.

9
Time-Limited Counseling and the Adjustment of New Admissions to Nursing Homes*

Lenore Powell, Ed.D.**

The idea of critical periods for resocialization (Bennett and Nahemow, 1965b) seems to necessitate that intervention occur at the very onset of admission to an institution. This intervention could possibly forestall the deleterious effects of the desocialization process and restore some vitality and meaning to the lives of the new residents.

A major purpose of this research was to study the effects of a brief, time-limited counseling intervention program with isolated elderly persons immediately upon their admission to a nursing home. The intervention was designed to make the adjustment to the home less stressful within the first month, thereby reducing the risk of relocation stress by enhancing the aged person's adjustment to the home. The program concentrated on (1) some aged designated as social isolates, who had either lived most of their adult lives in insolation or had become isolated just prior to entrance into the home; and (2) nonisolated aged, who had lived their adult lives in a nonisolated manner. Counseling had a twofold focus: One focus was on resocialization, which included discussion of feelings about being in an institution—fears, anxieties and apprehensions, and separation anxiety regarding friends and family; a second focus was on orientation to the home to promote socialization, and included discussion and reinforcement of approporiate behaviors, norms, rules and regulations regarding procedures in the home.

GENERAL AND SPECIFIC HYPOTHESES

The general hypothesis was that counseling aged, newly admitted residents to a nursing home would significantly improve their initial

*Part of an unpublished dissertation, Teachers College, Columbia University, 1978. Supported by AOA Dissertation Grant #90A-1199 (01).
**Consulting Gerontologist; Psychotherapist; Faculty, New York City Community College, Institute for Study of Older Adults.

adjustment and socialization to the home; it would also improve their attitudes toward old people and morale, prevent desocialization in social isolates and possibly reduce the risk of relocation stress during the first three months of institutional life.

Operational hypotheses were:

1. Morale would show significant improvement after counseling for the experimental groups.
2. Attitudes toward old people would show significant improvement after counseling for the experimental groups.
3. There would be significant gains in knowledge of social environment after counseling for the experimental groups.
4. There would be measurable changes in a positive direction in the combined measures of initial adjustment (which include measures of conformity, integration and evaluation of the social environment) for the experimental groups.
5. Those residents who attended some, but not all, of the counseling sessions would do better than the nontreated control group but worse than those who attended all of the counseling sessions.
6. Those residents who attended all of the counseling sessions would make a better adjustment than those who attended no sessions. Social isolates who were treated would make the most dramatic improvement.
7. Those residents subjected to treatment who had the most positive reaction to the therapist would make the best adjustment to the home.
8. Those residents subjected to treatment who had the most positive reaction to the group would also make the best adjustment to the home.

DEFINITION OF TERMS

Socialization: The ability to learn social norms and values and appropriate roles in an environment.

Resocialization: A renewed interest in self and others, with emphasis on making friends and socializing with other members of the group and of the nursing home or home for the aged.

Orientation: Knowledge of norms of the nursing home or home for the aged, including rules in dormitories, in the dining room and throughout the home.

Adjustment: For purposes of this study, the physical, mental, psychological and social adaptation to a nursing home or home for the aged, as measured by an attitude scale, a morale scale, a knowledge-of-the-social-environment scale and a behavioral-adjustment scale consisting of social cognition, independence and mental activity.

Time-Limited Counseling: Twelve sessions of 60 minutes each, distributed over four weeks and held three times per week.

Therapist-Leader: One who uses clinical skills and knowledge to reinforce appropriate behaviors of the group and also to help members manage their emotional tensions.

Social Isolate: One who has lived alone in adulthood or just prior to institutionalization and scores low on measures of social isolation described in earlier chapters.

Social Functioning: Appropriate social behaviors that are adaptive to the home, including greeting others, eating with social manners and interacting with others in a friendly way.

SAMPLE

The sample culled from two separate nursing homes, designated as A and B for the purpose of this study, consisted of 78 subjects originally. Several subjects dropped out because of illness, death or discharge from the nursing homes. (The average length of stay was three months.) Thus, a total of 64 persons participated in the study. All subjects were pre-tested before any were assigned to an experimental or control condition, in order to decrease bias. Initially only those subjects were eliminated who scored less than 3 on the MSQ (a test of mental status), that test being used as a screening device to eliminate very confused patients. Using a random group design, subjects were randomly assigned to either an experimental or a control group. A total of 31 subjects remained in the experimental group, and a total of 33 remained in the control group. The experimental and the control groups consisted of both men and women, although women predominated in a ratio of about 4 to 1. All of the subjects were age 65 or over.

Experimental Groups: A total of 31 subjects were in the experimental group. Four experimental groups, two in each home, were divided in the following manner: Experimental Groups I and III in

Nursing Home A had respectively 5 and 11 subjects; Experimental Groups II and IV in Nursing Home B had respectively 5 and 10 subjects.

Control Groups: There were two control groups, one in each nursing home. Nursing Home A had a total of 18 subjects; Nursing Home B had a total of 15 subjects.

On the basis of pre-testing and for the purposes of data analysis only, the subjects were divided into groups designated as social isolates and nonisolates. These categories are derived from measures of social isolation including an Adulthood Isolation Index (AII) and a Past Month Isolation Index (PMI). Pre-testing also included the following: a Mental Status Questionaire (MSQ), Attitudes Toward Old People scale, Knowledge of Social Environment scale and a Morale scale. (The means on the AII, PMI and MSQ are so close as to indicate a lack of bias on any of these variables.)

INSTRUMENTS

The following measures were administered to all the new residents participating in the study; this was done prior to the actual intervention. They were administered in the order in which they are described.

1. A *face sheet* of demographic variables, which included such descriptive characteristics as: age, sex, religion, country of origin, amount of education, former occupation, age of entry into the United States (if not born in the United States), residence prior to entry into the home, stated reasons for decision to enter the home.

2. *Mental Status Questionnaire* (MSQ) (Kahn et al., 1961), which has ten items that test for orientation to time, place and person, and general information. Each item is scored one point with a maximum score of 10.

The MSQ has been validated with other scales. Reliability is reported as .53.

3. *Social Isolation Indexes* (Bennett [Granick], 1962), described in Chapter 2 consisting of an Adulthood Isolation Index (AII), which is a measure of the lifetime social contacts with family, friends, work and organizations, and a Past Month Isolation Index (PMI), which is a measure of the number of social contacts in the past month prior to entrance into the home.

The Social Isolation Index has predictive validity, i.e., the index is effective in predicting a future outcome. The index has also been validated with other scales. Reliability is reported as .62. The AII taps the following nine areas: spouse, children, mother, father, siblings, relatives, friends, work and organizations, to determine the number of social contacts that the newcomer resident had in the past.

The Past Month Isolation Index includes number of visits with children, siblings, relatives and friends, number of meetings attended and recreation activities.

   4. *Knowledge of Social Environment or Socialization Index* (Bennett [Granick] and Nahemow, 1961), which was given to measure the resident's awareness of the rules, procedures and norms of the home. There are ten items with a theoretical range of scores from 0 to 10.

   5. *Attitudes Toward Old People* (Kogan, 1961). This scale has 34 items consisting of 17 positive and 17 negative attitudes about the aged. The subject is asked to answer true or false to each statement. The total positive maximum score is 18; the total negative maximum score is 17. Validity is reported as .46 for positive scale and .56 for negative scale. Odd/even reliability is reported as .66 for positive scale and .85 for negative scale.

   6. *Morale Scale* (Lawton, 1972). This scale has 22 items. A response indicating morale is scored 2. An example is, "I see enough of my friends and relatives." "Yes" is considered a response indicating morale and receives a score of 2. "No" would be considered a non-morale response and would be scored 0. Internal validity is reported, and test–retest reliability is reported as .75, .91, .80 on three different small samples.

All of the above-reported scales have been used in other studies, summarized in Chapters 2 and 3 and elsewhere above.

Following the group-counseling intervention, residents were post-tested on the Knowledge of Social Environment or Socialization Index, the Attitudes Toward Old People scale and the Morale scale to see if there were any significant changes in knowledge, attitudes, morale, and so on. In addition, post-counseling measures of Initial Adjustment (which included tests of Conformity, Integration and Evaluation of the Social Environment) were given as follows:

   7. *Conformity*, which is a measure used by Bennett and Nahemow (1967), described in Chapter 3 above.

This scale is used to gauge the resident's subscription to the rules of the home. This and the following two instruments have been used in other studies. Split half measures of reliability are .93 for all three measures.

8. *Integration Scale*, which is a measure of the resident's degree of social integration into the home.

9. *Evaluation of the Social Environment*, which is a measure of how the resident likes conditions in the home.

In addition to the above measures and post-group intervention, an adjustment scale was filled out by the staff of nurses so that they could evaluate the adjustment of the new resident. This measure (the MACC) was compared with the Initial Adjustment measures to see if they differ significantly.

10. The *MACC Behavioral Adjustment Scale.* This scale was devised by Ellsworth (1971) to measure the mood, adjustment, cooperation and communication and social contacts of the new residents as viewed by staff members. Validity is reported as .93 vis-à-vis other scales, and test–retest reliability is reported as .86.

11. A *Therapist–Group Evaluation Scale.* This measure was devised by the researcher because there were no specific scales extant to perform the desired measurement. It was designed to elicit the resident's feelings about the group and feelings about the therapist. The rationale for this evaluation is that positive feelings about the group and about the therapist contribute to the positive adjustment of the resident. This scale was administered by staff to residents as a post-test.

12. *Matching-Environments Questionnaire.* This instrument was devised by Kahana and Harel (1975), and was completed by the researcher for each home. The purpose of the questionnaire is to determine similarities and differences between nursing homes. The questionnaire is composed of three parts: items pertaining to the environment and staff, items that are a home description and items that pertain to the environmental characteristics. There are 95 questions.

THE PROCESS OF TIME-LIMITED COUNSELING AS A RESOCIALIZATION AND ORIENTATION TECHNIQUE WITH NEW RESIDENTS IN A NURSING HOME

1. There were 12 sessions of counseling of one hour's duration each. Sessions were held three times per week for a period of four weeks.

2. The sessions had two foci: (1) One focus was on resocialization, which included a discussion of feelings of the newcomers to being in the nursing home—their fears, anxieties, apprehensions and separation anxiety regarding family and friends, as well as feelings of abandonment; (2) a second focus was on orientation to the home to promote socialization and included discussion and reinforcement of appropriate behaviors, norms, rules and regulations regarding procedures in the home.

3. The therapist-leader of the group played an active role in helping the residents deal with their feelings and also an educative role in orienting the residents to the home. Through verbal and gestural as well as facial expressions, the therapist expressed warmth, empathy and kind firmness toward the members of the group, and also supported and reinforced appropriate behaviors.

4. A tape recorder was included in each session for purposes of collecting clinical data for the research study. It was carefully explained in advance that this was the only purpose of the tape recorder, that the confidentiality of the group sessions would be maintained and that the identity of each group member would be protected in reporting the data or recounting sessions.

5. Residents were told in advance of the nature of the group and that they were part of a research project. Some discussion of feelings about being part of a study were elicited prior to the onset of the group in pre-counseling interviews with each patient.

Based on the psychoanalytic premise that the reduction of fear and anxieties frees an individual from tensions and compulsions, each group session started with a discussion of feeling; e.g., "What did it feel like when you decided to come into the home? How did it feel to leave your friends, neighborhood, etc.? Were you sad, relieved, fearful, etc.?"

Confidentiality of each member's contribution to the group was stressed. The issue of confidentiality touches areas of trust, shame, the fear of disclosure and the degree of commitment to the group. Thus there was initial reluctance expressed as verbal resistance by Mrs. B., "There's no one here to talk to," to which the therapist responded, "You seem to feel lonely and isolated here." Mrs. M. offered: "These people are not my type," to which the therapist commented, "Perhaps you are worried that no one here will understand you."

Nonverbal resistance was shown through frequent lateness to the meetings, absences or sometimes illness. Each resistance was confronted by the group and the therapist through an attempt at an empathic understanding of the member's situation. As the group built up cohesiveness and trust, members revealed more and more about themselves, shared their symptoms and found similarity among themselves. By the third session Mrs. M. and Mrs. B. were waiting for each other at the elevator to go together to the group meeting, which took place on another floor.

Orientation procedures dealt with the location of things, key people who are sources of assistance or persons to whom complaints can be delivered without retaliation, rules and regulations of the home, procedures regarding excursions from the home or receiving visitors, available activities and patient councils. Behavior that the institution and/or the group could not tolerate was openly discussed. For example, the whining and constant moaning of Mrs. A. during meals and during the group sessions was brought to her attention by several group members. They became angry at her, and told her how her crying made them want to run away from her. The therapist asked Mrs. A. if she wanted to share something with the group but felt it was too painful to do so. While asking this, the therapist soothed Mrs. A several times with a light touch on her shoulder. After this she was able to relax more and share her painful feelings. The conditioning technique (reinforced by touching) and verbalizing her difficulties helped the patient to feel quieter internally so that she could verbalize her distress to the group.

The schema always followed the following format: (a) Feelings that the patients brought with them were discussed; (b) appropriate behaviors were discussed, as well as rules and regulations; (c) residents' feelings about the rules were discussed, followed by closure or resolution of those feelings, and alternative solutions to problem-solving or new ways of looking at things.

The therapist actively sought to maintain interaction among the group members, clarified what the group expressed so that it was understandable to all, helped the group express their discomfort, embarrassment and guilt feelings by asking what the group was feeling in the present, kept the discussion dispersed so that one person did not dominate and so that more timid members were not shut off, and accepted reports of progress in an accepting way, always emphasizing the ego autonomy of the individual, i.e., that the person had done something for himself or herself, which implies mastery and competence and the capacity for continued growth (Rosenbaum and Berger, 1963). For example, in one session the group was given an exercise in which patients were asked to talk to each other for five minutes. They were timed and stopped. The results of the exercise was that Mrs. G. and Mrs. M. were facing each other and putting their hands on each other's wheelchairs during their animated discussion; Mrs. S. and Mrs. B. were animatedly discussing their respective families with some intimacy. The therapist's observation, which she verbalized to the group, was that they had derived some comfort from each other, and were deterred from their earlier feelings of isolation and loneliness about which they had complained earlier in the session.

Another example comes from the fifth session, in which Mr. M., a difficult and very dissatisfied patient who was angry at his children for putting him in the home complained that "One father can take care of ten children, but ten children can't take care of one father." A pizza baker prior to having a stroke that paralyzed his leg and one arm, Mr. M. seemed interested when Mrs. O. advised him of the cooking class she attended. However, Mr. M. was too proud to attend the class on his own. Realizing that Mr. M. needed a special invitation, Mrs. O. extended the invitation to Mr. M. In the next session the group learned that Mr. M. had made pizza for the entire cooking class and that it was received with high acclaim. The shared feeling of caring for one another and attending to the feelings of each other gave each group member a feeling of self-gratification from helping others. The group and the therapist acknowledged those feelings.

An example of the therapist's flexibility in being able to move into an area that seemed to be bogged down by the patient's resistance comes from a session in which Mrs. T. F. began the session by complaining about her fears of going to her granddaughter's wedding. She feared being envious of the other guests' ability to dance while she was confined to her wheelchair (she had cancer of the bones). Mrs. T. F. verbalized her anguish that other people would feel sorry for her. The therapist suggested that this was perhaps Mrs. T. F.'s feelings about herself. Then the group began to work on Mrs. T. F.'s problem. They indicated that they understood her feelings and suggested valid reasons to attend the wedding even if she couldn't dance. After several minutes of discussion and heavy verbal resistance on the part of Mrs. T. F., the therapist spontaneously (and based on her own intuitiveness) asked Mrs. T. F. if she could move her head. "Of course," was the terse reply. Could she move her arms, the therapist asked. Again a nod of agreement amidst puzzlement. However, now she was engaged; and at this point the therapist asked if Mrs. T. F. could move in time to music with the top half of her body—whereupon the therapist began to hum a tune and asked Mrs. T. F. if she would like to dance. The therapist pushed the wheelchair in time to the music, to Mrs. T. F.'s bewilderment and the group's amazement and delight. Several weeks later Mrs. T. F. reported on what a lovely time she had at the wedding.

The next example shows the friendships that the group sessions helped to create, which generalized to other areas of the homes including the wards. The group talked about their attempts to make the best of their lives on the wards and in the institution as a whole. Supporting each other morally was one way to generalize their friendships from the group sessions to the ward. Doing as much as they could for themselves was another way to keep up their spirits ("96% proof," added Mr. R.). Socializing in the institution was another way of making the best of their current situations. Activities were made meaningful and enjoyable when patients looked forward to sharing them with their new friends.

The morale-boosting nature of the group was attested to by most of the patients as they tried to manipulate things so that the group would not end. The ending of the group was a real loss for the patients and the therapist, and was so expressed by each individually and collectively. There were more shared intimacies, remembering meaningful and exciting past group events, reminding each other of gains made over the 12 weeks and mourning in the form of expressed anger over the loss of the group. Some patients came to decisions about remaining in the home, and others about leaving and returning to former life styles with children. Mrs. C. B. asked the therapist to come and visit her so that she could meet her son, who was a bachelor. The group had in some way revived her long-dormant interest in playing matchmaker. Closure was brought about by reinforcing the idea that each group member could use another member for support and to share grief and sorrow as well as positive feelings. A review of the meaningful insights accomplished during the 12 sessions was further reinforced by the therapist. Along with positive features of the home, the therapist reiterated the mechanisms for change that could be utilized by the patients.

DATA ANALYSIS

Descriptive Statistics

The descriptive phase of the data analysis consisted of the following descriptive and correlational statistics on the independent measures.

1. Means and standard deviations of pre- and post-counseling measures were computed for the first six scales (as described in the instruments). Means and standard deviations were computed for each scale and used to describe the experimental and control groups.

2. The following correlations were computed: (a) The AII was correlated with PMI, Attitudes Toward Older People, MSQ, Knowledge of Environment scale and Morale scale. (b) PMI was correlated with Attitudes Toward Old People, Knowledge of Environment scale, MSQ, and Morale scale. The Pearson product moment correlation coefficients between these variables were computed.

Analytic Statistics

These calculations were used to test the hypotheses as follows:

1. Morale, Attitudes Toward Old People and Knowledge of the Social Environment were tested by comparing the means between the experimental and control groups in each of the nursing homes with separate t tests.

2. A comparison of all of the social isolate groups was done pertaining to attendance. Attendance was measured by dividing the groups into high, low and no-attenders. Means for each of the groups were computed. The means of the high attenders and the low attenders were compared with a t test for the variables of morale and knowledge of social environment. Means of the high attenders were also compared with a t test for the same variables.

3. Means of the experimental groups of the four isolate categories were compared with reference to attendance. The mean differences of these isolate groups were compared with t tests on the variables of morale and knowledge of social environment. This was done to test the hypothesis that old age isolates would improve the most of all of the treated groups.

4. (a) A comparison of the individual number of responses to the group and the individual number of responses to the therapist among

the isolate groups was made. This was done by comparing the means of an isolate group with the other three isolate groups. (b) The individual number of positive and negative responses to both the group and the therapist was also computed and turned into percentages for comparison.

5. Combined measures of Adjustment were computed for the experimental and control groups by comparing the means of each group with a t test for each nursing home separately.

Some Statistical Findings and Results of Hypotheses Tested

On the pre- and post-test measures for experimental and control groups, the means of the experimental group increased between pre- and post-test measures of Morale.

Within the entire experimental and control groups regarding the four dependent variables (morale, knowledge of the social environment, positive and negative attitudes toward old people), the experimental groups showed increases in the variables, whereas the control groups went down drastically.

Comparing the two nursing homes as indicated in Table 9.1, the morale of the experimental groups increased sharply while that of the control groups decreased sharply. Positive attitudes improved significantly in one nursing home; negative attitudes increased significantly in the other. There was an increase in the experimental group's knowledge of the social environment and a slight decrease in the control group in the expected direction. Conformity showed a marked increase in both nursing homes between experimental and control groups. Integration showed a significant increase in Home A only; however, the experimental group increased, and the control group decreased. One might speculate that the experimental group developed a sense of cohesiveness in the therapy group that generalized to the nursing home. The control groups did not identify with any particular group and therefore did not feel a common attraction to a group. The latter is implicit in any group cohesiveness (Coleman, 1969)—hence the lack of integration into the home by the control group. Evaluation of the social environment showed significant increases in both homes. The MACC did not show any significant differences between nursing homes.

Table 9.1. Experimental and Control Comparisons in Two Nursing Homes on Selected Measures[a]

		NURSING HOME A		NURSING HOME B	
		Exper.	Control	Exper.	Control
Morale	N	34	30	34	30
	$\overline{X}$	8	-10	8	-3
	σ	6.8	7	6.5	4.2
	t	7.35***		2.38*	
		$(df=62)$		$(df=62)$	
Positive attitudes	N	34	30	34	30
	$\overline{X}$	4	-2	1	-.4
	σ	5.3	3.5	4.9	6.9
	t	3.82***		.62	
		$(df=62)$		$(df=62)$	
Negative attitudes	N	34	30	34	30
	$\overline{X}$	-1	-.1	-2	4
	σ	5.6	5.9	4.3	4
	t	.54		3.75***	
		$(df=62)$		$(df=62)$	
Knowledge of social environment	N	34	30	34	30
	$\overline{X}$	2	0	3	-.4
	σ	1.7	2	1.7	1.7
	t	3.13**		5.40***	
		$(df=62)$		$(df=62)$	
Conformity	N	34	30	34	30
	$\overline{X}$	15	10	11	7
	σ	2.4	.7	4.2	4
	t	4.95***		2.50*	
		$(df=62)$		$(df=62)$	
Integration	N	34	30	34	30
	$\overline{X}$	3	1	3	-.9
	σ	1.5	1	1.7	1.4
	t	4.35***		.12	
		$(df=62)$		$(df=62)$	
Evaluation of social environment	N	34	30	34	30
	$\overline{X}$	16	9	15	7
	σ	3	3.3	3	3.9
	t	6.25		6.06***	
		$(df=62)$		$(df=62)$	
MACC	N	34	30	34	30
	$\overline{X}$	57	59	55	48
	σ	10.6	11.4	11.8	12.3
	t	-.51		1.45	
		$(df=62)$		$(df=62)$	

[a] $\overline{x}$ = mean; σ = standard deviation.
*$p < .05$.
**$p < .01$.
***$p < .001$.

COMPARISON OF FOUR ISOLATE GROUPS ON MORALE AND KNOWLEDGE OF SOCIAL ENVIRONMENT

A comparison of the four isolate groups was made in the following way: The data were used in two ways, (a) to compare each isolate group with its corresponding control group to see if the differences between these two groups were significant, and also (b) to compare the experimental groups with each other to see if these group comparisons were significant.

The hypothesis that was being tested stated that social isolates who are treated would make the most dramatic improvement of all the treated groups. That hypothesis was confirmed. On the average, all of the experimental groups increased, and the control groups decreased on both Morale and Knowledge of Social Environment. However, the largest increase on both of these variables was in the involuntary isolate group as predicted; the means on Morale for the experimental and control groups were 14 and -4.5, respectively, with a t of 6.3 ($df = 15, p < .001$), whereas the means for the experimental and control groups on Knowledge of Social Environment were 3 and -1 with a t of 3.36 ($df = 15, p < .01$), as shown in Table 9.2.

Contrary to expectations, the integrated group of experimental subjects showed small average increases in Morale that were significant, whereas the control group showed decreases. The means were 2 and -11 for the experimental and control groups with a t of 4.48 ($df = 11, p < .001$). Also the nonisolated group showed some small increases in Morale that were significant. The means were 3 and -8, respectively, for the experimental and control groups, with a t of 2.3 ($df = 8, p < .05$). Although these increases in the above two groups were not predicted, it would not be unreasonable to speculate that group therapy helped to improve the Morale of these groups, although not as dramatically as for the old age isolates.

As expected, the lifelong isolate group did not respond to the treatment with a significant difference between experimental and control groups, although the means indicated that the experimental group increased in Morale, and the control group decreased in Morale. (Means were 9 and -5.6 for experimental and control groups with a t of 1.00, $df = 22$.) The tendencies of the differences were in the same direction as in the other groups.

One might speculate that the group therapy sessions did not have as great an effect on the lifelong isolate group as it did on the other

Table 9.2. Four Isolate Groups with Means, Standard Deviations and Significance on Two Measures by Whether Experimental or Control Group

CATEGORY		MORALE		KNOWLEDGE OF SOCIAL ENVIRONMENT	
		Exper.	Control	Exper.	Control
I Integrated	$\overline{X}$	2	−11	2	−.14
individual	σ	3.26	5.7	2	2.6
$N=13$	t	4.48***		1.42	
		($df=11$)		($df=11$)	
II Involuntary	$\overline{X}$	14	− 4.5	3	−1
isolate[a]	σ	6.27	5.2	1.6	3
(O.A.I.)	t	6.3***		3.36**	
$N=17$		($df=15$)		($df=15$)	
III Lifelong	$\overline{X}$	9	−5.6	2	.3
isolate	σ	6.4	7.5	1.5	.87
(L.L.I.)	t	1.00		.24	
$N=24$		($df=22$)		($df=22$)	
IV Old age	$\overline{X}$	3	−8	4	−.6
nonisolated	σ	5.2	8	1.4	.45
$N=10$	t	2.3*		−2.8	
		($df=8$)		($df=8$)	
TOTAL $N=64$					

[a]Also known as old age isolate.
 *$p \leq .05$.
**$p \leq .01$.
*** $p < .001$.

groups, because of the lifelong patterns of isolations that permeated the life styles of these individuals. Therefore, because these life styles are integrated into the personality structure, amelioration or changes would entail long-term psychotherapy of a reconstructive nature.

In comparing the various experimental groups among themselves, there were no significant differences between any of the pairs within the four groups of isolates. Most of the groups had small N's, making it harder to achieve statistical significance.

COMPARISON OF MEANS OF EXPERIMENTAL GROUP BY ISOLATE CATEGORY

To test the hypothesis that social isolates who are treated would improve the most after counseling, and that the group designated as old age isolates would improve the most, the means of all of the four isolate groups of high and low attenders were computed. N is small for each group because the total group comprised only 31 individuals. However, the means show that the old age isolates ($N = 9$) improved the most on Morale and Knowledge of Social Environment; the means were 14 and 3, respectively. This is in the predicted direction. The lifelong isolates ($N = 11$) had the next highest mean, 6.91 for Morale and 2.27 for Knowledge of Social Environment. The old age non-isolated group ($N = 5$) had the same means for both variables; the means were 2.8. The integrated group ($N = 6$) had the lowest means on both variables; the means were 0.33 and 1.5.

A comparison of the mean differences between the old age isolate group and the lifelong isolate group indicates a significant difference on Morale, with a t of 3.42 ($df = 18, p < .01$) as shown in Table 9.3. The mean differences between the old age isolates and lifelong isolates on Knowledge of Social Environment are not significant.

On the basis of the above-reported results, the hypothesis that social isolates who are treated would improve the most after counseling, and that the group designated as old age isolates would improve most of all, is confirmed.

SUMMARY OF RESEARCH

Subjects over the age of 65 and with a mean age of 78.5 who were new residents within a month of admission to two different nursing homes, and who were comparable on background characteristics of age, sex, amount of education and place of birth, were pre-tested with several measures of adulthood and recent social isolation scales as well as with a scale of mental status, a morale scale, a knowledge of social environment scale and an attitude scale. These subjects were then randomly divided into experimental and control groups. There were two experimental groups and one control group in each of the nursing homes.

The nursing homes were similar in capacity and services rendered to the patients; they differed with respect to attitudes of the staff, the ethnic composition of nursing personnel and the setting and location of each home. However, the homes were essentially similar, as indicated by a matching environments scale.

Table 9.3. Comparison of Mean Differences in Experimental Group on Two Measures by Isolation Categories

ISOLATE CATEGORY	N	MORALE	KNOWLEDGE OF SOCIAL ENVIRONMENT
Integrated	6	0.33	1.5
Lifelong isolated	11	6.91 ⎤	2.27 ⎤
		⎥ t 3.42*	⎥ t -1.3
Old age nonisolated	5	2.8 ⎦ (df=18)	2.8 ⎦ (df=18)
Old age isolates	9	14	3
TOTAL N =	31		

*p <.01.

Each of the four experimental groups was involved in a group intervention of time-limited counseling sessions for a total of 12 sessions. The control group did not receive counseling. The sessions lasted one month. After the sessions, all of the subjects were post-tested with the same instruments of the pre-test with the addition of three measures of adjustment. Nurses rated subjects on a behavioral scale; social workers pariticpated in rating the therapist and the group by administering an evaluation scale that tapped the positive and negative reactions to both the group and the therapist.

Findings of the study indicated that the morale of the subjects in the experimental group was considerably improved as compared with the control group. The experimental group's knowledge about the nursing home was also greater in comparison with the control group.

Combined measures of adjustment, which included measures of conformity, integration and evaluation of the social environment, were significant in terms of the experimental group's improved adjustment over the control group.

Attendance was a factor in the adjustment of residents known as social isolates, especially for the old age isolate group. Although the group and therapist evaluations were not statistically significant, the individual responses indicated that positive reactions to the group, and especially to the therapist, contributed to the improved adjustment of the residents.

A summary of the findings of the study indicates that five out of eight of the hypotheses tested were confirmed. The three hypotheses that were not confirmed may be accounted for on the basis of the small N of the study.

Discussion of the findings and conclusions suggests that adjustment of new residents to a nursing home is positively affected by a time-limited group intervention that occurs early in the resident's admission to the home. Recommendations, limitations of the study, implications of the study and suggestions for further research are included below.

SUMMARY OF THE FINDINGS

The following hypotheses were made and either confirmed or disaffirmed:

1. The hypothesis that morale would show significant improvement for the four experimental groups after counseling was confirmed.

2. The hypothesis that attitudes toward old people would show significant improvement for the experimental groups after counseling was not confirmed. Significant increases occurred in one of the nursing homes but not in the other.

3. The hypothesis that there would be significant gains in knowledge of social environment for the four experimental groups after counseling was confirmed.

4. The hypothesis that there would be measurable changes in a positive direction in the combined measures of adjustment (conformity, integration, evaluation of the social environment) was confirmed.

5. The hypothesis that the residents who attend some but not all of the counseling sessions will do better than the nontreated control group was confirmed. The hypothesis that the residents who attend some sessions would do worse than those who attend all of the sessions was not confirmed.

6. The hypothesis that social isolates who are treated will make the most dramatic improvement of all the treated groups was confirmed. This was especially true for the involuntary or recent social isolates.

7. The hypothesis that those residents who are treated and have the most positive reaction to the therapist will make the best adjustment to the home was not confirmed statistically, probably owing to the lack of variance in each group. A look at the individual scores indicates that 80% of the experimental group had a positive reaction to the therapist.

8. The hypothesis that those residents subjected to treatment who have the most positive reaction to the group will also make the best adjustment to the home was not confirmed. In the experimental groups 55% reacted negatively to the group, and 45% reacted positively. What is interesting to note, however, is that the isolate group with the highest number of positive responses to the group was the old age isolates. This was in the predicted direction.

DISCUSSION OF THE FINDINGS

An increase in the scores between pre- and post-testing measures indicated that there were significant differences between the four experimental groups and the control group with reference to an improvement in Morale and Knowledge of Social Environment. The subjects were newcomer residents to a nursing home who had been taken into the study within the first month of their admission to the nursing home.

Improvement in scores was used as a criterion of positive adjustment and decline as a criterion of negative adjustment. An investigation of the various groups of social isolates in the experimental and control groups showed that of the treated groups those isolates designated as involuntary isolates (or old age isolates) made the most dramatic improvement. As expected, the group known as lifelong isolates did not respond to treatment significantly. An unexpected result was that the integrated group responded with small average increases on the Morale scale that were significant. Also, the old age nonisolated group responded to treatment with increases in Morale that were significant. Thus, with the exception of the lifelong isolates, the group counseling sessions had an impact on all of the other members of the experimental groups. It is reasonable to expect that the integrated and old age nonisolated groups would also derive some benefit from counseling; however, the old age isolates seemed to derive the most benefit, as predicted, and the lifelong isolates the least benefit, as expected. The old age isolates probably needed the group to help them to deal with their feelings about recent losses and feelings of isolation, whereas the lifelong isolates have either used the defense mechanism of isolation to protect themselves from the emotional impact of felt isolation, or isolation has become an integral part of their personality structure with which they have had much experience in coping.

An increase in morale suggests that the residents were able to cope with being relocated from hospitals, their own homes and other nursing homes with minimum discomfort. Increases in Knowledge of Social Environment suggest the residents were able to understand the rules and regulations of the home and accept them. The decline of the control groups showed that these groups did not accept their current life situation and were not able to become integrated into the home.

The fact that positive attitudes increased in one nursing home while negative attitudes increased in the second nursing home may indicate that there were some slight differences in the initial attitudes of the residents that contributed to increasing their negative attitudes. While the study also indicates that it is possible to match homes and residents by utilizing specific scales designed for the evaluation of the home, adjustment of the residents with reference to their attitudes may also be influenced by the attitudes of staff toward residents as well as by residents' attitudes toward each other, which were not measured.

The study also suggests that although the frequency of sessions attended is not a significant factor, attendance in and of itself is important in making a positive adjustment to a nursing home. What seems apparent is that whether or not the isolates attended some or all of the counseling sessions, the sessions made a difference. An interpretation of this phenomenon may come from the "belief system" that is inherent in all psychotherapy patients and therapists as well. The belief is that patients' suffering, their chaotic inner worlds and their tortuous interpersonal relationships are all explicable and therefore governable by a set of principles that permit an ordered explanation (Yalom, 1970). One might speculate that it is this belief system that is operative in helping group members to become and feel part of the group regardless of the number of sessions they attend. More specifically, in this group the absence of group members was noted and discussed. Residents were inquired after when they did not appear for group sessions, and their return to the group was welcomed by the therapist and group members. Thus group cohesion would be a factor in explaining positive gains regardless of the number of sessions attended by the resident. Being a part of a group generalizes to feelings about the home itself and plays an important role in developing positive feelings toward the home.

Positive attitudes toward the groups or toward the therapist do not seem important in terms of adjustment to the home. However, most of the attitudes toward the therapist were positive (80%), whereas responses to the group were mostly negative. A study with a larger N would probably show that positive attitudes toward group and therapist are significant factors in the successful outcome of the patient's therapy.

The fact that the hypotheses regarding the group and therapist evaluation scales were not confirmed may also reflect the crudeness of the measuring instruments.

It is of interest to note that the lifelong isolate group had only two individuals who reacted negatively to the therapist. One might speculate that this group's positive reactions were promulgated by the feeling that the therapist was concerned about them, whereas they felt the group was not. Among lifelong isolated groups one tends to find both schizoid or withdrawn individuals and those narcissistic personalities who enjoy the attention of a one-to-one relationship. Within a group, the narcissistic person usually talks to the therapist alone and not to the group, and feels that the therapist is there for his or her needs alone, just as the attention of the baby focuses on the mother, who satisfies the infant's needs.

PATIENT-THERAPIST RELATIONSHIP

There is a tendency for patients who perceive their therapist with qualities of nonpossessive warmth and genuineness to improve more than other patients in psychotherapy; this also applies to behavior therapy patients.

In a study conducted by Sloane et. al. (1975) there was a tendency for patients to improve when they perceived their therapist with the qualities mentioned above and also as an empathic person though these findings did not reach statistical significance. The results of the present study suggest that the relationship between the patient and the therapist was critical.

CONCLUSIONS

Based on the findings, the following conclusions are offered:

The experimental group in this study showed improvement in social adjustment on the same scales used by Bennett and Nahemow (1965a). Conformity, Integration and Evaluation of the Social Environment were measures of social adjustment. The improvement was shown after the group counseling sessions and applied only to the experimental groups, not to the controls, who had not had counseling. This suggests a positive effect on adjustment as a result of the counseling sessions.

The study confirms the Bennett [Granick] (1962) and Bennett [Granick] and Nahemow (1961) studies with reference to critical periods of socialization. The first month seems to be a crucial time, in which most socialization occurs. It also confirms Bennett's hypothesis that desocialization may be stopped if timely intervention occurred within a month of the resident's admission to the home; the residents did not have the opportunity to maladapt by picking up things as they went along. From the outset, they knew what the expectations of the home were and were learning to deal with their feelings about being in the home.

The present study agrees with Howard and Wesley (1969) in their description of the goals of small groups. Residents who were in the group showed improvement in their personal grooming and etiquette, dressing up for the group sessions as if they were a special occasion. Residents showed a willingness to help each other, which generalized to the floors where they sought out other people and tried to help them. Increased camaraderie among the members of the group seemed to generalize to the other residents when the group members took the initiative. Stimulated interest in one another in the group also generalized to concern and interest about fellow roommates, dining room partners and same-floor and other-floor occupants. There seemed to be increased communication between patients and personnel, which was less childish and more adult in terms of requests. Also, residents seemed to take a greater interest in the life of the home itself.

The present study also agrees with Anderson (1967) in that the impact of institutionalization is mediated by interpersonal relationships.

The research indicates that group counseling of a time-limited nature is an effective way of improving the adjustment of new residents to a nursing home by changing their behavior.

RECOMMENDATIONS BASED ON FINDINGS

With the present system of nursing home care, it is recommended that each nursing home employ a highly skilled psychotherapist with a background in gerontology who would be able to run group counseling sessions for residents new to the home.

Other suggestions for research by future researchers include the following ideas:

1. It would be interesting to compare the results of the therapy administered at different points in time (for example, before entry, upon entry and three months after entry into the institution) to study the differences in terms of critical intervention periods.

2. There is a need to study the impact of time-limited individual therapy sessions for new residents of a nursing home or home for the aged. These sessions would have to be conducted by a skilled psychotherapist trained in both psychotherapy and gerontology. By use of measures of adjustment similar to the ones used in the present study, the morale and knowledge about the environment could be compared in those new residents who have individual counseling and those new residents who do not have individual counseling, or who are in a group counseling program. Then the effects of individual counseling and group counseling on the adjustment of new residents could be established. Individual counseling would take the same number of sessions, and thus the time would be comparable to that of the group sessions. However, it would be more costly to work on a one-to-one basis than it is to use a group technique.

3. Another interesting study would be to compare the elderly institutionalized aged in different settings; for example, rural as opposed to urban. Rural people are more accustomed to isolation than urban people, and their attitudes toward their isolation might be quite different. These attitudes in turn could affect how they adjusted to institutional life.

4. Because socialization starts in the home with the family actively or passively socializing young infants to the structure of the family, it seems appropriate that other forms of resocialization should also begin in the family. Families who have advance knowledge of the institutionalization of a member of that family could be prepared, and the individual about to be admitted could be prepared in the home to eventually leave for another home. The implication is that people who are waiting on lists to go into nursing homes or to homes for the aged would be appropriate subjects for socialization.

Although the logistics of getting such a population together might be somewhat unwieldy, it could be done with several investigators acting together. Prior to entrance into the home, a small group of potential new admissions could be gathered together, to meet at the prospective home and participate in group counseling sessions. The present study could then be duplicated, but with an orientation to the future rather than the present. The counseling sessions would help the prospective residents to deal with their feelings in the same way they helped new residents in the present study. Knowledge of institutional life might encourage those who can adjust to an institution, and discourage other individuals who choose not to or cannot adjust to an institution so that they would find other, more appropriate alternatives.

5. Family counseling for relatives of waiting-list individuals and for new admissions to nursing homes is a vital aspect of any introduction into institutional life and should also be an important part of any relocation program. Family counseling can be done either with groups of families together or with individual families. The process of counseling needs the skill of a trained family therapist who is also a gerontologist. It would be interesting to study the effect of family counseling on the adjustment of residents who have families. A hypothesis could be formulated that those residents whose families have received time-limited family therapy will make a better adjustment to a nursing home or home for the aged than those residents whose families are merely interviewed when their family member is admitted to the home. These families could also be compared with the resident on a measure of adjustment such as morale. Three different groups could be set up in which families having counseling and residents having counseling could be compared with families where residents only are counseled, to see the impact of the three different types of situations and their effect on the morale of both the patient and the patient's family.

The study implies that the morale and knowledge of the environment of new residents in a nursing home can be improved through a group intervention process known as group counseling. The time limit of the group seemed appropriate and did not in any way limit the results of the study, since it was built-in from the beginning.

A highly skilled therapist who is aware of the particular needs of this type of population is able to work with this population only with the total cooperation of the entire institution because group counseling becomes an integral aspect of therapeutic activities in the home and must be seen as such.

Group counseling is a relatively economical way of attending to the needs of individual patients so that more patients are reached within a day than would be possible if the therapy were conducted on a one-to-one basis.

The group counseling process may be applied in other types of settings such as housing developments, hospitals or other long-term care facilities. It can be utilized when any type of relocation is being contemplated. The process is also appropriate for short-term relocation projects such as transferring patients within a facility to a new ward or a new floor or building.

Such a therapeutic process should be an integral part of any institutional facility that purports to offer rehabilitation, medical care or housing to individuals who by virtue of aging must endure life away from familiar surroundings, bereft of loved ones and friends, without status or employment or the few creature comforts that help to give us a sense of identity, dignity and purpose.

REFERENCES

Anderson, N. Institutionalization and self-esteem. *J. Gerontol.,* 1967, *22,* 313–317.

Bennett [Granick], R., and Nahemow, L. Preadmission Isolation as a Factor in Adjustment to an Old Age Home in Hoch, P. and Zubin J. (Eds.), *Psychopathology of Aging,* New York: Grune and Stratton, 1961, pp. 285–302.

Bennett, R., and Nahemow, L. Institutional totality and criteria of social adjustment in residences for the aged. *J. Soc. Issues,* 1965a, *21,* 44–77.

Bennett, R., and Nahemow, L. The relations between social isolation, socialization and adjustment in residents of a home for the aged. In M. P. Lawton and F. Lawton (Eds.), *Mental Impairment in the Aged.* Philadelphia: Maurice Jacob Press, 1965b, 90–108.

Bennett [Granick], R., Social isolation experienced prior to entry as a factor in the adjustment of residents of a home for the aged. Unpublished doctoral dissertation, Columbia University, 1962.

Cohen, D. Assessment and behavior modification. *Gerontologist,* 1967, *14,* 221–225.

Coleman, J. C. *Psychology and Effective Behavior.* Glenview, Ill.: Scott, Foresman and Co., 1969, 272–300.

Ellsworth, J. *The MACC Behavioral Adjustment Scale,* rev. ed. Los Angeles: Western Psychological Services, 1971.

Howard, J., and Wesley, W. Group approach in nursing rehabilitation of geriatric psychiatric patients. *J. Am. Geriatr. Soc.,* 1969, *17,* 1147–1148.

Kahana, E., and Harel, Z. Matching environments to needs of the aged. In J. Gubrium (Ed.), *Late Life: Recent Developments in Sociology of Aging*. Springfield, Ill.: Charles C. Thomas, 1975.

Kahn, J., Goldfarb, A., Pollack, T., and Peck, A. Brief objective measures for the determination of mental states of the aged. *J. Chron. Dis.*, 1961, *9*, 220–233.

Kogan, N. Attitudes toward old people. *J. Abnorm. Soc. Psychol.*, 1961, *62*, 46–47.

Lawton, M. P. The Dimensions of Morale. In D. P. Kent, R. Kastenbaum, and S. Sherwood (Eds.), *Research, Planning and Action for the Elderly*. New York: Behavioral Publications, 1972.

Rosenbaum, J., and Berger, L. *Group Psychotherapy and Group Function*. New York: Basic Books, Inc., 1963.

Sloane, R., Staples, F., Cristol, A., Yorkston, N., and Whipple, D. *Psychotherapy versus Behavior Therapy*. Cambridge, Mass.: 1975.

Yalom, I. *The Theory and Practice of Group Psychotherapy*. New York: Basic Books, Inc., 1970.

PART IV
ISOLATION AND AGING STUDIES: PAST, PRESENT AND FUTURE

10
Summary and Concluding Remarks
Ruth Bennett, Ph.D.

Our first study of over 20 years ago was one in which 100 case records of a home for the aged were used to identify those characteristics that differentiated residents who were transferred to a mental hospital from those who were not. Fifty residents of the Home who were transferred were compared to controls matched for age, sex and length of residence who remained in the Home. The findings showed that poor scores on a combined index of social isolation experienced prior to entering the Home were related to inability to get along with staff members and other residents and sometimes resulted in transfer to a mental hospital.

Given the limitations of case-record studies, a direct survey was undertaken of 100 elderly residents, two-thirds of whom were women in their late seventies. One hundred consecutive admissions to the Home were interviewed three times, once on admission and again at one- and two-month intervals. Data on six-month adjustment were collected from social work case records and from interviews with recreation workers in the Home.

In this research, social isolation experienced prior to entry as well as during adulthood was studied in relation to socialization, integration (participation), evaluation and conformity. Social isolation was found to be inversely and significantly related to socialization and integration. There was no significant relation between isolation and evaluation (a concept similar to morale) or conformity after either one or two months of residence in the Home. With time, however, there was an increase in the inverse relation between isolation and conformity. As length of residence in the Home increased, isolated aged persons engaged in deviant behavior. One explanation for this delay may be that it took time to learn to deviate or learn the forms of deviance in the Home.

Isolation related to socialization, and early or rapid socialization, rather than socialization per se, related best to adjustment. That is, those with accurate perceptions of life in the Home in the first month adjusted better than those who subsequently became socialized.

After two years, a follow-up study of the process of long-term social adjustment of residents of the Home was undertaken. Changes in adjustment patterns over time, interrelations between components of adjustment, relations between early and late adjustment and the relations between socialization and both early and later adjustment were studied. Forty-five residents who had been seen two years earlier were interviewed once more. Findings showed that the relation between one-month socialization and integration was stable over time. There was a systematic decrease in the correlation between socialization and evaluation with time, mainly because evaluations became differentiated. There was a continued increase in the relation of socialization to conformity, which had been indicated by the six-month social workers' adjustment report.

Four patterns of isolation were differentiated. They were: nonisolation, old age nonisolation, recent or involuntary isolation and lifelong or voluntary isolation.

The lifelong isolate might describe himself as a loner: his life style might be considered marginal; he might drink a lot.

The involuntary isolate might be someone who was outgoing and social early in life but has now been taken out of circulation, for example, because of needing to care full time for an ill spouse.

The early isolate might be a bit of a character; typically female and single, she is isolated early in life but is discovered to be a remarkable person by nieces or nephews late in life—a sort of Auntie Mame type.

The lifelong integrated person is fully involved and may even work in old age.

These patterns were studied in relation to socialization. Findings show that all patterns of isolation had negative effects on socialization, in contrast to nonisolation. The score differences between the nonisolated and the group next in line were greater than between any two types of isolates.

Although the lifelong (voluntary) isolates (who were, perhaps, mentally ill) did worst of all, they were not much worse than involuntary or 'recent isolates. However, the gap widened between involuntary isolation and early isolation, and widened most between early isolation and no isolation at all. The findings suggest there may be critical periods for isolation, and that it may have more negative consequences for socialization if it occurs late in life and is uncompensated.

From the series of studies described above, it was concluded that the consequences of isolation are such that socialization and social adjustment to a home for the aged are impaired. Age, sex, physical status and other background factors did not relate systematically to isolation, nor did they explain the findings obtained.

This led to the suspicion that there were two, or possibly more, "syndromes" related to similarly maladjusted behavior found among the elderly: One was mental disorder, which probably resulted in hospitalization; the other has since been termed the "isolation–desocialization" syndrome, for want of a better name. The isolation–desocialization syndrome is a process that may look somewhat like this: An old person in the community becomes isolated, then desocialized; he enters a home for the aged or some other setting, misperceives the norms and blunders socially soon after entry; others single him out, perhaps labeling him a "troublemaker," and avoid him; he then becomes involved in overt conflict with staff members and/or other residents. Presumably, long experience with social isolation would not be as great a handicap to an old person who remained in the community as it is to one who is relocated and must adjust socially. However, also presumably, the effects of social isolation may be remediable, whereas those resulting from mental disorders of the senium may be more difficult to treat.

It was not clear from our just-described early studies whether some of the maladjusted behavior observed was the result of the "isolation–desocialization" syndrome or of mental disorder. It was our good fortune to have working with us a visiting psychiatrist, trained in Britain, who wanted to study in a nonclinical manner the relationship between social isolation, mental disorder and social adjustment in the aged. Fifty-three successive admissions who had been studied two years earlier were independently evaluated by the psychiatrist using a crude standard diagnostic form he designed to determine presence or absence of organic or functional mental disorder. This measure was designed to exclude data on early social isolation or social adjustment, and was based largely on current cognitive functioning. Findings showed no relationship between social isolation and mental disorder.

Residents suffering from senile and/or arteriosclerotic dementia were differentiated from those with functional psychiatric disorders by their social adjustment patterns. Those with mild dementia adjusted to the institutional environment much as normal residents did. Those with functional disorders behaved much like social isolates; they were unhappy and did not live up to the expectations and requirements of other residents. Neither group of mentally disordered residents participated in the home's activities, in contrast to the normal residents. In this sense, they resembled the isolates.

This study was then extended into four other settings ordered by degree of totality. A mental hospital was seen as the most totalistic institution; an apartment project for senior citizens was seen as the least totalistic. It had been hypothesized that isolation would impede socialization and adjustment in all settings but that those isolates in the apartment project would be worst-off because the rules that govern behavior would be least likely to be spelled out; thus those in least contact with others would be least able to learn the norms and would be least adjusted.

The experience of pre-entry isolation appeared to have a negative effect on socialization in all but one residential setting. The experience of isolation immediately prior to entry was a better predictor of poor socialization than isolation experienced during an individual's entire adulthood. The correlations between pre-entry isolation and integration were generally smaller than those between socialization and integration. The correlations of both isolation and socialization with integration, while positive throughout, were generally higher in the moderately total institutions than in settings at both extremes of totality. Thus, a new admission to a nursing home, home for the aged or apartment residence who had been either isolated or unsocialized usually did not become well integrated into the home's activities. On the other hand, in the mental hospital and housing development, integration was not as affected by prior isolation or poor socialization.

Socialization seemed only slightly related to mental status. Possibly, use of a more comprehensive psychiatric-status instrument would have strengthened this finding. The high degree of socialization found among residents of a public housing development in no way was related to their social adjustment. Normative knowledge and, possibly, its internalization did not appear to be a prerequisite for adjustment in residential settings at either extreme of the totality continuum. It was related positively and significantly only in institutions of the middle range of totality. Perhaps only in the middle totality range is how well you do socially a clear reflection of what you know, a relationship that may be explained by size or degree of cohesion in institutions of the middle range, where adjustment criteria were found to be explicit and clearly communicated. This finding was thought to reflect the needs of such institutions, which are structured like small communities and which serve as permanent homes for their residents. Perhaps such institutions rely most heavily on an individual's learning and possible internalization of norms so that he may be able to regulate his conduct. Thus, an individual who was not socialized early in such settings was seriously disadvantaged in adjusting.

At the extreme high and extreme low ends of the totality continuum were a state hospital and a public housing development. Neither seemed much of a community, and both were large. Nor is it clear whether those who run them think of themselves as working in institutions serving as permanent communities for residents. In such settings many intervening factors may play a role in the relation between socialization and adjustment. There may be a large difference between one's knowing what's expected of him and his doing it. The factors of personality and pathology may play a greater role in a large and anonymous setting than in a smaller, more personal one. Those who know what to do may feel less inclined to do it in a setting in which they don't feel personally committed to the community norms. Such residential settings may, therefore, rely more heavily on external agents and sanctions to enforce and uphold norms than on individual internalization of norms. In order to determine whether the correlation between socialization and social adjustment stems from the value placed on community and the principle of permanency in institutions of the middle range or some other aspect of their structure, it was thought that future research on this problem should involve a comparison of institutions within a single category. Thus, for example, a comparision should be made of two homes for the aged of approximately equal size and totality, one of which serves as a community and a permanent residence and one of which does not.

At one point we thought that although isolation led to poor socialization and social adjustment, it might have some salutary social psychological effects. Possibly isolation would result in attitudinal independence, in the rugged individualist willing to do battle against society. In order to determine if this were so, 96 residents, all those who had been residing in a home for one to three years, were interviewed twice. Persuasibility was defined as the tendency to agree with contradictory opinions expressed by two interviewers. One salient measure and one topic-free measure of persuasibility were used. Social integration was measured sociometrically by using staff members' reports about the activities engaged in by the residents and the friendship choices of other residents in the home. The hypothesis that the socially isolated residents would be highly persuasible was supported. Paradoxically and unexpectedly, the socially integrated residents were both attitudinally independent and socially conforming. Therefore, the relationship between conformity to social norms, persuasibility and counternormative persuasion was also intensively studied. In general, while the residents were highly persuasible and some were clearly more persuasible than others, no relationship was found between the tendency to be persuaded by the interviewers and conformity to the norms of the home. Furthermore, highly conforming residents were found to be most resistant to counternormative persuasive appeals.

Conforming individuals evaluated the home positively and tended to regard it as a positive reference group while simultaneously indicating a lack of interest in people and events outside the home. It was concluded that conformity was less dependent upon a general compliance tendency than upon commitment to normative standards of the home.

Thus, we found that isolation is bad for the aged; it desocializes them, hampers adjustment and reduces attitudinal independence. It is not correlated with age, sex, mental status or education. It is not synonymous with mental disorder though it may result in similar behavioral patterns. Its effects may be reversible through resocialization processes described in this book. On the other hand, if not compensated for in time, its effects may lead to serious cognitive, social and emotional impairment. At the core of our experimental resocialization programs was the belief that it was important to reduce isolation in any settings in which the aged were found. In order to try to reduce isolation, we began on an experimental basis the Friendly Visitor Program in the Morningside Health Catchment Area, from which residents of the homes studied in earlier work were drawn.

The Morningside Health Catchment Area of New York City is an area that contains about 20,000 elderly persons aged 65 and over. In order to extend this visiting program both to other parts of New York City and, conceivably, to other large cities, it was necessary to determine first if such a program had an impact on the social functioning and mental state of a sample of the elderly. Thus, the emphasis of this research was on the systematic evaluation of a friendly visiting program using a fairly standard method of evaluation research design.

Much of our own earlier research tried to deal with the problem of differentiating social isolation from some of its presumed mental and behavioral consequences. By intervening socially, that is, by providing old people with the opportunity to interact with friendly visitors, we expected to determine if we are able significantly to reduce the behavioral as well as mental deterioration that seems attributable to social isolation. The Friendly Visitor Program was, therefore, designed as a social experiment to determine if there is a causal relationship between social isolation and mental disorder, poor social adjustment and cognitive impairment in the aged. The Friendly Visitor Program represents an effort to base a large-scale social service program on social gerontological theory and to evaluate the program's effects.

A friendly visitor program reduces social isolation by reconnecting the elderly to others, by indicating an awareness of their presence in the community and by showing concern with their well-being. We expected the Friendly Visitor Program to result in improved morale initially, as well as in improved social and personal adjustment and mental state as the program progressed. The friendly visitors would not only be expected to help reduce isolation but also attendant feelings of abandonment, as well as feelings of loneliness, depression and anxiety. Moreover, by providing opportunities to engage in discussion we expected to bring about improvement in some cognitive aspects of the mental state of the elderly respondents.

It was expected that friendly visits, even if only from student volunteers, would have a positive effect on mental status. However, these visits were thought to have only a temporary effect because they brought no assurance of help to those visited, and the elderly visitees were not encouraged to initiate requests for help.

In order to determine if the Friendly Visitor Program has any lasting effects, a follow-up visit was conducted after the program terminated. Findings showed observable differences in communicativeness, sociability, the condition of the apartment and personal grooming between the first and the succeeding visits. On follow-up, it was found that isolation was reduced in those visited.

We believed it was important to reduce isolation in any setting in which the aged were found. Thus, in a medical clinic at Coney Island Hospital they were grouped and placed experimentally in a resocialization group. Those who were in such a group improved on a variety of measures of socialization and adjustment as compared with control groups.

Although isolation may not necesarily predispose one to poor adjustment in a community in which one is already settled, it may have negative consequences if one is moved into an institution. Therefore, several resocialization experiments were undertaken with residents of institutions in order both to develop ways of working with groups of elderly maladjusted residents and to determine if some patterns of isolation were found to be more amenable to treatment than others.

Remotivation turned out to be very successful as a group resocialization form with the elderly. However, it was not clear that this format would work in all settings.

Type of group leadership made a difference too. Chiefly, professional group leaders were more effective than elderly persons in resocialization efforts in DIPHA homes.

In an experiment utilizing time-limited group therapy methods, it was found that some patterns of isolation were more treatable than others. Involuntary isolates were found to be most responsive to group resocialization efforts. It was thought that it might be effective to target involuntary isolates for group resocialization efforts in the future.

To summarize, from our studies of social isolation described above, we have found that isolation has a negative impact on the aged; it desocializes them, hampers social adjustment and seems to reduce independence. At the present time, isolation in the aged does not seem to be correlated with the usual demographic factors in institutions though we have found that old women in the community are more readily rejected than men when they age. Isolation is not synonymous with mental disorder in the aged though it may result in some behavior patterns associated with mental disorder, specifically poor social adjustment and poor cognitive functioning. If not compensated for in time, the effects of isolation may lead to serious and possibly irreversible cognitive and other impairments. However, unlike senile mental disorders, the effects of isolation may be reversible through resocialization, remotivation and friendly visiting programs. Measures of isolation, specifically the PMI, can be used to detect isolates as is indicated in our friendly visitor study. The PMI is also sensitive to changes in social interaction as is indicated in the same study, where after a course of visiting PMI scores went up.

Currently we are investigating the phenomenon of social isolation cross-nationally. The United States–United Kingdom cross-national study of health, mental health and social problems in the community-based elderly and a one year follow-up gave us, among other things, the opportunity for the first time to look at how isolation distributes in random samples of the elderly in New York and London, and how it correlates with mental health, physical health and social problems. We found the need, in this study, to utilize multiple measures of isolation.

Two new scales have been developed. In addition to AI and PMI we have developed the following two measures:

1. Measure of Subjective Isolation, which measures feelings of loneliness, desire for more contact, desire to withdraw from others, etc. This scale seems to be a component of depression.
2. Enlarged Measure of Present Isolation, which is similar to Past Month Isolation (PMI) but contains more items.

Both of these measures are reliable. AI, PMI and the Enlarged Measure of Present Isolation are correlated with each other; however, none is correlated with the measure of Subjective Isolation, which may well be an index of depression, morale or anomia rather than an expression of isolation.

For correlations of all isolation measures with various measures of impairment such as dementia, depression, physical illness, environmental disadvantage, etc., measures of present isolation, especially the scales of Subjective Isolation and Present Isolation show higher correlations with both mental and physical impairment, than do measures of past isolation. Correlations increase with the Enlarged Measure of Present Isolation though the direction of the relationships remain the same as with the PMI.

On the four measures of isolation, by selected background characteristics, females are more isolated than males on objective measures but not on subjective measures. In other words, they are actually more isolated but feel less bothered by it, which is a surprising finding and runs counter to stereotypes of women. On all isolation indexes, living alone is related to isolation, whereas living with others is not.

However, again these differences are more dramatic and significant when the enlarged measure of current isolation is used.

Current findings are encouraging because they indicate that there is some external validation for the isolation measures. One would expect older females to be more isolated on any objective measures. There is, however, no reason to believe that females would feel more subjectively isolated, that is, have low morale or experience feelings of anomia. One would also expect those who are living alone to be more isolated, though it is too soon to tell if the single item, living alone, is as good a predictor of present isolation as is an index of present isolation.

Our current studies do not include all measures used in earlier institutional studies, but many measures of health, mental health and social problems that we thought would distinguish different types of isolates were included.

For the New York City sample, the group that seems most mentally, socially and physically impaired is the group that early in life showed an inclination to be social but who, for many reasons, became socially isolated late in life—the group called involuntary or recent isolates. This group also uses more services than do the others. This is not inconsistent with the findings of our earlier research, which suggest that involuntary isolates are good targets for social programs because they improve when offered help.

Voluntary or lifelong isolates were also found to be socially disadvantaged in New York City.

Early isolates seem to be fairly independent, unmarried, poor females who are lowest on service use.

Those who are socially integrated throughout life appear to be best-off, as would be expected.

Thus, a consistent finding has been that involuntary or recent isolates are a good group to target for delivery of services and programs. They make use of these programs when they are available, and show improvements after such services and programs are delivered. Persons in this category were found to improve after institutionalization as well as after experiencing time-limited therapy. Given scarce resources such as services and resocialization programs, it might be useful to target the recent or involuntary isolate for such services because he stands to improve the most.

Of course, in the best of all possible worlds such services and programs should be offered to all of the elderly in the hope of preventing the sorts of crises and episodes that result in institutionalization or in declining ability to care for oneself.

Such programs as friendly visiting, delivered regularly, are reassuring to the elderly. They know that they are not alone or forgotten, that someone will be looking in on them and will discover whether or not they are ill, and that they will be cared for if there is such a need. Thus far, such programs are not available to the elderly on any large-scale basis.

Such programs seem as necessary for the urban as they are for the rural aged. Many of the urban elderly live in isolation and fear in declining neighborhoods, just as many rural elderly find that as they get older, they get more cut off from their neighbors. Certainly, the sense of fear, isolation and lack of stimulation cannot be good for the elderly, and this idea is a central focus for our continuing studies of both the community and the institutionalized aged.

Resocialization, remotivation and psychotherapy groups seem to be effective means of reconnecting and resocializing the institutionalized elderly and should be used more widely than they currently are. They are particularly effective with those who have been involuntarily isolated and who have the desire, but perhaps have lost the ability, to interact with others. These persons seem to flourish when given the opportunity and encouragement to get to know and, perhaps, assist other people.

Index

Index

Index